The Philosophy of Punishment

By the same author

THE ILLUSION OF THE EPOCH: MARXISM-LENINISM AS A PHILOSOPHICAL CREED (1955)

WHAT MARX REALLY SAID (1967)

The Philosophy of Punishment

A COLLECTION OF PAPERS

edited by H. B. ACTON
Professor of Moral Philosophy in the University of Edinburgh

Macmillan

St Martin's Press

© Selection and editorial matter
H. B. ACTON 1969

First published 1969 by
MACMILLAN AND CO LTD
Little Essex Street London WC2
and also at Bombay Calcutta and Madras
Macmillan South Africa (Publishers) Pty Ltd Johannesburg
The Macmillan Company of Australia Pty Ltd Melbourne
The Macmillan Company of Canada Ltd Toronto
St Martin's Press Inc New York
Gill and Macmillan Ltd Dublin

Library of Congress catalog card no. 73–97179

Printed in Great Britain by
WESTERN PRINTING SERVICES LTD
Bristol

Contents

ACKNOWLEDGEMENTS

The editor and publishers wish to thank the following for their kindness in granting permission for the use of copyright material: Mr K. G. Armstrong, for 'The Retributivist Hits Back', from *Mind* (October 1961); Professor K. E. Baier, for 'Is Punishment Retributive?', from *Analysis*, vol. 16, no. 2 (December 1955); The Clarendon Press, for *The Responsibility of Criminals*, by Professor William Kneale; Professor Giorgio Del Vecchio, for *The Struggle against Crime*, translated by Professor A. H. Campbell; Professor James F. Doyle, for 'Justice and Legal Punishment', from *Philosophy* (January 1967); Professor Antony Flew, for 'The Justification of Punishment', from *Philosophy*, vol. XXIX, no. iii (October 1954); Mr J. D. Mabbott, for 'Punishment', from *Mind*, vol. XLVIII, no. 190 (1939) and for 'Professor Flew on Punishment', from *Philosophy* (July 1955); Professor C. W. K. Mundle, for 'Punishment and Desert', from the *Philosophical Quarterly*, vol. IV, no. 16 (July 1954); Mr Anthony M. Quinton, for 'On Punishment', from *Analysis*, vol. 14, no. 6 (June 1954); Professor John Rawls, for 'Two Concepts of Rules', from the *Philosophical Review*, vol. LXIV (January 1955); Mrs Alwynne Smart, for 'Mercy', from *Philosophy* (October 1968); and Mr J. E. R. Squires, for 'Blame', from the *Philosophical Quarterly* (January 1968). The editor and publishers also thank the editors of the above-mentioned journals.

⅀ *Contributors*

H. B. ACTON Professor of Moral Philosophy, University of Edinburgh

K. G. ARMSTRONG Lecturer in Politics, University of Melbourne

K. E. BAIER Professor of Philosophy, University of Pittsburgh

GIORGIO DEL VECCHIO Formerly Rector of the University of Rome

JAMES F. DOYLE Professor of Philosophy, University of Missouri

ANTONY FLEW Professor of Philosophy, University of Keele

WILLIAM KNEALE Formerly White's Professor of Moral Philosophy, University of Oxford

J. D. MABBOTT President of St John's College, University of Oxford

C. W. K. MUNDLE Professor of Philosophy, University College of North Wales, Bangor

ANTHONY M. QUINTON Fellow of New College, University of Oxford

JOHN RAWLS Professor of Philosophy, Harvard University

ALWYNNE SMART Lecturer in Philosophy, La Trobe University

J. E. R. SQUIRES Lecturer in Logic and Metaphysics, University of St Andrews

I ✑ *Introduction: The Philosophy of Punishment*

H. B. ACTON

I

Most of those whose papers are published in the present volume have worked out their views within the philosophical tradition of the English-speaking world. Their conceptions of punishment, of course, must have been influenced by the prevailing penal system and by the ideas and activities of penal reformers, but the philosophical discussions of punishment from which they spring – often by way of reaction – are those of the British Idealists, F. H. Bradley, T. H. Green and Bernard Bosanquet, and of their non-idealist or realist critics, Hastings Rashdall, A. C. Ewing and Sir David Ross. Our first task, therefore, in introducing the papers printed in this volume, will be to give some indication of the main accounts of punishment that were before the philosophical public in 1939 when the first of the papers was published.

F. H. BRADLEY

In the first essay, entitled 'The Vulgar Notion of Responsibility', of *Ethical Studies* (1876), Bradley set himself against what he says is J. S. Mill's view that punishment is justifiable only as a means of benefiting the offender and protecting others. Bradley also objected to Mill's idea that punishment is a sort of 'medicine'.[1] Such views, Bradley held, conflict with the conviction of ordinary men that what justifies punishment is the guilt, the 'criminal desert' of the offender. According to Bradley, although benefiting the offender and protecting other people are desirable concomitants of

[1] Bradley's references are to ch. xxvi ('The Freedom of the Will') of Mill's *Examination of Sir William Hamilton's Philosophy*, 2nd ed. (1872). Mill's view is much more complex than Bradley gives it credit for, since Mill gives 'securing the just rights of others' as an aim of punishment (p. 597).

punishment, its essential characteristic is 'the destruction of guilt, whatever be the consequences'. Its essence, therefore, is retribution. Plain men also believe, says Bradley, that punishment can only be rightly inflicted upon responsible individuals, on individuals who freely will their acts and maintain their identity through the series of their acts. Bradley thought that Mill, like Hume before him, had a theory of human will and personality that was incompatible with the ordinary man's conception of agency. In particular, 'our people', according to Bradley, do not believe that the world of human action is the determinist's world of 'mechanism', of 'tractions and compositions of forces'. In face of the objection that perhaps the common sense of plain men is wrong, Bradley refers to the Hegelian conception of 'a philosophy which *thinks* what the vulgar believe'. Bradley does not here think of philosophy as something that could alter the beliefs of ordinary men.

Bradley also discussed punishment in an article in *The International Journal of Ethics* (1894).[2] By this time he had been influenced by Darwinism and had come to believe that the older view of punishment should be subordinated to 'the principle of social surgery', according to which punishment is a reaction of the whole community against conduct that weakens it. If this view is accepted, he argues, then 'the connexion between punishment and guilt' is broken. Furthermore, as morality becomes more inward, with stress upon disposition and intention rather than upon merely external performance, it becomes more difficult to ascertain and assess the moral responsibility of the accused. Hence, verdicts and sentences based on external actions may not be 'genuinely moral'. Bradley also argues that it may be necessary to 'remove the innocent' in spite of the injustice of doing so. He admits that it may not be right to *call* this punishment, but 'the thing being justified I will not pause to consider the name'. In consequence, he continues, 'the sacred rights of innocence have become a thing conditional'. The conclusion Bradley draws is that the justice of retributive punishment may have to be overridden by the superior moral principle of 'the good of the social organism', just as any subordinate moral principle may have to give way before a superior one. In this connection Bradley says that 'the sacredness of human life seems largely a Christian idea', and it is clear that, in this particular, Bradley thought that Darwin had superseded Jesus.

[2] Reprinted in *Collected Essays*, vol. 1 (1935).

T. H. GREEN

T. H. Green discusses punishment by the State in the context of state action generally, in his *Lectures on the Principles of Political Obligation* delivered in 1881. His central idea is that punishment is justifiable on account of the wrongdoer's violation of someone else's rights. This, he holds, distinguishes punishment in principle from any sort of private vengeance or retaliation. Public indignation against a wrongdoer 'borrows the language of private revenge, just as the love of God borrows the language of sensuous affection', but it is essentially the demand 'that the criminal should have his due, should be dealt with according to his deserts, should be punished justly'. Punishment by the State presupposes a system of publicly supported rights which some individuals may deliberately violate. When someone thus contravenes the rights of others, punishment is just to the extent that it is necessary to maintain the rights of all. In such circumstances a criminal 'sees that the punishment is his own act returning on himself, in the sense that it is the necessary outcome of his act in a society governed by the conception of rights, a conception which he appreciates and to which he does involuntary reverence'. Green holds that punishment is preventive as well as retributive in the sense just mentioned, but what it should aim to prevent is not any general diminution of happiness (as Bentham had thought), for this would justify all sorts of interferences that are not punishment, but encroachments on the rights that it is the business of the State to uphold. By associating violation of rights with the terror of punishment, the importance of rights is emphasised and their maintenance is strengthened.

Green also argues that it is not possible to make 'the pain of punishment commensurate with the guilt of the criminal' and hence that no attempt should be made to do so. What is possible is to 'associate terror with the contemplation of the crime in the mind of others who might be tempted to commit it'. Furthermore, the degree of such terror should be associated with the degree of importance of the rights that are violated. Public indignation varies in accordance with its view of the relative importance of the rights that have been interfered with. This is a very different sort of judgment from that which an individual's conscience delivers on his own actions. In punishment the State 'looks not to virtue and vice but to rights and wrongs'. Punishment should be '*justly* preventive of *injustice*'. It may help to reform a criminal, but if it does, this is 'an incident of its preventive function, as regulated by the consideration of what is just to the criminal as well as to others'.

BERNARD BOSANQUET

Bosanquet, like Green, discusses punishment in the context of the State and its functions. Like Green, too, he sees punishment as the State's maintenance of rights by the use of force. In discussing punishment in *The Philosophical Theory of the State* (1899), he presents a view much like that of Green, except that he is at pains to attack the idea that punishment is a sort of therapy. This is an insult to wrongdoers and would justify taking any man who is thought capable of improvement and forcibly ameliorating him. Those who regard punishment as retribution, he maintains, at least take the wrongdoer seriously.

Bosanquet returned to the subject of punishment in 1918 in his *Some Suggestions in Ethics*, chapter viii of which is entitled: 'On the growing repugnance to punishment'. Here he argues that punishment is essentially the 'annulment' of the wrong act, its 'undoing' or 'cancellation'. Why *should* the wrong act be annulled? Because if things were left just as they were after the crime had been committed, the criminal act would have been allowed to become a bad precedent. How *can* the wrong act be annulled? Bosanquet gives a number of examples to show this. A man who has wrongfully erected a fence can be made to be present at its removal, a man who has told a damaging lie can be made to tell the truth publicly, a resolution of the House of Commons can be expunged, a wrongdoer can be brought to court and condemned. He must be publicly arraigned and made to suffer 'some visible and sensible deprivation of personality' because he has failed to respect the rights of others. It may be said that this would be pointless if the wrongdoer were not to be reformed by it, but according to Bosanquet this objection 'betrays a deep-seated individualism'; the point of the annulment is that it 'maintains the moral standard of the general mind and will'. In cancelling the wrong act punishment 'negates' the bad will of the criminal. Bosanquet also argues that deterrence and reformation are not separate ends of punishment but 'expansions, outgrowths of its central character, the negation of the evil will'. Punishment is perverted into therapy or cruelty if reformation or deterrence are allowed to become independent ends. They are acceptable in so far as they are aspects of the act of retribution, annulment and negation.

HASTINGS RASHDALL

In an article in *The International Journal of Ethics* (1891) and in book 1, chapter 9 of *The Theory of Good and Evil* (1st ed. 1907, 2nd ed. 1924) Rashdall took issue with the retributive justification of punishment. He argued in the first place that if pains are to be matched with sin or moral guilt there must be some means of equating an amount of the one with an amount of the other. This, however, is quite impossible. 'There is absolutely no commensurability between the two things.' In the second place, even if they were commensurable, any addition to the pain for purposes of deterrence or reform would be unjust, so that room could only be found for them by inflicting an unjustly small amount of punishment. A third objection to the retributive view is that if it were accepted it would imply that forgiveness is always wrong. Rashdall considers the argument that forgiveness is compatible with punishment in so far as the victim may cease to show or feel resentment after the punishment has been inflicted. But he nevertheless concludes that this is an unsatisfactory view of forgiveness; fundamentally 'forgiveness is opposed to punishment'. All that remains of retribution, once the moral difficulties in it are exposed, is the requirement that punishment should only be inflicted on the guilty. Rashdall also allows that the infliction of pain may sometimes lead to moral improvement and that the criminal law 'has an important work to do in giving expression to the moral sense of the community'. Rashdall obviously feels that there is something unchristian in the retributive view. He denies that the view defended by Bosanquet in *The Philosophical Theory of the State* is, properly speaking, a defence of retribution at all, and says that 'there is much in all this talk about involuntary and impenitent submission to an unreformatory punishment being really the work of the person's own will, which is quite as unintelligible and ethically objectionable as the crudest form of the retributive theory'.

A. C. EWING

Dr Ewing's *The Morality of Punishment* (1929) is a detailed and comprehensive discussion that cannot be adequately summarised in a paragraph. Ewing does not think that reform and deterrence could provide the main justification for punishment, but he finds difficulties in the retributive view as well. Like Rashdall he argues that since the State cannot match pain with moral guilt, then on the retributive view it commits an injustice almost every time that it punishes. It would be better, therefore, if it did not punish at all. If 'punishment' means 'inflict pain or harm', it can hardly be maintained that no one should be punished, i.e. be given pain or harm, unless he had committed some crime, for this would prohibit surgery. If 'punishment' means 'inflict pain *for* the commission of a crime', then the injunction not to punish the innocent 'becomes little more than a tautology, since they have *ex hypothesi* not committed a crime'.

Ewing's own view is that punishment is essentially an expression of moral condemnation. A man cannot be rightly condemned unless he has committed a wrongful act, and hence, Ewing argues, this view conforms with the central element in the retributive view that only the guilty can be justly punished. When wrong actions are condemned in proportion to the degree of wrongness, the wrongdoer and others are being educated in morality. They are being deterred by fear of receiving the emphatic condemnation that punishment consists of, and they are being educated in so far as they come to recognise the wrongness and the degrees of wrongness of the sorts of action they are being deterred from doing. The moral aim of punishment as such, he writes, 'is to make people think of a certain kind of act as very bad, but, if it were inflicted otherwise than for a bad act, it would either produce no effect of this sort at all or cause people to think an act bad which was not really bad...'.

W. D. ROSS

In appendix ii to chapter ii of *The Right and the Good* (1930) Sir David Ross argues for the view that punishment by the State is justified on account of the wrongdoer's violation of the rights of others. Retribution by the State would require happiness and unhappiness to be made proportionate to moral worth, but the State is not equipped to do any such thing. What it should try to do is to protect 'the most important rights of individuals, those without which a reasonably secure and comfortable life is impossible'. A man who has violated someone else's rights has put himself into a different position from that of people who have not. The State is no longer obliged to protect him to the extent that it is obliged to protect innocent people. 'It is morally at liberty to injure him as he has injured others, or to inflict any lesser injury on him, or to spare him, exactly as consideration both of the good of the community and of his own good requires'. Hence it is justifiable, with a view to the general interest, to inflict deterrent or reformatory punishment on an individual who has violated the rights of others. The criminal law is 'a threat to the guilty', but also 'a promise to the injured person and his friends and to society'. It is also a promise to all members of society that if they do not break the law they will not be punished. According to Ross, therefore, the State's right to punish is justified in two ways. In the first place, the State has a right to punish criminals in the public interest. It has a right to injure any of its members in the public interest, but, because the criminal has injured others, it has a special right to injure him. In the second place, in punishing a criminal the State is keeping a promise which, in the very fact of establishing the criminal law, it makes to any victim and to anyone in its jurisdiction. Thus Ross rejects retribution but justifies punishment by the State in terms of promise-keeping as well as in terms of the general good.

Some Problems Raised in the Foregoing

The philosophers we have considered have discussed punishment by the State.

Retribution is supported by Bradley, and in a modified form by Green and Bosanquet, on the ground that it is just. All three Idealists hold that deterrence and reform, considered apart from retribution, entail using individuals as mere means. Bosanquet thinks that it is insulting to the criminal to regard him as a patient who needs to be cured. Bradley and Bosanquet (following Hegel) try to explain retribution in such terms as annulment, cancelling, negating.

Although Bradley is generally taken as an upholder of retribution, he argued in his 1894 article that it can be overridden in the public interest, so that an innocent man might rightly be punished although this would be unjust. This, Bradley says, would be a case of a superior moral principle overriding an inferior one.

Green, Bosanquet and Ross say that what justifies punishment by the State is the fact that the criminal has violated the rights of others. They give different accounts, however, of how this justification is to be made.

All these philosophers – even Bradley, in his 1894 essay – consider it impossible to match pain to moral guilt. They therefore reject any form of the retributive view that assumes that this is possible. Green and Bosanquet, however, do not reject retribution altogether, but try to give some acceptable account of it. Rashdall opposes retribution because he thinks that it goes against Christian forgiveness. Green, on the contrary, argues that punishment by the State is essentially different from personal vengeance or retaliation.

There is some discussion of scales of punishment. Green and Ross suggest that the degree of severity of punishments marks society's estimate of the degree of violation of rights committed in various types of criminal act. Green argues that deterrence, in the context of punishment by the State, is not merely a means of diminishing the general pain or increasing the general happiness, but also a means of instilling a proper regard for the rights of otthers. This begins to approach the idea that punishment is educative, a view also held by Ewing, who links with it the notion of punishment as public condemnation.

When Bradley says that it might be justifiable to 'punish' an innocent man, he notices that this might be thought to be a misuse of the verb 'to punish'. Ewing notices that if 'punish' means 'inflict pain for the commission of a crime', the injunction not to punish the innocent 'becomes little more than a tautology'. Both of these philosophers (and, I think, Rashdall too) have therefore distinguished between a merely verbal and a moral justification of punishment.

II

In what follows I shall consider the principal ways in which the above arguments have since been elaborated or criticised both in the papers printed in this book and in others it has not been possible to include in it. We must start with some comments on

Mr Mabbott's paper of 1939 which has determined to a considerable degree the course of subsequent discussion.

MABBOTT, 1939

Mabbott says he is defending a retributive view, which he opposes to the utilitarian objectives of reform and deterrence. He also says that what he is concerned to justify is 'the punishment of some particular person'. His starting-point, therefore, is the commission of a wrong by an individual. But what sort of wrong? If some bystander in a country where animals are not protected by law sees a man misusing a horse he is not entitled to punish that man, since the man has not committed a legal wrong, and, even if he had, the mere bystander is not authorised to punish. If punishment is to be justified, therefore, there must be laws administered by some sort of judicial authority. It is clear that Mabbott has the State chiefly in mind, although he mentions schools and colleges as well.[3] This arrangement he calls 'a legal system', and he considers alternatives to it, such as a system of honour, a system of sporadic mob violence against individuals who wrong others, and a system in which individuals are treated, not punished, for such wrongs, while social preventive measures are constantly being taken. If there is to be a legal system, there must be police, courts and judges (or some equivalent), and if individuals break the law they bring their punishment upon themselves. 'Punishment is a corollary not of law but of law-breaking.' Mabbott makes it clear that whether there should be a system of law, and if so, what laws there should be, are questions to be settled on grounds of utility. Deterrence, if it occurs, is not itself punishment, but a concomitant of any publicity that the punishment receives. Nor is reformation punishment either, although it may be sought in the process of imprisonment or probation. Mabbott thinks that his account of what justifies punishment has the support of intelligent and articulate criminals, and he quotes from a book by one of them: ' "To punish a man is to treat him as an equal. To be punished *for an offence against rules* is a sane man's right." ' According to Mabbott, punishment is retribution for a crime, not for 'moral baseness'. In taking this view he seems to be

---

[3] In his reply to Flew's criticisms Mabbott expresses doubt whether punishment in his sense should be regarded as including non-state authorities. (Below, p. 119).

avoiding the difficulties raised by Rashdall about the possibility of matching pain with degrees of moral guilt.

CRITICISMS OF MABBOTT: MISS GLOVER, FLEW, MUNDLE, QUINTON, RAWLS

Soon after the appearance of Mabbott's paper Miss M. R. Glover objected that it contained primarily 'logical and legal arguments'.[4] She admitted that it might be unconstitutional or illogical for a judge or juryman to refuse to convict someone whose offence was established even if the law was bad, but that nevertheless it might be right. Legislation itself, she pointed out, is subject to moral assessment, so that Mabbott's distinction between criminal and moral guilt might not be easy to sustain. She thought, too, that he gave too much weight to the views of criminals and headmasters. Mabbott's article came up for more detailed criticism, however, at a meeting of the Scots Philosophical Club in 1953, where his point of view was discussed by Professors Flew and Mundle (see Papers 5 and 4 below). Flew gives an analysis of the standard case of punishment under the auspices of an authority which comes fairly close to that assumed by Mabbott. But Flew also argues that Mabbott is not clear whether he is defending the retributive view on the basis of the meaning of the word 'punishment' – this would be a *logical* justification – or whether he is putting forward the *ethical* argument that retribution is morally right. Mundle argued that Mabbott's view is not really retributive at all, and formulated what he considered to be a genuinely retributive account. Mr Quinton in an article published about the same time (see Paper 3 below) argued that if a pain is only punishment if it is inflicted on the guilty, then retribution is part of the very meaning of the word 'punishment', whereas it is utilitarian considerations that determine when it is morally permissible or morally obligatory to punish. A little later Professor Rawls (see Paper 6) distinguished between justifying a practice and justifying an action falling under it, and pointed out that this distinction is 'fundamental to J. D. Mabbott's important paper'.

MABBOTT, 1955

In his reply to Flew (see Paper 7), Mabbott also took the occasion to comment on Miss Glover's and Mr Quinton's criticisms

[4] 'Mr Mabbott on Punishment', in *Mind* (Oct 1939).

of his 1939 paper. These three critics had all said that Mabbott was not clear whether he was arguing (*a*) that retribution is logically bound up with punishment, in that pains deliberately inflicted on an innocent person are not punishment at all, or (*b*) that it is morally permissible or morally obligatory to punish the guilty. Mabbott, however, does not admit that he was confused at all. He did intend to assert that 'a reference to past guilt is included in the meaning of punishment'. But he also asked the moral question: 'Ought persons to suffer injury or loss for breaking laws?' He answered it too, saying that a judge, having voluntarily accepted his office, and recognising 'the value of a legal system which has rules with penalties', is morally bound to pass sentence on guilty men in accordance with the law. Now Quinton had argued that in cases where the judge has discretion to pass a higher or a lower sentence for a class of crime, his decision 'must be determined by reference to considerations of utility'. But Mabbott objects that when the judge has discretion to sentence within limits, he exercises it, not for utilitarian ends, but in the light of 'the degree of guilt (in the past) or the degree of responsibility (also in the past)'. The judge, he points out, considers such things as whether the convicted man was or was not careless, whether he was sorely tempted, and so on. If he were sorely tempted, he might receive a lesser sentence, whereas on utilitarian grounds the greater the temptation, the greater the punishment required in order to deter. Thus Mabbott holds that the backward-looking retributive feature of punishment is essential not only in determining who should be punished but also in determining the severity of the penalty.

Mabbott accepts Miss Glover's point that if the law or legal system is very bad indeed it might be the duty of judge or jury to go against it by acquitting people who are guilty of breaking the law. His account of such situations is that in them the jury's and judge's '*prima facie* obligation' to convict and pass sentence is overridden by another, stronger obligation, although he does not say what this is. We have already seen (p. 10) that Bradley held that 'the sacred rights of innocence' might properly be overriden by the higher principle of 'the good of the social organism'. Whether Bradley believed that any judge would be entitled to do this at any time, or whether he believed that laws should be enacted to make this legitimate, is not clear. But although both Bradley and Mabbott allow the possibility that the claims of a superior moral principle might on occasion justify interference with the jury's or judge's *prima facie* duty, Mabbott conceives of this as involving *not* punishing the man who has broken a bad law, while Bradley conceives of it as *punishing* a man who has not broken a law at all. One thing that emerges from what is said by Miss Glover, and by Quinton and by Mabbott, is that punishing the innocent is logically and morally very different from not punishing the guilty.

MUST UTILITARIANS DEFEND PUNISHING THE INNOCENT?

Mabbott brings a well-known argument against the utilitarian view that punishment is for purposes of deterrence. The argument is that someone who believes this would, if he were consistent, advocate the punishment of an innocent man if he knew it was necessary to prevent a destructive riot or a serious increase in crime. If the deceit became known, of course, then it might make matters worse, but this possibility would make it all the more necessary to keep it dark. Professor Rawls does not think that this argument is as strong as it has been made out to be. How, he asks, could such a deceit be carried out? It would need some institutional arrangement to make it possible, and this he calls 'telishment'. But is telishment a workable institution? It would have to enable certain officials to decide when the circumstances called for telishment, to decide who was to be selected as the victim, and what sort of evidence was to be brought forward. He concludes that, in view of the difficulty of keeping the arrangements dark and of the problems created by the presence of both guilty and 'telished' prisoners in the same jail, 'it would serve no useful purpose. A utilitarian justification for this institution is most unlikely.' We may think, however, that Rawls is creating unnecessary difficulties in trying to describe an *institution* for 'telishment'. Would not *ad hoc* decisions by existing officials in the light of the needs of the moment be sufficient? Mr T. L. S. Sprigge[5] considers this possibility in some detail. He doubts whether anyone could know that any particular frame-up would have the desired consequences, and gives grounds for believ-

[5] *Inquiry*, vol. 8 (1965), pp. 276 ff. Mr Sprigge's article is a criticism of Professor H. J. McCloskey's 'A Non-Utilitarian Approach to Punishment' in the same issue. See also S. I. Benn, 'An Approach to the Problems of Punishment', *Philosophy* (Oct 1958), p. 331.

ing that it would be reasonable to expect that the bad consequences for the innocent man and his friends and relations are likely to outweigh any possible good consequences for others. What does seem clear is that there are good, if not decisive arguments against the possibility or utility of punishing an innocent man for the good of the people.

WHAT IS RETRIBUTION? MUNDLE, QUINTON, BAIER

According to Mundle, Mabbott's view is non-utilitarian but not really retributive. Mundle says that if the punishing of an offender is to be retributive it must be for a moral offence and in proportion to the moral gravity of the offence. He also says that to be just punishment must be deserved,[6] and uses the expression 'deserved for morally wrong actions'. It does appear that Mabbott has not used the word 'desert' in his account of punishment. The nearest he comes to the idea is in his assertion that the heaviest penalties should be inflicted for 'what are socially the most serious wrongs'. It would be natural to suppose that this means that some one who commits a murder deserves to be punished much more severely than someone who steals a sheep. Perhaps, too, something like desert is meant when Mabbott says that the criminal brings his punishment on himself. Mabbott does not make the point, but it seems that if we take the view that an offender brings his punishment on himself by performing the prohibited action, then we are committed to a legal view of the matter. For if someone commits a moral wrong that is not prohibited by a positive law, then he does not bring any legal punishment upon himself because there is none. What would it mean, then, to say that, although he has incurred no legal penalty, he nevertheless *deserves* to be punished? If we leave divine punishment out of the question, we seem to be left with the idea that it is a pity that there is no law that would enable him to be punished for what he has done. Yet we might not think it right for the sort of thing he has done to be legally prohibited. We might think, for example, that that sort of thing could never be proved in a court of law, or that if it could be, legal prohibition of it would

[6] The importance of desert is also emphasised by A. R. Manser in 'It serves you right', in *Philosophy* (Oct 1962) and by H. J. McCloskey in 'The Complexity of the Concepts of Punishment', in *Philosophy* (Oct 1962) and in his article in *Inquiry* (1965) referred to above.

allow courts to enquire further into people's lives than is advisable. Perhaps, then, when we say someone deserves to be punished even though he has broken no law, we are really giving emphatic expression to our disapproval of what he has done, and disapprobation is certainly not punishment and could exist if there were no punishment at all. We may suggest, therefore, that it is because the types of conduct that are prohibited by the criminal law are *also* morally wrong that we are inclined to link punishment with moral wrong as well as with infringements of the law. Does, then, a man who commits a murder morally deserve a heavier punishment than a man who steals a sheep? Certainly he has done more harm and has brought the heavier punishment upon himself. He has infringed a more basic right than the sheep-stealer has. But it does not follow that his *moral* guilt is greater in the same proportion as the permissible punishment is. There may be all sorts of circumstances that would diminish his moral guilt, just as there might be all sorts of circumstances that could make an act of sheep-stealing morally degrading to a very high degree. Indeed, it has been suggested that moral guilt, in the sense of moral failure, is not something that could be susceptible of degrees at all.[7]

Yet in spite of these arguments there does seem to be one respect in which the attempt is made to achieve some matching between the penalty and the moral guilt. This is the procedure mentioned above (p. 19) by which a judge may, within the prescribed legal limits, vary the sentence in accordance with the temptation, provocation, degree of carelessness, etc. If these considerations are not deterrent or reformative, must they not imply judgments on the degree of *moral* desert, or the amount of *moral* guilt? All I can suggest here is that accused persons are regarded as responsible beings with such knowledge of the laws and of right and wrong as is relevant to the ordinary conduct of their lives. Although, therefore, the criminal law is concerned with criminal deeds rather than with the characters and dispositions from which they spring, those who administer it are bound to deal with criminals as responsible persons inhabiting the same moral world as non-criminals. The permitted variations in sentences for the same crime would then give expression to this.

[7] By Professor W. G. Maclagan in 'Punishment and Retribution', in *Philosophy* (July 1939), p. 290. Maclagan does not accept Mabbott's view of punishment. See pp. 286–7.

Quinton probes further into the concept of retribution, and briefly considers it in terms of annulment, of making the punishment fit the crime (*lex talionis*), and of giving the offender his right. The first and third, as we have seen, have been defended during the last hundred years, but the *lex talionis* was exploded by Blackstone in the eighteenth century when he showed the impossibility of requiting fraud by fraud, forgery by forgery, or even death by death.[8] Annulment, Quinton argues, is really concerned with the future, for it tries 'to bring about a state of affairs in which it is as if the wrongful act had never happened'. This he says, leaves only the guilty act – essential to punishment by its very meaning – as the past item to which punishment looks back. If what I have said earlier is correct, we may also look back to those moral circumstances of the guilty act which may justify some modification of the punishment within the legally prescribed range. Bosanquet's account of annulment as a refusal to allow the guilty act to set a precedent has merit, but it obviously refers to the future as well as to what has been done. The resolution is expunged from the records of the House of Commons, for example, not only because it was wrong, but in order that it shall not be referred to in the future as justification for future acts of that sort. It is unusual, even if striking, to say that a wrongdoer has a *right* to be punished, and Quinton brings this out when he says: 'It is an odd sort of right whose holders would strenuously resist its recognition.' I suggest, however, that what is meant by it is that in being punished instead of being treated or cured or used *in terrorem*, an offender is being regarded as a responsible person. He will not *like* imprisonment, but he may think it less humiliating than being sent to hospital to have something done to his brain or his testicles.[9] Ruth Ellis, who was hanged

[8] *Commentaries on the Laws of England* (1765), book IV, section headed 'Of the Proportion of Punishments'. 'Nor is death always an equivalent for death . . . the execution of a needy decrepit assassin is a poor satisfaction for the murder of a nobleman in the bloom of his youth and full enjoyment of his friends, his honour, and his fortune.' As to 'an eye for an eye', Blackstone asks what should be done with a two-eyed sighted man who knocks out the only healthy eye of a one-eyed man. Similar difficulties arise in the Code of Hammurabi. For example, when the penalty for killing someone else's daughter is to have one's own daughter killed, problems arise in the case when the killer has no daughter, quite apart from the daughter's innocence.

[9] See D. Sington and G. Playfair, *Crime, Punishment and Cure* (1965) ch. vii.

for murder, refused to try to save her life by pleading insanity because she thought it would have been degrading to do so.

THE PUNISHMENT 'GAME'

Professor Baier throws further light on the nature of punishment in the course of criticising an aspect of Quinton's paper. Quinton suggested that, whereas it makes perfectly good sense to say: 'He punished him for something he had not done', it is as senseless to say 'I am punishing you for something you have not done' as to say 'I promise to do something which is not in my power.' (The influence of J. L. Austin's account of 'performatory utterances' is apparent here.) According to Baier, however, the executioner, if he believes the man to be innocent, *could* meaningfully whisper into his ear on the scaffold: 'I am punishing you for something you have not done.' The basis of Baier's criticism here is his account of what he calls 'the game' – the influence of Wittgenstein's *Philosophical Investigations* is apparent in the choice of the word – in which punishment finds its place. The 'game' involves the making of rules, the attachment of penalties to breaches of them, a system of detecting these breaches and apprehending suspects, putting on trial, reaching verdicts, passing sentence, carrying out the sentence.[10] This last act is 'administering punishment', and it 'cannot be performed unless things have gone according to the rules until then'. Therefore, a judge who says: 'I sentence you to three years' imprisonment' when the verdict was 'not guilty' is not really pronouncing sentence at all. I should like to add that were a judge to say: 'I am sentencing you for something you have not done', this could indicate that he disagreed with the verdict but was nevertheless passing the sentence that the verdict required. Baier was doubtful whether 'I am sentencing you for something you have not done' is absurd or meaningless (he writes: 'Quinton's account is not true of punishing but at best of sentencing'), and I think he was right to have this doubt.

[10] Baier recognises differences between punishment by the State and punishment by parents and teachers, but does not appear to consider that they are more than differences of detail necessitated by the differences of circumstance. This view is opposed by C. H. Whiteley, 'On Retribution', in *Philosophy* (Apr 1956) and by H. J. McCloskey 'The Complexity of the Concepts of Punishment', in *Philosophy* (*Oct* 1962).

UTILITARIANISM AND RETRIBUTION.
BENN, HART AND ARMSTRONG

The arguments of Flew and Quinton had pointed in the following direction. The distinction is drawn between particular acts of punishment on the one hand, and the institution of punishment on the other. To inflict pain on someone who had not committed an offence would not be punishment at all. For a pain or deprivation to constitute an act of punishment it must be inflicted on someone who has committed an offence. There is therefore no punishment without guilt. This is a verbal or logical point, but it meets the retributivist's demand that punishment requires pain to be inflicted for guilt. But what the retributivist is granted is not the moral justification of punishment he sought for, but rather a phantom definition that can only engender tautologies. The definition is: 'Punishment is pain or deprivation inflicted on an offender for his offence, i.e. upon a guilty man.' The tautology is: 'Punishment requires guilt and is inflicted in respect of it.' Mr S. I. Benn, in his article 'An Approach to the Problems of Punishment' (*Philosophy*, Oct 1958), pursues this idea, and tries to show that there is nothing more than this in the retributive justification of particular acts of punishment. He recognises that it would appear that the *amount* of punishment is proportioned to the 'seriousness' of the crime, but he argues that what constitutes 'seriousness' and the degrees of it, is itself determined on utilitarian, primarily deterrent, grounds. He recognises, however, that judges appear to use what discretion they are allowed by applying such moral criteria as degree of temptation, provocation and the like. But he argues that leniency in these circumstances is allowed only because it is not likely to reduce the general deterrent effect of the law. He argues too that blame plays in morality a similar role, that of 'a technique for discouraging undesirable conduct', to that which punishment plays in law, so that morality and law are not likely to conflict with one another very often.

Professor H. L. A. Hart goes over this ground too in his 'Prolegomenon to the Principles of Punishment' (*Proceedings of the Aristotelian Society*, 1959–60[11]). He here introduces some useful terminology. We need to consider, he suggests, three main topics,

[11] Reprinted in *Punishment and Responsibility* (Oxford, 1968).

viz. the definition of punishment, the general justifying aim of punishment, and the distribution of punishment. Distribution, in its turn, comprises (i) liability, that is, *who* should be punished, and (ii) amount, that is, *how much* punishment each should get. Now as to liability, Hart points out that it has been generally held that insane people, children, and people who have been coerced are not liable to be punished. To be liable to be punished an individual must have acted with *mens rea*, with what Blackstone called 'a vitious will'. Utilitarians have given a rather different account of this. They have argued that the reason why insane people and children are not liable to legal punishment is that the threat of punishment cannot influence them – Benn's 'technique for discouraging undesirable conduct' does not work on them – so that there is nothing to be gained by punishing them. Hart objects, however, that on strictly utilitarian grounds it could be argued that, although threats of punishment do not influence *insane* people, punishment actually carried out on them probably does influence *other* people, who might be deterred from crime thereby. It is possible, that is, that punishing insane people would have good consequences on the whole because of its effects on sane people. Hart considers, therefore, that it is 'a requirement of Justice', independent of utilitarian considerations, that men should not be punished for crimes they did not sanely and freely choose to commit. Justice requires, too, that 'like cases should be treated alike' and that punishments should be graded in severity in proportion to 'a commonsense scale of gravity'. This he calls 'retribution in distribution'. This last requirement he appears to accept not, at least not primarily, on grounds of justice, but because in departing from the commonsense scale in which severity is matched with gravity 'there is a risk of either confusing common morality or flouting it and bringing the law into contempt'.

RETRIBUTION DEFENDED. K. G. ARMSTRONG

Mr Armstrong's paper was written before Professor Hart's was published but in time for him to utilise and to comment upon some of Hart's terminology. Armstrong points out, for example, that while Hart's distinction between definition, general justifying aim, and distribution of punishment is incontestable, the phrase 'general justifying aim' is ambiguous, and might mean 'the actual aim or point of a practice' (for example, the aim or point of torture is to get information), or its moral justification. What is particularly interesting in Armstrong's paper – apart from his denial of real importance to the verbal points about definition made by Flew and Quinton – is the claim that the general justifying aim of punishment, in the sense of the moral justification of the practice, may be understood in retributive terms. This extends the retributive justification beyond the legal sphere in which Mabbott had placed it. According to Armstrong, the great merit of a retributive account of the general justifying aim is that it connects punishment with desert and hence with justice. What, he asks, would be a just deterrent, if it were not one that is retributively just? Furthermore he argues that the retributive justification of the practice connects punishment 'with the deep-seated general conviction we all have that to strike back and to strike first are two very different things, morally speaking, irrespective of the results they may produce or be intended to produce.'

The idea behind this suggestion that the practice or institution of punishment should receive its moral justification in terms of retribution must be that a reason for setting up or maintaining the institution of punishment, quite independent of its utility, is that it enables people to get their deserts and endeavours to contrive things so that aggressors are treated differently from non-aggressors. But this raises the question, which so exercised Hobbes, of how desert and aggression can be understood apart from some existing legal system. Can we conceive of desert and aggression except in terms of laws or rules broken or conformed to, and can we conceive of aggression apart from rights? If we can, perhaps we need the notion of natural law sporadically enforced, as Locke imagined, by victims and their friends. But I suggest that it is significant that in our moral language there are expressions that seem to be most at home in legal contexts. Even if we regard the language of conscience, with its verdicts, appeals and punishments, as untypical or unnecessary, it would be wrong to ignore the legal bearing of such words as 'rights', 'duties', and, indeed, of 'justice' itself. If the concepts and institutions of positive law have, so to say, flowed back into morality and renewed or impregnated it, a moral justification of an element or practice in positive law may not do very much to reinforce or justify it. This difficulty, it seems to me, is additional to the general difficulty of justifying a practice or institution, the difficulty that we must make a dogmatic stop somewhere or else go on *ad infinitum*. Deep-seated social institutions may be criticised as inconsistent or in terms of other institutions, and it may be noticed that they are in process of changing. But attempts to justify, or to abolish them in the light of such abstractions as Utility or Justice may be difficult only because they are futile.

THE SOCIAL CONTEXT OF PUNISHMENT.
JAMES F. DOYLE

We have seen that Baier brought out in some detail the place of punishment in the 'game' in which legislators, law-breakers, police, judges and prison officers all play their parts. Professor Doyle (Paper 10), developing this style of approach still further, goes on to show the place of the 'game' of punishment in the social order within which it is played. He considers what should be done to satisfy all the legitimate claims of all the parties involved, when a member of the community has deliberately broken the criminal law. The offender himself has a just claim to 'the preservation at all times of his worth and dignity as a person, whatever deprivation or coercion may be necessary'. The victims may justly claim that the offender should be apprehended, that they should be protected from him in the future, and that they should be recompensed for their loss. The State, as representing the community, can claim such powers and conditions as are necessary to save law-abiding people from being interfered with. When, however, the State endeavours to prevent crime, perhaps by means of deterrence, it should exercise its authority as far as possible with reason as well as with force, and see to it that the citizens understand and accept as just the laws they may be punished for breaking. It follows that the State should have authority to educate the people in its rules and to deliver public censure and reprobation of wrongs committed against the public.

We are not told precisely where in this scheme the institution of punishment is itself to be found. There is deterrence, but without naked terror; there is prevention, but by methods that are generally regarded as just; there is reform, but by way of expiation rather than by cure; there is education, both in knowledge of the laws themselves and in the need to recognise the rights of others; and there is public denunciation too. It will be remembered that, according to Bosanquet, deterrence and reform should not be considered in abstraction from retribution. Professor Doyle likewise endeavours to link together the various 'abstract' aims of punishment and to relate them to the rights and interests of all whose lives are regulated by law.[12]

III

So far we have been considering the views of philosophers who have taken punishment more or less as it is and have attempted to analyse and justify it. Bradley objected to Mill that he was really trying to alter punishment rather than to elucidate it, and many subsequent philosophers have followed Bradley in preferring acceptance and analysis to criticism. Yet even in the nineteenth century the institution of punishment itself had its critics, such as Fourier and Marx, and in the twentieth century, and especially during the last ten years, legislative and administrative changes have encouraged critics who wish to alter or to abolish it. Professor Hart called his Aristotelian address of 1959 a 'prolegomenon' because in it he did not discuss 'modern sceptical doubt about the whole institution of punishment'. It is no longer merely a question of what the punishment 'game' is, nor merely of how it fits in with the other games we play, but whether its rules should be drastically altered, or whether indeed we should cease to play it altogether.

SCIENTIFIC SENTENCING

In *Crime and the Criminal Law* (1963) Lady Wootton, disturbed by the way in which different courts impose very different

---

[12] It is interesting to compare Mr Nigel Walker's treatment of the philosophy of punishment in his *The Aims of a Penal System* (1966). He examines, one by one, the principal aims that have been suggested – protecting offenders, retribution (which he considers to be the same as atonement), denunciation and prevention – and gives reasons for rejecting them one by one until he is left with the prevention of crime by methods that are as humanitarian as possible. The inadequacy of this mode of argument is shown when he says that if denunciation were all that is required, then the denunciatory ritual could be completed without any need for a penalty – as if denunciation could stand alone. Perhaps denunciation is not just a means of giving people 'real satisfaction' (p. 27) like that which they may get, according to Mr Walker, from listening to a sermon in which they hear 'condemnations of conduct of which they already disapprove'. Perhaps, however, the denunciation of crime is a corollary of the loyalty that citizens give to their community and its laws.

sentences for the same sort of offence, and convinced that it is impossible to ascertain what is going on in the minds of accused men, proposes fairly radical changes in the punishment game. The prevalent view, among lawyers and laymen alike, is that before an accused person can justly be pronounced guilty he must have a guilty mind (*mens rea*), that is, he must have been a sane adult who had deliberately done what he was accused of doing and could have refrained from doing it. In some cases – increasing in number under modern circumstances and legislation – this requirement does not obtain. These are called cases of 'strict liability' or 'absolute liability'. It is no excuse for a man accused of driving while under the influence of drink to say that he did not know that the drink would affect him in this way. Nor is it an excuse for the manufacturer of adulterated food to say that he did not know that the food had been tampered with. Some writers have expressed alarm at this tendency,[13] but Lady Wootton welcomes it and would like to see it extended. She thinks that once a court has established that the accused committed the crime for which he was indicted, the question of what sentence should be imposed should be settled by another body composed of experts in criminal statistics (supported perhaps – Lady Wootton is not enthusiastic about them – by psychiatrists and psychologists). This body would impose treatment or punishment in accordance with the probable effect on the offender. She does not think that the deterrent effect on other people, even if there is one, can at present be ascertained. She thinks that as this modified or new sort of game comes to be played, the difference between punishment and treatment would get blurred. Both prisons and mental hospitals, she thinks, 'will be simply "places of safety" in which offenders receive the treatment which experience suggests is most likely to evoke the desired response' (p. 80). The distinction is already breaking down, as under present legislation there is now a 'genuinely hybrid institution' (p. 81), and the Home Secretary is entitled to 'treat as sick persons' people whom the courts 'have sentenced to imprisonment and presumably regard as wicked' (p. 82).

Now in 'The Responsibility of Criminals' (Paper 11 below) Professor Kneale, while sympathising with Lady Wootton's aims,

[13] J. Ll. J. Edwards, *Mens Rea in Statutory Offences* (1955), Lord Devlin, *Samples of Law Making* (1962), and Hart, *Punishment and Responsibility*, containing earlier papers.

wishes to retain the idea that punishment should be inflicted on those who deserve it. Like her, however, he does not think that the courts of law are fitted to establish whether or not anyone is fully responsible, and he therefore agrees that where there is any doubt it should be decided through her system of 'reform commissioners'.[14] It is not clear that Lady Wootton wishes to make *all* criminal liability strict. If she does, then, if an accused person is fit to plead, the court would only have to decide whether he did what he is accused of, and would not need to consider even whether he intended it or whether it was an accident. Kneale objects that this can and ought to be decided by a court of law, and that if it were left to some other body there would be grave danger of 'arbitrary interference', the very thing that courts of law are expected to protect people from.

DESERT AND RESPONSIBILITY

We saw above (pp. 21–2) when we discussed Mundle's view that *moral* desert is required if punishment is to be just, that a view which makes punishment a strictly legal concept has to give a legal account of desert. This may be attempted by saying, as Mabbott did, that the offender brings the punishment on himself by breaking the law. But since there are breaches of moral (or natural) law which bring no legal punishment, we can hardly, in those cases, speak of *deserving* punishment, for if there is no punishment for the act, the doer of it does not bring punishment on himself by doing it. Furthermore, is there anything *moral* in the desert that consists simply of having brought the penalty on oneself by one's illegal act ? Kneale attempts to deal with these difficulties. He accepts the view that the offender brings the punishment on himself, and he says that this is what desert is, but he introduces an indirect moral reference by saying that, for the punishment to be deserved, it must not only have been brought on the offender by his own free will but must have been imposed under a 'positive law that is just'. Thus, a man would not deserve to be punished if the law were iniquitous. (But suppose the law is only *rather* bad ?)

What are we to say then about non-punishable wrongs that are offences against moral and natural law? Those who commit them

[14] Professor Kneale's references are to a lecture to the Cambridge Institute of Criminology reported in *The Times*, 13 Feb 1960.

are, according to Kneale, liable to blame. Someone is justly blamed, he considers, if he 'did wrong in circumstances when he could have chosen to act otherwise'. Blame, therefore, is a matter of judgment and of truth, and is rightly imposed when those who blame are correct in thinking that the individual they are blaming did wrong and could have done right. It is one thing to blame, another thing to blame someone *to his face*, and another thing again to *publish* the blame generally. It can only be right to blame a man to his face if there is some prospect of his thereby being induced to rectify his own shortcomings and defects of character. A person who is able to be affected in this way when he is blamed to his face has what Kneale calls '*full* moral responsibility'. Someone with full moral responsibility can exercise 'self-censure' and is said to have a conscience and to be susceptible 'to influence by moral considerations'.

PROPOSED ALTERATIONS

The most drastic proposal – we need not ask whether it is precisely what Lady Wootton intended – would consist in this: the criminal law would not provide ranges of penalties for each specific crime, but would merely prohibit the crimes and say what sorts of punishment and what sorts of treatment offenders are liable to for committing any crime whatsoever, making no distinction between intentional and unintentional acts. Thus the 'reform commissioners' would have a completely free hand, and potential offenders would have only the vaguest idea of what they would be bringing on themselves by committing a crime. According to our present ideas this would be unjust, for it would mean that unintentional offenders would suffer the shame of conviction and only then be released. (Or perhaps they would have to have lessons in care and concentration.)

If intention is to be considered in the court, then the 'reform commissioners' would be left to 'sentence' psychotics, neurotics, psychopaths, and people with 'full moral responsibility' who had deliberately broken the law. But would it not be better, in view of the last three classes, to publish specific penalties in the criminal statutes? This might have some deterrent effect, and the last class of people might think they are entitled to have some idea of what is in store for them. We should then be left with the decisions: who are abnormal? who have full moral responsibility? Treatment (and perhaps some punishment) would follow for the former, and punishment for the latter. The distinction between treatment and punishment would thus be maintained, and 'hybrid institutions' would be unjust. If, however, there are to be no hybrid institutions, how should the penal institutions differ from the therapeutic? Should allowance be made in sentencing for the fact that 'normal' people censure themselves and suffer from remorse? These are matters that need elucidation and should not be left to be decided by so-called experts.

PUNISHMENT AND TREATMENT

Sir James Fitzjames Stephen[15] maintained that an important feature of punishment by the State is that it gives justified expression to hatred of the criminal. Potential criminals, he argued, contemplate punishment in an essentially different way from that in which they would contemplate unpleasantnesses that stem from natural causes. '... how many people,' he asks, 'would be deterred from stealing by the chance of catching a bad fever?' Deterrence and reprobation, like retribution, are conscious reactions to *deeds*, not natural consequences of *events*. In being 'taught a lesson', or even in being used as an example to deter others, a man is being faced by other men and is colliding with their wills on account of what he has *done* rather than because of something that has *happened* to him. Just because committing a crime does not seem to him at all like an illness, suffering a penalty does not seem at all like receiving treatment.[16] His rights are not violated when he suffers an illness, nor does his illness violate the rights of others – it is only he who can do that. Hence the very notion of a mental illness needs careful examination. In many contexts, no doubt, it is acceptable and necessary, but it may be extended in such a way as to threaten the distinction between deeds on the one hand and mere passivities on the other.[17]

---

[15] *History of the Criminal Law of England*, vol. II (1883), p. 81.

[16] It seems to me that Mr Mabbott was right to consider the criminal's view of punishment, and that Miss Glover was wrong to question the relevance of this.

[17] See Dr Vinit Haksar, 'The Responsibility of Psychopaths', in *The Philosophical Quarterly* (1965), and 'A Scientific Morality', in *Philosophy* (Jul 1967).

REPARATION RATHER THAN PUNISHMENT

Professor Del Vecchio's suggestion for the reform of the institution of punishment is very different from anything we have so far considered. He does not wish in any way to water down the notion of personal responsibility, but on the contrary he is anxious to strengthen the accountability of the criminal to his victim and to society. He does not think this can be done by punishment, for he is convinced that punishment does little to prevent crime, and that it even provides opportunities for criminals to learn from one another to commit crimes more effectively. Because the criminal has violated the rights of others, he should be required to pay compensation to his victims. Because he has violated the laws, he should be expected to pay compensation to the State that established them for the protection of individuals. But there is no reason why this should involve him in suffering nor why he should be incarcerated so as to make his family suffer for what he has done. Del Vecchio proposes, therefore, that the extent of the personal and public damage he has done should be assessed and be regarded as a debt that he must pay. He should be expected to pay this debt from the proceeds of his own work, and he would be left free as long as he continued to do this. Surveillance or loss of freedom would only be needed if he failed to work and pay according to his capacity.

There are serious practical difficulties in this idea. Many criminals are not good workers, and find it difficult to earn an ordinary wage, let alone a wage sufficient to leave a margin for compensation payments. Damages would generally have to be assessed in terms of the capacities of the offender rather than in terms of the harm to victims and society. Offenders who persistently refused to work or to make restitution would have to be dealt with, presumably by means of imprisonment. Although, therefore, the number of exercises of penal sanctions might be reduced, punishment could hardly be eliminated altogether. Nevertheless, the idea goes some way towards meeting the case of those who consider imprisonment to be ineffective and wasteful, without eroding conceptions of justice that are essential to civilised life. An offender might see more sense in being made to pay a proportion of his income as reparation to those he has injured, than in being forced to live among other offenders in conditions which make productive work difficult or impossible.

IV BLAMING

In considering the morality of punishment we have also had to examine such important associated concepts as desert and responsibility.[18] Closely associated, too, is the notion of blame, which Benn regarded as 'a technique for discouraging undesirable conduct'. Kneale, it will be remembered, considers that blame is a sort of knowledge, which may or may not be published. If someone blames without giving public expression to his blame, then he may not be discouraging the man he is blaming, who may have no idea that he is being blamed at all. It might be argued, nevertheless, that if someone does not want to be blamed even if the blame is not published, he would be discouraged from performing actions which he believes he would be blamed for performing. If people know that unpublished blaming goes on, their conduct is likely to be influenced by this knowledge. Utilitarians, however, have tended to think of blame, as Bentham did, as a sort of sanction, and so as a kind of punishment. J. S. Mill, for example, in chapter iv of *On Liberty* gives a series of reactions running from punishment by the State, through 'moral reprobation' and making the offender's life uncomfortable, to 'reproach' and 'standing aloof' from him. Mr Squires (Paper 13), like Kneale, regards blame as an opinion about someone's conduct that may be true or false, and as such it could only fit into Mill's sequence after the very last item, that of 'standing aloof'. Even if reproach and standing aloof can be regarded as techniques of discouragement or as sanctions, this hardly seems to be the central feature of unpublished blame, which is primarily a taking note of someone's failure, judging, as Squires puts it, 'that he is responsible for an undesirable upshot, that he has done what he ought not'. It would be possible, indeed, for someone to publish his blame without wanting or intending to discourage the blamed person, if blaming is merely correctly or incorrectly attributed. Even so, however, blaming, whether published or unpublished, does seem to go beyond mere judgment or statement, and to constitute *criticism*,[19] and criticism, even when directed on statements or theories, is an attempt to secure correction.

[18] There is a detailed discussion of responsibility in Hart's *Punishment and Responsibility*, ch. ix.

[19] Mr John Charvet in his interesting 'Criticism and Punishment', in *Mind* (Oct 1966) suggests that punishment is a sort of criticism. What-

We do sometimes say such things as that someone was or was not blameworthy, or deserved or did not deserve to be blamed.[20] On the Kneale-Squires view this would mean that someone who deserves to be blamed is someone who has done what he ought not to have done. To blame someone who did not deserve it would merely be to think or to say that he had done what he ought not to have done when in fact he had not so failed. Now if we adopt the view that to deserve punishment is to bring punishment upon oneself by breaking a positive law, then we may ask whether someone brings blame on himself when he acts as he ought not to have acted. If blame is a sort of criticism, does he bring the criticism on himself? It would seem that there is a big difference between bringing on oneself the published criticism of other people and bringing on oneself one's own criticism. Other people's criticisms, published or even unpublished, may act as a sort of sanction. But one may not know or care what view others will take of one's action, but one is seldom in doubt and can hardly not care about one's own attitude towards it. One may reject other people's criticism as unacceptable, but one's own criticism of oneself has to be ultimate. Self-blame and remorse appear to be the same, and to be a form of self-criticism. Published or unpublished blame by other people may act as a sanction, but self-blame or remorse is different in that the desire to avoid it presupposes that the individual accepts the rule that he blames himself for breaking.

MERCY

If punishment is dispensed by an authority, and is understood primarily in terms of punishment by the State, then retaliation[21] is not of its essence and forgiveness is not directly related to it, for just as it is the injured man who retaliates, so it is he, and not a judge, who forgives. What a judge can do is pardon or exercise mercy, but why should he give less than the punishment prescribed

---

ever the truth of this, blame, when applied to human conduct, is hardly separable from criticism. Perhaps it is no accident that punishment has been called 'correction' as in the phrase 'houses of correction'.

[20] See Dr L. Kenner's 'On Blaming', in *Mind* (Apr 1967), pp. 247–9.

[21] When Mr Armstrong says that 'to strike back and to strike first are two very different things' he appears to assume that retaliation is somehow related to retribution.

by law? Mrs Smart gives three answers. First, she says that justice requires sentences to be brought into closer correspondence with the details of each crime than strict adherence to the prescribed penalties can secure. She says that this, however, is justice rather than mercy. Second, the judge should concern himself with any unfortunate effects the prescribed sentence might have on innocent people such as the children of the offender. Third, she thinks that when the offender is only discovered long after the crime was committed, and has lived an inoffensive and useful life in the meantime, it would be wrong to exact the full penalty. One reason why it would be wrong is that over a long period of time the offender may have become a very different person, so that punishing him would not be punishing the original offender.

Exercising mercy, therefore, is not being jolly or easy-going, but rather attending to all the morally relevant circumstances of the offence and not exclusively to what is in the lawbook. As a member of what we may call the Melbourne Retributive School (Professor McCloskey and Mr Armstrong are other members of it) Mrs Smart argues that the rightness of being merciful is explicable on retributive principles but not on utilitarian grounds. Mercy requires one principle (e.g. upholding the law) to give way before another (say, support for the innocent relations of the offender). But the Utilitarian has only one principle, that of maximising good, and a utilitarian judge could never think it right to be merciful when this was not the way to maximise the good. Whether a rule-Utilitarian would fare better than an act-Utilitarian in justifying mercy she does not say.

V

We have had to pick our way through a rather complex set of arguments. At the beginning there was Mabbott's defence of retribution as essential in the punishment of individuals, and of rule-Utilitarianism in the justification of the institution of punishment. Some critics in the early fifties, impressed by the distinction between logical and ethical justification, thought they could take the heat and importance out of retribution by making guilt part of the meaning or definition of punishment. But it became clear that there are difficulties in the way of regarding the varying severity of punishments as means of deterrence or reform as utilitarians require.

Then the Wittgensteinian idea of exploring the rules of a 'language-game' was applied to punishment, and later punishment itself was looked at in the light of other social activities. Wittgenstein's influence was not as hostile to retribution as logical positivism had been. Within the still more recent view of philosophy as an exploration of concepts, such adjacent notions as blame and mercy have been distinguished and analysed. Although administrators and practical reformers are much opposed to retribution – which, however, they do not always distinguish from either retaliation or revenge – there is more support for it in the philosophical literature, especially when it is pointed out that retribution does not necessarily involve pain though it does and must involve dissatisfaction.

However hard philosophers may try, they cannot wholly withdraw the question of punishment from its connections with practical reform. Thus the modern tendency to substitute therapy for punishment and to push this process forward as far as possible has been vigilantly and somewhat apprehensively scrutinised by Professor Hart, and Professor Kneale has tried to show how far the process should go and how responsibility should be defined. Professor Del Vecchio has given some moral arguments for replacing punishment by reparation. I have suggested, however, that when, as seems inevitable, some offenders refuse to make the reparation that they owe, punishment cannot be avoided and hence appears to be inseparable from the very continuance of the State.

2 ⚜ *Punishment*

J. D. MABBOTT

I propose in this paper to defend a retributive theory of punishment and to reject absolutely all utilitarian considerations from its justification. I feel sure that this enterprise must arouse deep suspicion and hostility both among philosophers (who must have felt that the retributive view is the only moral theory except perhaps psychological hedonism which has been definitely destroyed by criticism) and among practical men (who have welcomed its steady decline in our penal practice).

The question I am asking is this. Under what circumstances is the punishment of some particular person justified and why? The theories of reform and deterrence which are usually considered to be the only alternatives to retribution involve well-known difficulties. These are considered fully and fairly in Dr Ewing's book, *The Morality of Punishment* (1929), and I need not spend long over them. The central difficulty is that both would on occasion justify the punishment of an innocent man, the deterrent theory if he were believed to have been guilty by those likely to commit the crime in future, and the reformatory theory if he were a bad man though not a criminal. To this may be added the point against the deterrent theory that it is the threat of punishment and not punishment itself which deters, and that when deterrence seems to depend on actual punishment, to implement the threat, it really depends on publication and may be achieved if men believe that punishment has occurred even if in fact it has not. As Bentham saw, for a utilitarian apparent justice is everything, real justice is irrelevant.

Dr Ewing and other moralists would be inclined to compromise with retribution in the face of the above difficulties. They would admit that one fact and one fact only can justify the punishment of this man, and that is a *past* fact, that he has committed a crime. To this extent reform and deterrence theories, which look only to the consequences, are wrong. But they would add that retribution can determine only *that* a man should be punished. It cannot determine ow or how much, and here reform and deterrence may come in. Even Bradley, the fiercest retributionist of modern times, says 'Having once the right to punish we may modify the punishment according to the useful and the pleasant, but these are external to the matter; they cannot give us a right to punish and nothing can do that but criminal desert.' Dr Ewing would maintain that the whole estimate of the amount and nature of a punishment may be effected by considerations of reform and deterrence. It seems to me that this is a surrender which the upholders of retribution dare not make. As I said above, it is publicity and not punishment which deters, and the publicity though often spoken of as 'part of a man's punishment' is no more part of it than his arrest or his detention prior to trial, though both these may be also unpleasant and bring him into disrepute. A judge sentences a man to three years' imprisonment not to three years *plus* three columns in the press. Similarly with reform. The visit of the prison chaplain is not part of a man's punishment nor is the visit of Miss Fields or Mickey Mouse.

The truth is that while punishing a man and punishing him justly, it is possible to deter others, and also to attempt to reform him, and if these additional goods are achieved the total state of affairs is better than it would be with the just punishment alone. But reform and deterrence are not modifications of the punishment, still less reasons for it. A parallel may be found in the case of tact and truth. If you have to tell a friend an unpleasant truth you may do all you can to put him at his ease and spare his feelings as much as possible, while still making sure that he understands your meaning. In such a case no one would say that your offer of a cigarette beforehand or your apology afterwards are modifications of the truth, still less reasons for telling it. You do not tell the truth in order to spare his feelings, but having to tell the truth you also spare his feelings. So Bradley was right when he said that reform and deterrence were 'external to the matter', but therefore wrong when he said that they may 'modify the punishment'. Reporters are admitted to our trials so that punishments may become public and help to deter others. But the punishment would be no less just were reporters excluded and deterrence not achieved. Prison authorities may make it possible that a convict may become physically or morally better. They cannot ensure either result; and the punishment would still be just if the criminal took no advantage of their arrangements and their efforts failed. Some moralists see this and exclude these 'extra' arrangements for deterrence and reform. They say that it must be the punishment *itself* which reforms and deters. But it is just my point that the punishment *itself* seldom reforms the criminal and never deters others. It is only 'extra' arrangements which have any chance of achieving either result. As this is the central point of my paper, at the cost of laboured repetition I would ask the upholders of reform and deterrence two questions. Suppose it could be shown that a particular criminal had not been improved by a punishment and also that no other would-be criminal had been deterred by it, would that prove that the punishment was unjust? Suppose it were discovered that a particular criminal had lived a much better life after his release and that many would-be criminals believing him to have been guilty were influenced by his fate, but yet that the 'criminal' was punished for something he had never done, would these excellent results prove the punishment just?

It will be observed that I have throughout treated punishment as a purely legal matter. A 'criminal' means a man who has broken a law, not a bad man; an 'innocent' man is a man who has not broken the law in connection with which he is being punished, though he may be a bad man and have broken other laws. Here I dissent from most upholders of the retributive theory – from Hegel, from Bradley, and from Dr Ross. They maintain that the essential connection is one between punishment and moral or social wrong-doing.

My fundamental difficulty with their theory is the question of *status*. It takes two to make a punishment, and for a moral or social wrong I can find no punisher. We may be tempted to say when we hear of some brutal action 'that ought to be punished'; but I cannot see how there can be duties which are nobody's duties. If I see a man ill-treating a horse in a country where cruelty to animals is not a legal offence, and I say to him 'I shall now punish you', he will reply, rightly, 'What has it to do with you? Who made you a judge and a ruler over me?' I may have a duty to try to stop him and one way of stopping him may be to hit him, but another way may be to buy the horse. Neither the blow nor the price is a punishment. For a moral offence, God alone has the *status* necessary to punish the offender; and the theologians are becoming more and more doubtful whether even God has a duty to punish wrong-doing.

Dr Ross would hold that not all wrong-doing is punishable, but only invasion of the rights of others; and in such a case it might be thought that the injured party had a right to punish. His right, however, is rather a right to reparation, and should not be confused with punishment proper.

This connection, on which I insist, between punishment and crime, not between punishment and moral or social wrong, alone accounts for some of our beliefs about punishment, and also meets many objections to the retributive theory as stated in its ordinary form. The first point on which it helps us is with regard to retrospective legislation. Our objection to this practice is unaccountable on reform and deterrence theories. For a man who commits a wrong before the date on which a law against it is passed, is as much in need of reform as a man who commits it afterwards; nor is deterrence likely to suffer because of additional punishments for the same offence. But the orthodox retributive theory is equally at a loss here, for if punishment is given for moral wrong-doing or for invasion of the rights of others, that immorality or invasion existed as certainly before the passing of the law as after it.

My theory also explains, where it seems to me all others do not, the case of punishment imposed by an authority who believes the law in question is a bad law. I was myself for some time disciplinary officer of a college whose rules included a rule compelling attendance at chapel. Many of those who broke this rule broke it on principle. I punished them. I certainly did not want to reform them; I respected their characters and their views. I certainly did not want to drive others into chapel through fear of penalties. Nor did I think there had been a wrong done which merited retribution. I wished I could have believed that I would have done the same myself. My position was clear. They had broken a rule; they knew it and I knew it. Nothing more was necessary to make punishment proper.

I know that the usual answer to this is that the judge enforces a bad law because otherwise law in general would suffer and good laws would be broken. The effect of punishing good men for breaking bad laws is that fewer bad men break good laws.

[*Excursus on Indirect Utilitarianism.* The above argument is a particular instance of a general utilitarian solution of all similar problems. When I am in funds and consider whether I should pay my debts or give the same amount to charity, I must choose the former because repayment not only benefits my creditor (for the benefit to him might be less than the good done through charity) but also upholds the general credit system. I tell the truth when a lie might do more good to the parties directly concerned, because I thus increase general trust and confidence. I keep a promise when it might do more immediate good to break it, because indirectly I bring it about that promises will be more readily made in future and this will outweigh the immediate loss involved. Dr Ross has pointed out that the effect on the credit system of my refusal to pay a debt is greatly exaggerated. But I have a more serious objection of principle. It is that in all these cases the indirect effects do not result from my wrong action – my lie or defalcation or bad faith – but from the publication of these actions. If in any instance the breaking of the rule were to remain unknown then I could consider only the direct or immediate consequences. Thus in my 'compulsory chapel' case I could have considered which of my culprits were law-abiding men generally and unlikely to break any other college rule. Then I could have sent for each of these separately and said 'I shall let you off if you will tell no one I have done so.' By these means the general keeping of rules would not have suffered. Would this course have been correct? It must be remembered that the proceedings need not deceive everybody. So long as they deceive would-be law-breakers the good is achieved.

As this point is of crucial importance and as it has an interest beyond the immediate issue, and gives a clue to what I regard as the true general nature of law and punishment, I may be excused for expanding and illustrating it by an example or two from other fields. Dr Ross says that two men dying on a desert island would have duties to keep promises to each other even though their breaking them would not affect the future general confidence in promises at all. Here is certainly the same point. But as I find that desert-island morality always rouses suspicion among ordinary men I should like to quote two instances from my own experience which also illustrate the problem.

(i) A man alone with his father at his death promises him a private and quiet funeral. He finds later that both directly and indirectly the keeping of this promise will cause pain and misunderstanding. He can see no particular positive good that the quiet funeral will achieve. No one yet knows that he has made the promise nor need anyone ever know. Should he therefore act as though it had never been made?

(ii) A college has a fund given to it for the encouragement of a subject which is now expiring. Other expanding subjects are in great need of endowment. Should the authorities divert the money? Those who oppose the diversion have previously stood on the past, the promise. But one day one of them discovers the 'real reason' for this slavery to a dead donor. He says 'We must consider not only the value of this money for these purposes, since on all direct consequences it should be diverted at once. We must remember the effect of this diversion on the general system of benefactions: We know that benefactors like to endow special objects, and this act of ours would discourage such benefactors in future and leave learning worse off.' Here again is the indirect utilitarian reason for choosing the alternative which direct utilitarianism would reject. But the immediate answer to this from the most ingenious member of the opposition was crushing and final. He said, 'Divert the money but keep it dark.' This is obviously correct. It is not the act of diversion which would diminish the stream of benefactions but the news of it reaching the ears of benefactors. Provided that no possible benefactor got to hear of it no indirect loss would result. But the justification of our action would depend entirely on the success of the measures for 'keeping it dark'. I remember how I felt and how others felt that whatever answer was right this result was certainly wrong. But it follows that indirect utilitarianism is wrong in all such cases. For its argument can always be met by 'Keep it dark'.]

The view, then, that a judge upholds a bad law in order that law in general should not suffer is indefensible. He upholds it simply because he has no right to dispense from punishment.

The connection of punishment with law-breaking and not with wrong-doing also escapes moral objections to the retributive theory as held by Kant and Hegel or by Bradley and Ross. It is asked how we can measure moral wrong or balance it with pain, and how pain can wipe out moral wrong. Retributivists have been pushed into holding that pain *ipso facto* represses the worse self and frees the better, when this is contrary to the vast majority of observed cases. But if punishment is not intended to measure or balance or negate moral wrong then all this is beside the mark. There is the further difficulty of reconciling punishment with repentance and with forgiveness. Repentance is the reaction morally appropriate to moral wrong and punishment added to remorse is an unnecessary evil. But if punishment is associated with law-breaking and not with moral evil the punisher is not entitled to consider whether the criminal is penitent any more than he may consider whether the law is good. So, too, with forgiveness. Forgiveness is not appropriate to law-breaking. (It is noteworthy that when, in divorce cases, the law has to recognise forgiveness it calls it 'condonation', which is symptomatic of the difference of attitude.) Nor is forgiveness appropriate to moral evil. It is appropriate to personal injury. No one has any right to forgive me except the person I have injured. No judge or jury can do so. But the person I have injured has no right to punish me. Therefore there is no clash between punishment and forgiveness since these two duties do not fall on the same person nor in connection with the same characteristic of my act. (It is the weakness of vendetta that it tends to confuse this clear line, though even there it is only by personifying the family that the injured party and the avenger are identified. Similarly we must guard against the plausible fallacy of personifying society and regarding the criminal as 'injuring society', for then once more the old dilemma about forgiveness would be insoluble.) A clergyman friend of mine catching a burglar red-handed was puzzled about his duty. In the end he ensured the man's punishment by information and evidence, and at the same time showed his own forgiveness by visiting the man in prison and employing him when he came out. I believe any 'good Christian' would accept this as representing his duty. But obviously if the punishment is thought of as imposed *by* the victim or *for* the injury or immorality then the contradiction with forgiveness is hopeless.

So far as the question of the actual punishment of any individual is concerned this paper could stop here. No punishment is morally retributive or reformative or deterrent. Any criminal punished for any one of these reasons is certainly unjustly punished. The only justification for punishing any man is that he has broken a law.

In a book which has already left its mark on prison administration I have found a criminal himself confirming these views. *Walls Have Mouths*, by W. F. R. Macartney, is prefaced, and provided with appendices to each chapter, by Compton Mackenzie. It is interesting to notice how the novelist maintains that the proper object of penal servitude should be reformation,[1] whereas the prisoner himself accepts the view I have set out above. Macartney says 'To punish a man is to treat him as an equal. To be punished

[1] p. 97.

for an offence against rules is a sane man's right.'[2] It is striking
also that he never uses 'injustice' to describe the brutality or provocation which he experienced. He makes it clear that there were
only two types of prisoner who were *unjustly* imprisoned, those
who were insane and not responsible for the acts for which they
were punished[3] and those who were innocent and had broken no
law.[4] It is irrelevant, as he rightly observes, that some of these innocent men were, like Steinie Morrison, dangerous and violent characters, who on utilitarian grounds might well have been restrained.
That made their punishment no whit less unjust.[5] To these general
types may be added two specific instances of injustice. First, the
sentences on the Dartmoor mutineers. 'The Penal Servitude Act . . .
lays down specific punishments for mutiny and incitement to
mutiny, which include flogging. . . . Yet on the occasion of the only
big mutiny in an English prison, men are not dealt with by the Act
specially passed to meet mutiny in prison, but are taken out of gaol
and tried under an Act expressly passed to curb and curtail the
Chartists – a revolutionary movement.'[6] Here again the injustice
does not lie in the actual effect the sentences are likely to have on
the prisoners (though Macartney has some searching suggestions
about that also) but in condemning men for breaking a law they
did not break and not for breaking the law they did break. The
second specific instance is that of Coulton, who served his twenty
years and then was brought back to prison to do another eight years
and to die. This is due to the 'unjust order that no lifer shall be
released unless he has either relations or a job to whom he can go:
and it is actually suggested that this is really for the lifer's own
good. Just fancy, you admit that the man in doing years upon years
in prison had expiated his crime: but, instead of releasing him, you
keep him a further time – perhaps another three years – because
you say he has nowhere to go. Better a ditch and hedge than prison!
True, there are abnormal cases who want to stay in prison; but
Lawrence wanted to be a private soldier, and men go into monas-
teries. Because occasionally a man wants to stay in prison, must
every lifer who has lost his family during his sentence (I was doing
only ten years and I lost all my family) be kept indefinitely in gaol
after he has paid his debt?'[7] Why is it unjust? Because he has paid
his debt. When that is over it is for the man himself to decide what

[2] p. 165. My italics.   [3] pp. 165–6.   [4] p. 298.
[5] p. 301.   [6] p. 255.   [7] p. 400.

is for his own good. Once again the reform and utilitarian arguments are summarily swept aside. Injustice lies not in bad treatment or treatment which is not in the man's own interest, but in restriction which, according to the law, he has not merited.

It is true that Macartney writes, in one place, a paragraph of general reflection on punishment in which he confuses, as does Compton Mackenzie, retribution with revenge and in which he seems to hold that the retributive theory has some peculiar connection with private property. 'Indeed it is difficult to see how, in society as it is today constituted, a humane prison system could function. All property is sacred, although the proceeds of property may well be reprehensible, therefore any offence against property is sacrilege and must be punished. Till a system eventuates which is based not on exploitation of man by man and class by class, prisons must be dreadful places, but at least there might be an effort to ameliorate the more savage side of the retaliation, and this could be done very easily.'[8] The alternative system of which no doubt he is thinking is the Russian system described in his quotations from *A Physician's Tour in Soviet Russia*, by Sir James Purves-Stewart, the system of 'correctional colonies' providing curative 'treatment' for the different types of criminal.[9] There are two confusions here, to one of which we shall return later. First, Macartney confuses the retributive system with the punishment of one particular type of crime, offences against property, when he must have known that the majority of offenders against property do not find themselves in Dartmoor or even in Wandsworth. After all, his own offence was not one against property – it was traffic with a foreign Power – and it was one for which in the classless society of Russia the punishment is death. It is surely clear that a retributive system may be adopted for any class of crime. Secondly, Macartney confuses injustice within a penal system with the wrongfulness of a penal system. When he pleads for 'humane prisons' as if the essence of the prison should be humanity, or when Compton Mackenzie says the object of penal servitude should be reform, both of them are giving up punishment altogether, not altering it. A Russian 'correctional colony', if its real object is curative treatment, is no more a 'prison' than is an isolation hospital or a lunatic asylum. To this distinction between abolishing injustice in punishment and abolishing punishment altogether we must now turn.

[8] pp. 166, 167.   [9] p. 229.

It will be objected that my original question 'Why ought X to be punished?' is an illegitimate isolation of the issue. I have treated the whole set of circumstances as determined. X is a citizen of a State. About his citizenship, whether willing or unwilling, I have asked no questions. About the Government, whether it is good or bad, I do not enquire. X has broken a law. Concerning the law, whether it is well devised or not, I have not asked. Yet all these questions are surely relevant before it can be decided whether a particular punishment is just. It is the essence of my position that none of these questions is relevant. Punishment is a corollary of law-breaking by a member of the society whose law is broken. This is a static and an abstract view but I see no escape from it. Considerations of utility come in on two quite different issues. Should there be laws, and what laws should there be? As a legislator I may ask what general types of action would benefit the community, and, among these, which can be 'standardised' without loss, or should be standardised to achieve their full value. This, however, is not the primary question since particular laws may be altered or repealed. The choice which is the essential *prius* of punishment is the choice that there should be laws. This choice is not Hobson's. Other methods may be considered. A government might attempt to standardise certain modes of action by means of advice. It might proclaim its view and say 'Citizens are requested' to follow this or that procedure. Or again it might decide to deal with each case as it arose in the manner most effective for the common welfare. Anarchists have wavered between these two alternatives and a third – that of doing nothing to enforce a standard of behaviour but merely giving arbitrational decisions between conflicting parties, decisions binding only by consent.

I think it can be seen without detailed examination of particular laws that the method of law-making has its own advantages. Its orders are explicit and general. It makes behaviour reliable and predictable. Its threat of punishment may be so effective as to make punishment unnecessary. It promises to the good citizen a certain security in his life. When I have talked to business men about some inequity in the law of liability they have usually said 'Better a bad law than no law, for then we know where we are.'

Someone may say I am drawing an impossible line. I deny that punishment is utilitarian; yet now I say that punishment is a corollary of law and we decide whether to have laws and which laws to have on utilitarian grounds. And surely it is only this corollary which distinguishes law from good advice or exhortation. This is a misunderstanding. Punishment is a corollary not of law but of law-breaking. Legislators do not *choose* to punish. They hope no punishment will be needed. Their laws would succeed even if no punishment occurred. The criminal makes the essential choice; he 'brings it on himself'. Other men obey the law because they see its order is reasonable, because of inertia, because of fear. In this whole area, and it may be the major part of the State, law achieves its ends without punishment. Clearly, then, punishment is not a corollary of law.

We may return for a moment to the question of amount and nature of punishment. It may be thought that this also is automatic. The law will include its own penalties and the judge will have no option. This, however, is again an initial choice of principle. If the laws do include their own penalties then the judge has no option. But the legislature might adopt a system which left complete or partial freedom to the judge, as we do except in the case of murder. Once again, what are the merits (regardless of particular laws, still more of particular cases) of fixed penalties and variable penalties? At first sight it would seem that all the advantages are with the variable penalties; for men who have broken the same law differ widely in degree of wickedness and responsibility. When, however, we remember that punishment is not an attempt to balance moral guilt this advantage is diminished. But there are still degrees of responsibility; I do not mean degrees of freedom of will but, for instance, degrees of complicity in a crime. The danger of allowing complete freedom to the judicature in fixing penalties is not merely that it lays too heavy a tax on human nature but that it would lead to the judge expressing in his penalty the degree of his own moral aversion to the crime. Or he might tend on deterrent grounds to punish more heavily a crime which was spreading and for which temptation and opportunity were frequent. Or again on deterrent grounds he might 'make examples' by punishing ten times as heavily those criminals who are detected in cases in which nine out of ten evade detection. Yet we should revolt from all such punish-ments if they involved punishing theft more heavily than blackmail or negligence more heavily than premeditated assault. The death penalty for sheep-stealing might have been defended on such deter-rent grounds. But we should dislike equating sheep-stealing with

murder. Fixed penalties enable us to draw these distinctions between crimes. It is not that we can say how much imprisonment is
right for a sheep-stealer. But we can grade crimes in a rough scale
and penalties in a rough scale, and keep our heaviest penalties for
what are socially the most serious wrongs regardless of whether
these penalties will reform the criminal or whether they are exactly
what deterrence would require. The compromise of laying down
maximum penalties and allowing judges freedom below these limits
allows for the arguments on both sides.

To return to the main issue, the position I am defending is that it
is essential to a legal system that the infliction of a particular punishment should *not* be determined by the good *that particular punishment* will do either to the criminal or to 'society'. In exactly the
same way it is essential to a credit system that the repayment of a
particular debt should not be determined by the good that particular
payment will do. One may consider the merits of a legal system or
of a credit system, but the acceptance of either involves the surrender
of utilitarian considerations in particular cases as they arise. This is
in effect admitted by Ewing in one place where he says 'It is the
penal system as a whole which deters and not the punishment of
any individual offender.'[10]

To show that the choice between a legal system and its alternatives is one we do and must make, I may quote an early work of
Lenin in which he was defending the Marxist tenet that the state is
bound to 'wither away' with the establishment of a classless society.
He considers the possible objection that some wrongs by man against
man are not economic and therefore that the abolition of classes
would not *ipso facto* eliminate crime. But he sticks to the thesis that
these surviving crimes should not be dealt with by law and judicature. 'We are not Utopians and do not in the least deny the possibility and inevitability of excesses by *individual persons*, and
equally the need to suppress such excesses. But for this no special
machine, no special instrument of repression is needed. This will be
done by the armed nation itself as simply and as readily as any
crowd of civilized people even in modern society parts a pair of
combatants or does not allow a woman to be outraged.'[11] This
alternative to law and punishment has obvious demerits. Any injury
not committed in the presence of the crowd, any wrong which

[10] *The Morality of Punishment*, p. 66.
[11] *The State and Revolution* (Eng. trans., 1933) p. 93. Original italics.

required skill to detect or pertinacity to bring home would go untouched. The lynching mob, which is Lenin's instrument of justice, is liable to error and easily deflected from its purpose or driven to extremes. It must be a mob, for there is to be no 'machine'. I do not say that no alternative machine to ours could be devised but it does seem certain that the absence of all 'machines' would be intolerable. An alternative machine might be based on the view that 'society' is responsible for all criminality, and a curative and protective system developed. This is the system of Butler's 'Erewhon' and something like it seems to be growing up in Russia except for cases of 'sedition'.

We choose, then, or we acquiesce in and adopt the choice of others of, a legal system as one of our instruments for the establishment of the conditions of a good life. This choice is logically prior to and independent of the actual punishment of any particular persons or the passing of any particular laws. The legislators choose particular laws within the framework of this predetermined system. Once again a small society may illustrate the reality of these choices and the distinction between them. A Headmaster launching a new school must explicitly make both decisions. First, shall he have any rules at all? Second, what rules shall he have? The first decision is a genuine one and one of great importance. Would it not be better to have an 'honour' system, by which public opinion in each house or form dealt with any offence? (This is the Lenin method.) Or would complete freedom be better? Or should he issue appeals and advice? Or should he personally deal with each malefactor individually, as the case arises, in the way most likely to improve his conduct? I can well imagine an idealistic Headmaster attempting to run a school with one of these methods or with a combination of several of them and therefore without punishment. I can even imagine that with a small school of, say, twenty pupils all open to direct personal psychological pressure from authority and from each other, these methods involving no 'rules' would work. The pupils would of course grow up without two very useful habits, the habit of having some regular habits and the habit of obeying rules. But I suspect that most Headmasters, especially those of large schools, would either decide at once, or quickly be driven, to realize that some rules were necessary. This decision would be 'utilitarian' in the sense that it would be determined by consideration of consequences. The question 'what rules?' would then arise and again the issue is utilitarian. What action must be regularised for the school to work efficiently? The hours of arrival and departure, for instance, in a day school. But the one choice which is now no longer open to the Headmaster is whether he shall punish those who break the rules. For if he were to try to avoid this he would in fact simply be returning to the discarded method of appeals and good advice. Yet the Headmaster does not decide to punish. The pupils make the decision there. He decides actually to have rules and to threaten, but only hypothetically, to punish. The one essential condition which makes actual punishment just is a condition he *cannot* fulfil – namely that a rule should be broken.

I shall add a final word of consolation to the practical reformer. Nothing that I have said is meant to counter any movement for 'penal reform' but only to insist that none of these reforms have anything to do with punishment. The only type of reformer who can claim to be reforming the system of punishment is a follower of Lenin or of Samuel Butler who is genuinely attacking the *system* and who believes there should be no laws and no punishments. But our great British reformers have been concerned not with punishment but with its accessories. When a man is sentenced to imprisonment he is not sentenced also to partial starvation, to physical brutality, to pneumonia from damp cells and so on. And any movement which makes his food sufficient to sustain health, which counters the permanent tendency to brutality on the part of his warders, which gives him a dry or even a light and well-aired cell, is pure gain and does not touch the theory of punishment. Reformatory influences and prisoners' aid arrangements are also entirely unaffected by what I have said. I believe myself that it would be best if all such arrangements were made optional for the prisoner, so as to leave him in these cases a freedom of choice which would make it clear that they are not part of his punishment. If it is said that every such reform lessens a man's punishment, I think that is simply muddled thinking which, if it were clear, would be mere brutality. For instance, a prisoners' aid society is said to lighten his punishment, because otherwise he would suffer not merely imprisonment but also unemployment on release. But he was sentenced to imprisonment, not imprisonment *plus* unemployment. If I promise to help a friend and through special circumstances I find that keeping my promise will involve upsetting my day's work, I do not say that I really promised to help him and to ruin my day's work. And if another friend carries on my work for me I do not regard him as carrying out part of my promise, nor as stopping me from carrying it out myself. He merely removes an indirect and regrettable consequence of my keeping my promise. So with punishment. The Prisoners' Aid Society does not alter a man's punishment nor diminish it, but merely removes an indirect and regrettable consequence of it. And anyone who thinks that a criminal cannot make this distinction and will regard all the inconvenience that comes to him as punishment, need only talk to a prisoner or two to find how sharply they resent these wanton additions to a punishment which by itself they will accept as just. Macartney's chapter on 'Food' in the book quoted above is a good illustration of this point, as are also his comments on Clayton's administration. 'To keep a man in prison for many years at considerable expense and then to free him charged to the eyes with uncontrollable venom and hatred generated by the treatment he has received in gaol, does not appear to be sensible.' Clayton 'endeavoured to send a man out of prison in a reasonable state of mind. "Well, I've done my time. They were not too bad to me. Prison is prison and not a bed of roses. Still they didn't rub it in. . . ".[12] This 'reasonable state of mind' is one in which a prisoner on release feels he has been punished but not *additionally* insulted or ill-treated. I feel convinced that penal reformers would meet with even more support if they were clear that they were *not* attempting to alter the system of punishment but to give its victims 'fair play'. We have no more right to starve a convict than to starve an animal. We have no more right to keep a convict in a Dartmoor cell 'down which the water trickles night and day'[13] than we have to keep a child in such a place. If our reformers really want to alter the system of punishment, let them come out clearly with their alternative and preach, for instance, that no human being is responsible for any wrongdoing, that all the blame is on society, that curative or protective measures should be adopted, forcibly if necessary, as they are with infection or insanity. Short of this let them admit that the essence of prison is deprivation of liberty for the breaking of law, and that deprivation of food or of health or of books is unjust. And if our sentimentalists cry 'coddling of prisoners', let us ask them also to come out clearly into the open and incorporate whatever starvation and disease and brutality they think necessary *into the sentences*

[12] p. 152. [13] Op. cit., p. 258.

they propose.[14] If it is said that some prisoners will prefer such reformed prisons, with adequate food and aired cells, to the outer world, we may retort that their numbers are probably not greater than those of the masochists who like to be flogged. Yet we do not hear the same 'coddling' critics suggest abolition of the lash on the grounds that some criminals may like it. Even if the abolition from our prisons of all maltreatment other than that imposed by law results in a few down-and-outs breaking a window (as O. Henry's hero did) to get a night's lodging, the country will lose less than she does by her present method of sending out her discharged convicts 'charged with venom and hatred' because of the additional and unconvenanted 'rubbing it in' which they have received.

I hope I have established both the theoretical importance and the practical value of distinguishing between penal reform as we know and approve it – that reform which alters the accompaniments of punishment without touching its essence – and those attacks on punishment itself which are made not only by reformers who regard criminals as irresponsible and in need of treatment, but also by every judge who announces that he is punishing a man to deter others or to protect society, and by every juryman who is moved to his decision by the moral baseness of the accused rather than by his legal guilt.

[14] 'One of the minor curiosities of jail life was that they quickly provided you with a hundred worries which left you no time or energy for worrying about your sentence, long or short. . . . Rather as if you were thrown into a fire with spikes in it, and the spikes hurt you so badly that you forget about the fire. But then your punishment would *be* the spikes not the fire. Why did they pretend it was only the fire, when they knew very well about the spikes?' (From *Lifer*, by Jim Phelan, 1938, p. 40.)

3 ᠭ *On Punishment*

ANTHONY M. QUINTON

I INTRODUCTORY

There is a prevailing antinomy about the philosophical justification of punishment. The two great theories – retributive and utilitarian – seem, and at least are understood by their defenders, to stand in open and flagrant contradiction. Both sides have arguments at their disposal to demonstrate the atrocious consequences of the rival theory. Retributivists, who seem to hold that there are circumstances in which the infliction of suffering is a good thing in itself, are charged by their opponents with vindictive barbarousness. Utilitarians, who seem to hold that punishment is always and only justified by the good consequences it produces, are accused of vicious opportunism. Where the former insists on suffering for suffering's sake, the latter permits the punishment of the innocent. Yet, if the hope of justifying punishment is not to be abandoned altogether, one of these apparently unsavoury alternatives must be embraced. For they exhaust the possibilities. Either punishment must be self-justifying, as the retributivists claim, or it must depend for its justification on something other than itself, the general formula of 'utilitarianism' in the wide sense appropriate here.

In this paper I shall argue that the antinomy can be resolved, since retributivism, properly understood, is not a moral but a logical doctrine, and that it does not provide a moral justification of the infliction of punishment but an elucidation of the use of the word. Utilitarianism, on the other hand, embraces a number of possible moral attitudes towards punishment, none of which necessarily involves the objectionable consequences commonly adduced by retributivists, provided that the word 'punishment' is understood in the way that the essential retributivist thesis lays down. The antinomy arises from a confusion of modalities, of logical and moral necessity and possibility, of 'must' and 'can' with 'ought' and 'may'. In brief, the two theories answer different questions: retributivism the question 'when (logically) *can* we punish?', utilitarianism the question 'when (morally) *may* we or *ought* we to punish?' I shall also describe circumstances in which there is an answer to the question 'when (logically) *must* we punish?' Finally, I shall attempt to account for this difference in terms of a distinction between the establishment of rules whose infringement involves punishment from the application of these rules to particular cases.

II THE RETRIBUTIVE THEORY

The essential contention of retributivism is that punishment is only justified by guilt. There is a certain compellingness about the repudiation of utilitarianism that this involves. We feel that whatever other considerations may be taken into account, the primary and indispensable matter is to establish the guilt of the person to be punished. I shall try to show that the peculiar outrageousness of the rejection of this principle is a consequence, not of the brutality that such rejection might seem to permit, but of the fact that it involves a kind of lying. At any rate the first principle of retributivism is that it is necessary that a man be guilty if he is to be punished.

But this doctrine is normally held in conjunction with some or all of three others which are logically, if not altogether psychologically, independent of it. These are that the function of punishment is the negation or annulment of evil or wrongdoing, that punishment must fit the crime (the *lex talionis*) and that offenders have a right to punishment, as moral agents they ought to be treated as ends not means.

The doctrine of 'annulment', however carefully wrapped up in obscure phraseology, is clearly utilitarian in principle. For it holds that the function of punishment is to bring about a state of affairs in which it is as if the wrongful act had never happened. This is to justify punishment by its effects, by the desirable future consequences which it brings about. It certainly goes beyond the demand that only the guilty be punished. For, unlike this demand, it seeks to prescribe exactly what the punishment should be. Holding that whenever wrong has been done it must be annulled, it makes guilt – the state of one who has done wrong – the sufficient as well as the necessary condition of punishment. While the original thesis is essentially negative, ruling out the punishment of the innocent, the annulment doctrine is positive, insisting on the punishment and determining the degree of punishment of the guilty. But the doctrine is only applicable to a restricted class of cases, the order of nature is inhospitable to attempts to put the clock back. Theft and fraud can be compensated, but not murder, wounding, alienation of affection or the destruction of property or reputation.

Realising that things cannot always be made what they were, retributivists have extended the notion of annulment to cover the infliction on the offender of an injury equal to that which he has caused. This is sometimes argued for by reference to Moore's theory of organic wholes, the view that sometimes two blacks make a white. That this, the *lex talionis*, revered by Kant, does not follow from the original thesis is proved by the fact that we can always refrain from punishing the innocent but that we cannot always find a punishment to fit the crime. Some indeed would argue that we can never fit punishment to wrong-doing, for how are either, especially wrong-doing, to be measured? (Though, as Ross has pointed out, we can make ordinal judgments of more or less about both punishment and wrong-doing.)

Both of these views depend on a mysterious extension of the original thesis to mean that punishment and wrong-doing must necessarily be somehow equal and opposite. But this is to go even further than to regard guilt and punishment as necessitating one another. For this maintains that only the guilty are to be punished and that the guilty are always to be punished. The equal and opposite view maintains further that they are to be punished to just the extent that they have done wrong.

Finally retributivism has been associated with the view that if we are to treat offenders as moral agents, as ends and not as means, we must recognise their right to punishment. It is an odd sort of right whose holders would strenuously resist its recognition. Strictly interpreted, this view would entail that the sole relevant consideration in determining whether and how a man should be punished is his own moral regeneration. This is utilitarian and it is also immoral, since it neglects the right of an offender's victims to compensation and of society in general to protection. A less extreme interpretation would be that we should never treat offenders merely as means in inflicting punishment but should take into account their right to treatment as moral agents. This is reasonable enough, most people would prefer a penal system which did not ignore the reformation of offenders. But it is not the most obvious correlate of the possible view that if a man is guilty he ought to be punished. We should more naturally allot the correlative right to have him punished to his victims or society in general and not to him himself.

III THE RETRIBUTIVIST THESIS

So far I have attempted to extricate the essentials of retributivism by excluding some traditional but logically irrelevant associates. A more direct approach consists in seeing what is the essential principle which retributivists hold utilitarians to deny. Their crucial charge is that utilitarians permit the punishment of the innocent. So their fundamental thesis must be that only the guilty are to be punished, that guilt is a necessary condition of punishment. This hardly lies open to the utilitarian counter-charge of pointless and vindictive barbarity, which could only find a foothold in the doctrine of annulment and in the *lex talionis*. (For that matter, it is by no means obvious that the charge can be sustained even against them, except in so far as the problems of estimating the measure of guilt lead to the adoption of a purely formal and external criterion which would not distinguish between the doing of deliberate and accidental injuries.)

Essentially, then, retributivism is the view that only the guilty are to be punished. Excluding the punishment of the innocent, it permits the other three possibilities: the punishment of the guilty, the non-punishment of the guilty and the non-punishment of the innocent. To add that guilt is also the sufficient condition of punishment, and thus to exclude the non-punishment of the guilty, is another matter altogether. It is not entailed by the retributivist attack on utilitarianism and has none of the immediate compulsiveness of the doctrine that guilt is the necessary condition of punishment.

There is a very good reason for this difference in force. For the necessity of not punishing the innocent is not moral but logical. It is not, as some retributivists think, that we *may* not punish the innocent and *ought* only to punish the guilty, but that we *cannot* punish the innocent and *must* only punish the guilty. Of course, the suffering or harm in which punishment consists can be and is inflicted on innocent people but this is not punishment, it is judicial error or terrorism or, in Bradley's characteristically repellent phrase, 'social surgery'. The infliction of suffering on a person is only properly described as punishment if that person is guilty. The retributivist thesis, therefore, is not a moral doctrine, but an account of the meaning of the word 'punishment'. Typhoid carriers and criminal lunatics are treated physically in much the same way as ordinary criminals; they are shut up in institutions. The essential difference is that no blame is implied by their imprisonment, for there is no guilt to which the blame can attach. 'Punishment' resembles the word 'murder', it is infliction of suffering on the guilty and not simply infliction of suffering, just as murder is wrongful killing and not simply killing. Typhoid carriers are no more (usually) criminals than surgeons are (usually) murderers. This accounts for the flavour of moral outrage attending the notion of punishment of the innocent. In a sense a contradiction in terms, it applies to the common enough practice of inflicting the suffering involved in punishment on innocent people and of sentencing them to punishment with a lying imputation of their responsibility and guilt. Punishment *cannot* be inflicted on the innocent, the suffering associated with punishment *may* not be inflicted on them, firstly, as brutal and secondly, if it is represented as punishment, as involving a lie.

This can be shown by the fact that punishment is always *for* something. If a man says to another 'I am going to punish you' and is asked 'what for', he cannot reply 'nothing at all' or 'something you have not done'. At best, he is using 'punish' here as a more or less elegant synonym for 'cause to suffer'. Either that or he does not understand the meaning of 'punish'. 'I am going to punish you for something you have not done' is as absurd a statement as 'I blame you for this event for which you were not responsible.' 'Punishment implies guilt' is the same sort of assertion as 'ought implies can'. It is not *pointless* to punish or blame the innocent, as some have argued, for it is often very useful. Rather the very conditions of punishment and blame do not obtain in these circumstances.

IV AN OBJECTION

But how can it be useful to do what is impossible? The innocent can be punished and scapegoats are not logical impossibilities. We do say 'they punished him for something he did not do'. For A to be said to have punished B it is surely enough that A thought or said he was punishing B and ensured that suffering was inflicted on B. However innocent B may be of the offence adduced by A, there is no question that, in these circumstances, he has been punished by A. So guilt cannot be more than a *moral* precondition of punishment.

The answer to this objection is that 'punish' is a member of that now familiar class of verbs whose first-person-present use is significantly different from the rest. The absurdity of 'I am punishing you for something you have not done' is analogous to that of 'I promise to do something which is not in my power'. Unless you are guilty I am no more in a position to punish you than I am in a position to promise what is not in my power. So it is improper to say 'I am going to punish you' unless you are guilty, just as it is improper to say 'I promise to do this' unless it is in my power to do it. But it is only *morally* improper if I do not *think* that you are guilty or that I can do the promised act. Yet, just as it is perfectly proper to say of another 'he promised to do this', whether he thought he could do it or not, provided that he *said* 'I promise to do this', so it is perfectly proper to say 'they punished him', whether they thought him guilty or not, provided that they *said* 'we are going to punish you' and inflicted suffering on him. By the first-person-present use of these verbs we *prescribe* punishment and *make* promises, these activities involve the satisfaction of conditions over and above what is required for *reports* or *descriptions* of what their prescribers or makers represent as punishments and promises.

Understandably 'reward' and 'forgive' closely resemble 'punish'. Guilt is a precondition of forgiveness, desert – its contrary – of reward. One cannot properly say 'I am going to reward you' or 'I forgive you' to a man who has done nothing. Reward and forgiveness are always *for* something. But, again, one can say 'they rewarded (or forgave) him for something he had not done'. There is an interesting difference here between 'forgive' and 'punish' or 'reward'. In this last kind of assertion 'forgive' seems more peculiar, more inviting to inverted commas, than the other two. The three undertakings denoted by these verbs can be divided into the utterance of a more or less ritual formula and the consequences authorised by this utterance. With punishment and reward the consequences are more noticeable than the formula, so they come to be sufficient occasion for the use of the word even if the formula is inapplicable and so improperly used. But, since the consequences of forgiveness are negative, the absence of punishment, no such shift occurs. To reward involves giving a reward, to punish inflicting a punishment, but to forgive involves no palpable consequence, e.g. handing over a written certificate of pardon.

Within these limitations, then, guilt is a *logically* necessary condition of punishment and, with some exceptions, it might be held, a morally necessary condition of the infliction of suffering. Is it in either way a sufficient condition? As will be shown in the last section there are circumstances, though they do not obtain in our legal system, nor generally in extra-legal penal systems (e.g. parental), in which guilt is a logically sufficient condition of at least a sentence of punishment. The parallel moral doctrine would be that if anyone is guilty of wrong-doing he ought morally to be punished. This rather futile rigorism is not embodied in our legal system with its relaxations of penalties for first offenders. Since it entails that offenders should never be forgiven it is hardly likely to commend itself in the extra-legal sphere.

V THE UTILITARIAN THEORY

Utilitarianism holds that punishment must always be justified by the value of its consequences. I shall refer to this as 'utility' for convenience without any implication that utility must consist in pleasure. The view that punishment is justified by the value of its consequences is compatible with any ethical theory which allows meaning to be attached to moral judgments. It holds merely that the infliction of suffering is of no value or of negative value and that it must therefore be justified by further considerations. These will be such things as prevention of and deterrence from wrong-doing, compensation of victims, reformation of offenders and satisfaction of vindictive impulses. It is indifferent for our purposes whether these are valued as intuitively good, as productive of general happiness, as conducive to the survival of the human race or are just normatively laid down as valuable or derived from such a norm.

Clearly there is no *logical* relation between punishment and its actual or expected utility. Punishment *can* be inflicted when it is neither expected, nor turns out, to be of value and, on the other hand, it can be forgone when it is either expected, or would turn out, to be of value.

But that utility is the morally necessary or sufficient condition, or both, of punishment are perfectly reputable moral attitudes. The first would hold that no one should be punished unless the punishment would have valuable consequences, the second that if valuable consequences would result punishment ought to be inflicted (without excluding the moral permissibility of utility-less punishment). Most people would no doubt accept the first, apart from the rigorists who regard guilt as a morally sufficient condition of punishment. Few would maintain the second except in conjunction with the first. The first says when you may not but not when you ought to punish, the second when you ought to but not when you may not.

Neither permits or encourages the punishment of the innocent, for this is only logically possible if the word 'punishment' is used in an unnatural way, for example as meaning any kind of deliberate infliction of suffering. But in that case they cease to be moral doctrines about punishment as we understand the word and become moral doctrines (respectively platitudinous and inhuman) about something else.

So the retributivist case against the utilitarians falls to the ground as soon as what is true and essential in retributivism is extracted from the rest. This may be unwelcome to retributivists since it leaves the moral field in the possession of the utilitarians. But there is a compensation in the fact that what is essential in retributivism can at least be definitely established.

VI RULES AND CASES

So far what has been established is that guilt and the value or utility of consequences are relevant to punishment in different ways. A further understanding of this difference can be gained by making use of a distinction made by Sir David Ross in the appendix on punishment in *The Right and the Good*. This will also help to elucidate the notion of guilt which has hitherto been applied uncritically.

The distinction is between laying down a rule which attaches punishment to actions of a certain kind and the application of that rule to particular cases. It might be maintained that the utilitarian theory was an answer to the question 'what kinds of action should be punished?' and the retributive theory an answer to the question 'on what particular occasions should we punish?' On this view both punishment and guilt are defined by reference to these rules. Punishment is the infliction of suffering attached by these rules to certain kinds of action, guilt the condition of a person to whom such a rule applies. This accounts for the logically necessary relation holding between guilt and punishment. Only the guilty can be punished because, unless a person is guilty, unless a rule applies to him, no infliction of suffering on him is properly called punishment, since punishment is infliction of suffering as laid down by such a rule. Considerations of utility, then, are alone relevant to the determination of what in general, what *kinds* of action, to punish. The outcome of this is a set of rules. Given these rules, the question of whom in particular to punish has a definite and necessary answer. Not only will guilt be the logically necessary but also the logically sufficient condition of punishment or, more exactly, of a sentence of punishment. For declaration of guilt will be a declaration that a rule applies and, if the rule applies, what the rule enjoins – a sentence of punishment – applies also.

The distinction between setting up and applying penal rules helps to explain the different parts played by utility and guilt in the justification of punishment, in particular the fact that where utility is a moral, guilt is a logical, justification. Guilt is irrelevant to the setting up of rules, for until they have been set up the notion of guilt is undefined and without application. Utility is irrelevant to the application of rules, for once the rules have been set up punishment is determined by guilt, once they are seen to apply the rule makes a sentence of punishment necessarily follow.

But this account is not an accurate description of the very complex penal systems actually employed by states, institutions and parents. It is, rather, a schema, a possible limiting case. For it ignores an almost universal feature of penal systems (and of games, for that matter, where penalties attend infractions of the rules) – discretion. For few offences against the law is one and only one fixed and definite punishment laid down. Normally only an upper limit is set. If guilt, the applicability of the rule, is established no fixed punishment is entailed but rather, for example, one not exceeding a fine of forty shillings or fourteen days' imprisonment. This is even more evident in the administration of such institutions as clubs or libraries and yet more again in the matter of parental discipline. The establishment of guilt does not close the matter, at best it entails some punishment or other. Precisely how much is appropriate must be determined by reference to considerations of utility. The variety of things is too great for any manageably concise penal code to dispense altogether with discretionary judgment in particular cases.

But this fact only shows that guilt is not a logically *sufficient* condition of punishment, it does not affect the thesis that punishment entails guilt. A man cannot be guilty unless his action falls under a penal rule and he can only be properly said to be punished if the rule in question prescribes or permits some punishment or other. So all applications of the notion of guilt necessarily contain or include all applications of the notion of punishment.

4 ⌇ *Punishment and Desert*

C. W. K. MUNDLE

My aim is to try to do justice to the so-called retributive theory of punishment, and to discuss *en route* the original features of the accounts of punishment advanced by Dr A. C. Ewing[1] and Mr J. D. Mabbott.[2] In Section I, I shall examine Ewing's attempt to provide a compromise between retributive and utilitarian principles. In Section II, I shall give my own analysis of what I take to be the essentials of the traditional retributive theory, and shall unfold the implications of this analysis by showing how it renders irrelevant various criticisms which have been considered decisive. In Section III, I shall examine what seems to me the most formidable objection to the traditional retributive theory, the difficulty of applying it to punishment by the State, and, after rejecting Mabbott's conclusions, I shall try to solve this problem. In the last section, I shall offer some reasons for accepting my version of the retributive theory.

I

Ewing presents his own theory after examining in turn each of the traditional theories of punishment – Retributive, Deterrent and Reformatory – and dismissing the claim of each to provide an adequate solution. His own theory, developed in chapter iv, is based on what he calls the 'educative function' of punishment, meaning by this its effectiveness in promoting the moral education of the community. This theory fills a gap between the reformatory and deterrent theories, as these are usually conceived and as they are defined by Ewing; for 'reformatory' is used to refer to the effects of punishment in promoting the moral education of the person(s) punished; 'deterrent' to refer to effects on other members of the community. Ewing's distinction between the deterrent and educative

[1] *The Morality of Punishment* (1929).   [2] Paper 2.

functions is that punishment is deterrent in so far as it makes people refrain from wrong actions through fear of punishment, and is educative in so far as it makes them refrain from such actions because they are thought wrong. In support of his view that a penal system has an educative influence, he argues that people tend to divide the actions they believe to be wrong into two classes – 'wrong' and 'very wrong indeed'; and that if a certain kind of wrong action is made punishable by law, this fact tends to make people put it into the latter class and regard it as something which 'simply must not be done'. Ewing attaches great importance to this function of punishment. He writes: 'The moral education of the community is a very important object indeed, and if it is desirable for the attainment of this object that crimes should be "annulled" by punishment, then surely we have found a fresh purpose to justify the latter' (p. 102). He even speaks of such moral improvement as being the 'special function' of punishment, and says: 'The moral object of punishment as such is to make people think of a certain kind of act as very bad' (p. 104). But although, in Ewing's view, the educative function is of primary importance, he finds a place in his theory for the claims of each of the traditional theories. 'The "educative" function of punishment must not be treated as the only one, but requires to be supplemented by the ordinary reformatory and deterrent views' (p. 120). Ewing's method of coming to terms with the retributive theory is probably the most original part of his theory. He rejects the retributive principle that it is fitting that a person guilty of a moral offence should suffer for it, that an offender *deserves* to suffer for his offence. In place of this principle he substitutes the following propositions – (*a*) that it is fitting that we should disapprove of moral badness, and (*b*) that the infliction of pain is 'a suitable way of expressing' our disapproval. Ewing maintains that the ideal state of affairs would be one in which the good effects normally produced by punishment could be produced by expressing disapproval without inflicting pain; and this ideal, he points out, may be progressively approached in practice, for the more sensitive we become to the disapproval of others, the less the pain which need be inflicted to produce the desired effects.

Ewing considers that this solution incorporates what is true and important in the retributive theory. 'But,' he says, 'our view still differs from the retributive theory, as usually interpreted, for

(1) It holds the valuable element in punishment to be not the

pain inflicted in proportion to desert but rather the moral disapproval implied thereby. . . .

(2) Without denying the intrinsic value of this attitude of disapproval or even of its expression in punishment, it justifies punishment rather as a means to good than as an end-in-itself. Punishment is valuable not chiefly because it expresses a right attitude of moral disapproval but because it has good consequences' (pp. 109–10).

One obvious criticism of Ewing's solution is that he is exaggerating the importance of the educative function of punishment. It is understandable that he should lay stress on this function, since it had not usually been emphasised by philosophers of the utilitarian school. I can, however, see no reason for describing it as 'the moral object' or 'special function' of punishment. We may agree that the moral education of the community is a very important object, but it seems debatable whether it is more important than those stressed in the deterrent theory – protecting the life, liberty and property of law-abiding people, or maintaining law and order. The achievement of these objects is after all necessary for the existence of a civilised society. Moreover, the efficacy of a penal system in promoting the moral education of the community seems much more uncertain than its efficacy in deterring anti-social behaviour through fear of penalties. I do not wish to dispute the contention (made previously by Rashdall[3]) that a penal system has a considerable influence on conventional estimates of the relative wrongness of different kinds of actions; but I do not understand why people should be said to be 'morally improved' if they come to regard an action as morally worse *solely* because it is made punishable by law, or because the penalty is increased. Presumably the purposes of moral education are to convey the reasons why certain actions are wrong and to strengthen the moral motive. The promulgation of a new penal law may further the first purpose *if* it is accompanied by an explanation of the harm caused by the prohibited behaviour. But in that case it is the explanation, not the threat of penalties, which performs the educative function. Concerning the second purpose of moral education, Ewing concedes that 'men commit crimes as a rule not because they do not know they are wrong, but because the consciousness of their wrongness is lacking in the power to influence action' (p. 100). Can we then have any confidence that the threat of

[3] *The Theory of Good and Evil*, vol. 1 (Oxford, 1907), pp. 296–7.

punishment strengthens the moral motive and does not merely provide a non-moral motive for avoiding the proscribed actions? It is, I imagine, on account of such difficulties that utilitarian philosophers have not usually stressed the 'educative' function of punishment, or distinguished it sharply from the deterrent function.

I do not propose to spend more time discussing the relative importance of the reformatory, deterrent and educative effects of punishment. We can readily understand the fact that practical people are often preoccupied with one or other of these functions (e.g. administrators with the prevention of crime, social workers with reform of wayward individuals) and are consequently inclined to justify punishments solely or primarily in terms of one such function. But, from a philosophical standpoint, reformatory, deterrent and educative theories of punishment are merely variations on the utilitarian theme. On utilitarian principles, the question whether a particular punishment, or system of punishments, is justified would depend on the *net* value of *all* its consequences. (And, incidentally, a penal system has consequences of social importance which are not usually taken into account by utilitarian philosophers, e.g. its economic effects on the level of employment, wages, etc.) The basic controversy is between those who maintain that punishment is to be justified by the value of its effects and the defenders of the retributive theory who deny this. Here Ewing attempts to compromise, by saying that punishment is justified partly because it expresses a right attitude of disapproval, but chiefly because it has good consequences.

Now we must keep in mind the reason why moralists have felt that punishment requires to be justified, namely the fact that punishment may be said to involve the 'deliberate infliction of pain'. This phrase suggests pictures of floggings or thumbscrews, so it is important to remember that the pain in question may, and usually does, consist mainly in the frustration of a person's desires, resulting from unwelcome restrictions on his liberty. In most contexts one could substitute 'constraint' or 'curtailment of rights or privileges' for 'infliction of pain' or 'making (a person) suffer'. Such a substitution would be inappropriate in cases of corporal punishment or the death-penalty, but the question whether penalties of these kinds are justifiable is independent of the question whether we should accept a utilitarian or a retributive theory of punishment. Now we would all, I think, admit that we have a duty not to inflict pain deliberately on another person; but we should also agree that this is not an unconditioned duty, since some other duty may provide a good or sufficient reason for inflicting pain. No one would deny that a sufficient reason for inflicting pain on a person may be provided by the fact that it is necessary for his own welfare or for that of others. Consider the things dentists do in the interests of the patient, or the unpleasant quarantine restrictions that are imposed on infectious people in the interests of others. The controversial question is whether the fact that a person has committed a moral offence constitutes a sufficient reason for inflicting pain on him. Though Ewing does not raise this question in this form, it seems clear from what he does say that he would answer this question in the negative. This is, I think, the main point of disagreement between Ewing and defenders of the retributive theory. Ewing attempts to conciliate the retributionists by conceding that punishment is justified *partly* on retributive (though chiefly on utilitarian) grounds. I am very doubtful, however, whether his modification of the retributive theory leaves this compromise open to him.

As we have seen, Ewing rejects the principle that it is fitting (i.e. morally fitting or right) that a person who commits a moral offence should be made to suffer solely on that account. He replaces this with the claims:

(*a*) that it is fitting that we should disapprove of moral badness, and (*b*) that the infliction of pain is a suitable way of expressing our disapproval. Ewing clearly intends (*a*) to be an ethical proposition, 'fitting' meaning morally fitting or right. The retributionist would have no complaint if (*b*) were also to be interpreted as an ethical proposition, namely, that it is morally fitting that we should express disapproval by the infliction of pain. In that case (*a*) and (*b*) would together imply the proposition they were introduced to replace. Ewing, however, intends (*b*) to describe a natural phenomenon – the fact that all or most human beings have a propensity to express disapproval by inflicting pain. This seems clear from his statement 'all my view presupposes is that in a given society a certain amount of pain is a suitable way of expressing a certain degree of disapproval, *just as one tone of voice may be a more suitable way of expressing it than another*' (p. 105, my italics). But on this interpretation the conjunction of (*a*) and (*b*) does not imply that punishment is morally justifiable. Given that we ought to disapprove of wrongdoing, and that we have a *natural inclination* to express our disapproval by inflicting pain, this does not warrant the conclusion that this way of expressing disapproval is morally permissible. For all that Ewing has said, the inclination in question might be one that we ought to inhibit, unless utilitarian considerations justify its expression. In view of this, Ewing ought surely to conclude that punishment is justifiable *solely* on utilitarian grounds.

Ewing makes another apparent concession to the retributive theory when he says that 'punishment implies guilt and must be retrospective, in so far as it is inflicted because of a past offence' (p. 44). He does not, however, treat this statement as a tautology, as I think it is. He says, for example: 'If the pain of punishment is educative, why not inflict it on the innocent? The answer is: because it is educative only for the guilty' (p. 91); and he proceeds to give arguments in support of this last contention. But surely such arguments are superfluous. All one need say in answer to his question is that to speak of 'punishing the innocent' is a contradiction in terms, *unless* it means 'inflicting pain on people because they are mistakenly believed to have committed an offence, or on the pretext that they have done so'. In that case the word 'punishing' is being used to mean 'intending (or pretending) to punish'. This view is confirmed by the fact that the *OED* defines 'punish' as 'to cause (an offender) to suffer for an offence'. Someone might protest that this definition is too narrow on the grounds that people often speak of punishing animals and infants, which are not deemed to be morally or legally accountable. I doubt, however, whether people who use 'punish' in such contexts intend to depart from the *OED* definition. Parents and animal-lovers often display a surprising confidence regarding the knowledge of their charges – 'he knows,' they will say, 'that he ought not to play with the poker (bring bones into the dining-room)'. If such people were persuaded to regard the chastising of infants or animals merely as a mechanism for inculcating socially desirable habits, merely as a process of 'conditioning', they would, I think, agree that their use of 'punish' was inappropriate, or at any rate metaphorical. Utilitarian philosophers are of course at liberty to recommend that we redefine 'punishment', e.g. as 'infliction of pain in order to inculcate socially desirable habits' or as 'infliction of pain in order to promote happiness'. But it is not difficult to show that such definitions do not correspond to current usage. The former definition is disposed of by the fact that we describe as a punishment the imprisonment of a hardened criminal, and even if no one believes that the sentence will improve his habits, we regard such punishment as justifiable; the latter by the fact that we do not regard the pain inflicted by a dentist as a punishment.

If the statement that punishment must be inflicted for a past offence is warranted on purely linguistic grounds, it contributes nothing to settling our ethical problem, concerning the *justification* of punishment. A utilitarian may accept the *OED* definition and still maintain that punishment can only be justified by the value of its after-effects. On the other hand, the meaning of 'punishment' may change; a time may come when its root meaning is, e.g., 'infliction of pain to inculcate desirable habits'. This eventuality would render it improper to call the retributive theory 'a theory of *punishment*', but the moral principles on which this theory is based would not thereby be invalidated.

II

I shall now offer an analysis of the retributive theory. It is doubtless true that some of its defenders have meant more by 'retribution' than is involved in my analysis, but I feel sure that none of them have meant less. If anyone considers that my analysis omits any essential element of the traditional theory, I should be happy to call my own account 'a moral desert theory'. The theory to be discussed involves three elements, two ethical claims and a verbal recommendation:

Claim 1, that the fact that a person has committed a moral offence provides a sufficient reason for his being made to suffer;

Claim 2 (or 'the principle of proportion') that if (or when) people are made to suffer for their offences, the suffering imposed ought to be proportionate to the moral gravity of their offences;

and the *verbal recommendation* that 'punishment' should be applied only to cases in which a person is made to suffer because (for the reason that) he deserves it on account of a moral offence.

My reasons for formulating the retributive theory in this way will, I hope, become clear in the ensuing discussion. The first points to notice are:

(i) that claims 1 and 2 are not analytic propositions, since they can be denied without contradiction, and the question whether they ought to be accepted cannot be settled simply by studying linguistic usage;

(ii) that although claims 1 and 2 are not usually clearly distinguished, they ought to be distinguished in ethical discussions, since to accept either claim does not commit us to accepting the other;

(iii) that claims 1 and 2 together provide an explication of the concept of *moral desert*;

(iv) that even if claims 1 and 2 are accepted, there are the further questions whether 'punishment' is *in fact* applied only to cases where a person is made to suffer on the ground that he deserves it, or, if not, whether its meaning *should* be restricted in this way. Defenders of the retributive theory must wish to answer at least one of these questions in the affirmative, since they call their view 'a theory of *punishment*'. Now, concerning actual usage, I have found that some people are somewhat undecided regarding the kind of reason for which an action must be performed in order to be called 'punishment'. I think it best, therefore, to avoid controversy about 'ordinary language' by interpreting the retributive theory as making a verbal recommendation. This, like any such recommendation, would be in one sense arbitrary; but, if the ethical claims are accepted, the recommendation would be a reasonable one; for it would involve using 'punishment' to mark a distinction which needs to be marked – between cases where people are made to suffer on the ground that they deserve it, and cases where they are made to suffer for other reasons.

The above analysis might, however, be said to be incomplete, on the grounds that claims 1 and 2 do not provide a complete explication of the concept of moral desert, and that for this purpose we need to add a further principle to the effect that for any particular offence there is a determinate kind and/or amount of suffering which is *the* just penalty ('claim 3'). Whereas claim 2 implies only that the worse the offence, the greater should be the penalty, claim 3 involves the notion of an absolute and precise equation between offence and penalty. Claim 3 seems to be implicit not only in formulae like 'an eye for an eye', but also, for example, in the view mentioned by Hegel when he says 'Reason cannot determine . . . any principle whose application could decide whether justice requires for an offence (i) a corporal punishment of forty lashes or thirty-nine, or (ii) a fine of five dollars or four dollars ninety-three, four, etc., cents. . . . And yet injustice is done at once if there is one lash too many, or one dollar or one cent . . . too many or too few' (*Philosophy of Right*, tr. T. M. Knox, p. 137).

I am not certain whether, or to what extent, claim 3 is implicit in the popular conception of moral desert, but I submit that whereas claim 2 is acceptable, claim 3 is not. In order to apply the principle of proportion, all that is necessary is that we should be able (*a*) to compare different offences in respect of their *relative* moral gravity, and (*b*) to compare different penalties in respect of their *relative* unpleasantness – and surely we can make such comparisons in many, if not all, cases. In order to apply the principle of claim 3, we should need to be able to discern an alleged equivalence between the moral gravity of each offence and some specific penalty – and in order to do this we should presumably have to assess, on an *absolute* scale, both the moral gravity of offences and the unpleasantness of penalties. The contention that it is meaningless to speak of such an equivalence, because, e.g., the terms of the equation are not commensurable, provides one of the commonest criticisms of the retributive theory. For example, the objection which Professor W. G. Maclagan[4] treats as decisive in refuting the retributive theory – 'the notion [of an equivalence between guilt and penalty] is, in fact, meaningless. . . . Thus there can be no meaning in saying that we ought to act retributively' – is based on treating claim 3 as an essential element in the retributive theory. An unusual variation of this sort of criticism is given by Ewing,[5] purporting to show that punishment by the State cannot be justified on a retributive theory. Ewing argues that the State will almost invariably fail to impose *the precise* penalty which an offender deserves; that 'every excess over the just amount must be in the same ethical position as punishment of "the innocent", an injustice which seems much worse than non-punishment of the guilty', and that too light a penalty is equally an injustice; and, he concludes, 'to do an injustice seems worse than to do nothing at all'. Ewing's argument presupposes that the retributive theory involves not only claim 3, but also (and this is indeed gratuitous) the principle that all penalties which deviate at all from *the* just penalty are equally unjust!

It might be said that by rejecting claim 3 we render the retributive theory incomplete, since this implies that the answer to the question – what is *the* just penalty for a given offence – is not in principle determinate. If this *is* an objection, it surely applies with equal force

---

[4] In his article 'Punishment and Retribution', in *Philosophy* (Jul 1939), pp. 290–2.
[5] *Morality of Punishment*, pp. 39–40.

against a utilitarian theory of punishment. A utilitarian who argues[6] that punishment could never be justified on retributive principles, because we cannot *know* the precise degree of the offenders' guilt, etc., is exposed to the reply that punishment could no more be justified on utilitarian principles. If we reject the retributive theory on the ground that God alone knows the extent of our moral guilt, we ought equally to reject a utilitarian theory on the ground that God alone knows what constitutes and conduces to our long-run welfare. We mortals can only have more or less confident beliefs concerning the welfare of others, and as to whether, and if so how, we can best promote this. In practice, it would appear that people responsible for imposing punishments can often be more confident in estimating what penalty is deserved, than they could be in solving the formidable problem of assessing the 'net welfare-productivity' of alternative penalties.

Now let us consider the implications of claim 1. To accept claim 1 does not imply, as Ewing seems to think,[7] that we should say that punishment is 'an end-in-itself' or that it has 'intrinsic value'. Ewing assumes that we must say this if we reject the utilitarian view. I suggest that the dichotomy – 'good-in-itself' or 'good-as-a-means' – is not applicable here. To say that punishment has intrinsic value would imply that the committing of an offence has instrumental value, but surely no one would embrace this paradox! We may say that the purpose of punishment is to avoid the *dis*-value of injustice, or that the state of affairs in which an offender is punished is less evil than that in which he goes unpunished.

To accept claim 1 does not imply Ewing's conclusion[8] that 'infliction of pain for pain's sake is what the retributive theory enjoins'. The retributionist would say 'for the sake of justice', not 'for pain's sake'. It may be argued that the psycho-analysts have explained the disposition to accept claim 1, have shown it to be a 'rationalisation' of sadistic (and/or masochistic) impulses. The retributionists may however retort that it is not difficult to find a psychological explanation of the disposition to reject what is really a principle of justice, since most of us would like to avoid the suffering we deserve! The issue can scarcely be settled by speculations about the unconscious motives of opponents.

To accept claim 1 does not imply that people responsible for

---

[6] Cf. Ewing, *Morality of Punishment*, pp. 37–8.
[7] Ibid., pp. 13–14.   [8] Ibid., p. 26 and cf. p. 29.

administering punishments should, when so doing, consider *only* retributive principles. Presumably everyone ought, in all his transactions, to consider, and, so far as his other duties permit, to promote the welfare of others. Judges, parents and teachers are not relieved of this duty on the occasions when they incur the duty to punish (which is, on the present view, the duty to impose deserved suffering). To grant that decisions concerning the nature of a penalty should be made in the light of its probable effects on the welfare of the offender and others, is perfectly compatible with claim 1. It does not follow that one reason for making a person suffer is not independently sufficient, simply because other reasons may also warrant such an action. Admittedly, utilitarian considerations sometimes conflict with retributive considerations and may warrant the remission (or an increase) of a deserved penalty. But I see no problem here. Claim 1 does not imply that the duty to punish is an unconditional duty, which could never be outweighed by the duties stressed in reformatory or deterrent theories. Moreover, the acceptance of claim 1 is compatible with widely different views concerning the relative importance of retributive justice and the goals stressed by utilitarians.

III

There remains, however, a formidable objection to the retributive theory. If the State had a duty to punish *moral* offences as such, the State ought to punish everyone, for which of us is without sin? Only moral offences which have been legislated against are punishable by the State, and, as Ewing puts it, 'it is obviously impracticable for the State to inflict pain . . . on everyone in accordance with their faults' (p. 43). This difficulty seems to warrant Ewing's conclusion that, so far as the retributive theory is concerned, the State ought not to punish at all. Now this is really the same difficulty as that which Mr Mabbott considers fatal to the retributive theory, as traditionally interpreted. He presents it as follows – 'It takes two to make a punishment, and for a moral or social wrong I can find no punisher. We may be tempted to say, when we hear of some brutal action, "that ought to be punished"; but I cannot see how there can be duties which are nobody's duties. If I see a man ill-treating a horse in a country where cruelty to animals is not a legal offence, and I say to him: "I shall now punish you", he will reply, rightly, "What has it to do with you? Who made you a judge and ruler over me?" ' (p. 41). The difficulty is that the facts seem to be incompatible with claim 1. We may want to insist that a man who commits what is a moral, but not a legal, offence deserves to suffer on that account, but if we treat this as implying that his offence is a sufficient reason for his being made to suffer, the question arises – by whom? By God perhaps; but neither the State nor any private citizen is thought to have a duty or a right to punish *an adult* for a moral offence *as such*. It looks as if the most that could be claimed for the retributive theory is that it applies to punishments inflicted by parents and teachers and by God.

Let us consider how Mabbott reacts to the above difficulty. He will have no truck with utilitarian considerations. 'The truth is that while punishing a man and punishing him justly, it is possible to deter others, and also to attempt to reform him, and if these additional goods are achieved the total state of affairs is better than it would be with just punishment alone. But reform and deterrence are not modifications of the punishment, still less reasons for it' (p. 40). So far, so good; but Mabbott proceeds to treat punishment as a purely legal matter. He holds that the breaking of a law constitutes the only sufficient reason for an act of punishment. Mabbott sums up his position by saying 'No punishment is *morally retributive* or reformative or deterrent. Any criminal punished for any one of these reasons is certainly unjustly punished. The only justification for punishing any man is that he has broken a law' (p. 45 my italics). Mabbott is, in effect, amending claim 1 by substituting 'legal offence' for 'moral offence'. Mabbott, however, claims to be defending a retributive theory of punishment. Thus Ewing and Mabbott meet the same difficulty in very different ways; Ewing by saying that punishment by the State cannot be justified on a retributive theory, Mabbott by adopting a position implying that only punishment by the State is justified, and that such punishment is retributive.

Obviously Mabbott is using 'retributive' in an unusual sense. (He is, I think, using it as equivalent to 'non-utilitarian'.) Neither of the claims which I have taken the retributive theory to be making is involved in Mabbott's theory. Since Mabbott's version of this theory is not based on moral principles, on what, we may ask, is it based? If it were defended as a tautology, on the grounds that 'punishment' *means* 'infliction of pain for a legal offence', its weakness would be transparent; for it is very common indeed for parents, teachers, clergymen, etc., to describe as 'punishment' the infliction of pain for moral offences which are not legal offences. Even if Mabbott were willing to extend his theory to cover breaches of rules promulgated by authorities other than the State, e.g. college authorities – and his examples on pages 42 and 51 suggest this – his theory would still be unsatisfactory. It would, for example, imply that it is always incorrect to describe a punishment as unjust, provided that the person punished has broken a law and that the penalty falls within the limits prescribed by the law. But this is to ignore something of fundamental importance. Surely a punishment which is legally correct may still be unjust, for example:

(i) where punishment is inflicted for actions which were morally and legally permissible when performed, but are later made punishable by retrospective legislation;[9]

(ii) where punishment is inflicted for breach of a law or order which prescribes a morally wrong action. The sort of case that requires Mabbott's attention is, e.g., that in which an army officer is punished for disobeying an order to kill or torture civilians;

(iii) where the statutory penalty for a legal offence is excessively severe in relation to the moral gravity of the offence, e.g. death for a starving man who steals a loaf.

It seems to me that even if the implications of Mabbott's position might satisfy a practising lawyer, they provide no answer to the questions concerning punishment which have exercised moralists. His position seems tantamount to a refusal to discuss questions concerning the *moral* justification of punishment; for it can, I think, be fairly described as being limited to the claim that punishment for a legal offence and only such punishment is *legally* justifiable.[10] Admittedly this claim cannot be denied without contradiction, but surely the same is true of the claim that punishment for a moral offence, and only such punishment, is *morally* justifiable. To ask if

[9] Mabbott discusses retrospective legislation on p. 42, but he considers only the situation in which the actions later made punishable were morally wrong when performed.

[10] If Mabbott claimed that punishment for a legal offence is alone and is always *morally* justifiable, I could not agree, since, apart from its arbitrary restriction of the meaning of 'punishment', this view implies that the law of the land is our only criterion, or at any rate our ultimate criterion, of moral justice.

a punishment is legally justified and to ask if it is morally justified is surely to ask two different questions.

We have now called attention to what is cogent in Ewing's criticism of the retributive theory, and what is unsatisfactory in Mabbott's statement of it. The position we have reached is this: the retributive theory breaks down if it is based solely on ethical principles involved in the concept of moral desert; yet if we divorce the theory from these principles we are left with a barren remnant which is of little or no interest to moralists. In view of these findings, is there any escape from the conclusion that punishment, if it *is* justifiable, must be justified on utilitarian grounds? I suggest that there is, provided that we combine the moral and the legalistic versions of claim 1 instead of regarding them as exclusive alternatives. As a *first* step we may replace claim 1, as originally formulated, by the following – 'if a person breaks a law, and if his action in so doing constitutes a moral offence, this is a sufficient reason for his being made to suffer'.

To prevent misunderstanding of this formula let me hasten to add that I do not mean by it that, to be justly punishable, an action must be intrinsically wrong, i.e. wrong independently of its being forbidden by law. I am assuming that citizens have a moral obligation to obey the laws of their State, an obligation which derives from the fact that regulation of their behaviour by law is a necessary condition of civilised life. The actions proscribed by law need not, of course, be intrinsically wrong, provided that there is some good reason for proscribing them. However – and this is the point which Mabbott's account ignores – the duty to obey one's State is not an unconditional duty. No problem arises in cases where the State proscribes intrinsically wrong actions, or enforces actions which, as such, are ethically neutral, e.g. the rules of the road. But if the State (or a duly appointed State official) commands one to perform an intrinsically wrong action, one is faced with a conflict of duties, and one's obligation to obey the State *may* be outweighed by one's obligation not to perform actions of the kind in question. In that case, if one disobeys the State one is not committing a *moral* offence, and although the State is *legally* justified in punishing one's disobedience, it would not be *morally* justified in so doing. I am not suggesting, however, that the opinion of a lawbreaker, as to whether it was right for him to break the law, is to be accepted as final! Opinions may differ as to whether a particular act of law-breaking was morally justified. My revised claim 1 involves no reference to the question who is to judge whether an act of lawbreaking constitutes a moral offence. If such reference *is* to be included in claim 1, it should read 'if a person A breaks a law, and if A's action in so doing is judged by B to be a moral offence, there will, in B's view, be a sufficient reason for A being made to suffer'. Here B is a variable which may refer to any individual, including A, or to any group of people, e.g. the Government or 'the general public'.

My amended version of the retributive theory implies that punishment of a person by the State is morally justifiable, if and only if he has done something which is both a legal and a moral offence, and only if the penalty is proportionate to the moral gravity of his offence. This seems to me to be satisfactory as far as it goes, but it does not go far enough. We must now extend our solution to make it applicable to punishment in the sphere of education. We can do this by expressing claim 1 in more general terms, i.e. instead of speaking of a *legal* offence or of breaking a *law*, we may speak of disobedience to, or breaking a rule laid down by, persons in authority. This is not an arbitrary step, for surely punishment by a parent or teacher is only justifiable if imposed for an action which is both a moral offence and the breach of a rule or command. Assuming that a child has a duty to obey its parents' commands, yet a breach of this duty would not, I think, be held to justify punishment, if the action commanded were morally wrong and the child disobeyed for this reason. Equally, punishment of a child for a morally wrong action would surely not be justified unless the child had previously been told that such actions were forbidden. If one chastised a child for doing something it had not been forbidden to do, the infliction of pain might be justified as a means of inculcating a desired habit, but, in that case, it should not, I think, be called 'a punishment'. Such a chastisement would no more be a just punishment than a case where the State penalised a past action on the strength of retrospective legislation. Furthermore, my proposed solution seems compatible with the concept of Divine Retribution. If, in this connection, theologians do not think it necessary to interpret claim 1 as specifying two distinct conditions (committing a moral offence *and* breaking a rule or law), this would presumably be because they identify our moral duties with laws or commands made by God.

IV

What I have tried to do, in the preceding sections, is so to formulate the retributive theory that it provides a consistent and comprehensive account of punishment which can be defended against the stock arguments of its critics. While I do not think that the ethical claims of the theory can be established by argument, I think I must say something about the acceptability of these claims.

The principle of proportion seems to me to be acceptable, to be a basic principle of justice and, moreover, to be incapable, as it is normally understood, of being derived from utilitarian principles. My reasons for this last statement are, briefly, as follows: (i) If the purpose of punishment were the reform of the offender, correlation between the painfulness of the cure and the gravity of the offence would be accidental. The most effective cure for poaching or drunkenness might be more painful than that for murder or treason. (ii) It is sometimes said that, on a deterrent theory, the severest penalties would be justified for minor offences. This, however, ignores Bentham's maxim[11] that we should be 'frugal' in inflicting penalties, since pain is an evil. But this is not to say that the principle of proportion, as it is normally understood, can be derived from a deterrent theory. If some people perform a prohibited action with calculated deliberation and others perform the same action on impulse or in passion, we regard the former as morally worse and as deserving a heavier penalty. The deterrent aim would require, however, that offences of the latter kind should be punished the more severely, since such offences could only be prevented (if at all) by a penalty greater than is needed to prevent deliberate offences. Such implications surely offend our sense of justice.

If one accepts the views given in the preceding paragraph, one cannot adopt an exclusively utilitarian account of punishment; but one might still adopt a predominantly utilitarian account, if one rejected claim 1. Many people nowadays would, apparently, reject claim 1, but I suspect that their attitude to this claim might be due to misunderstanding its implications. The retributive theory, as I have interpreted it, does not imply that any punishment, which is justified because it is deserved, is not also justifiable on account of

[11] *Introduction to the Principles of Morals and Legislation*, ch. xv, section xi.

the value of its after-effects. I doubt if we can point to any cases of *deserved* punishment which have no valuable effects of any kind for the persons punished or for others. This being so, it may appear to be a matter of indifference whether we adopt a retributive theory, or conclude that punishments are multiply justifiable, meaning by this that retributive considerations and utilitarian considerations *each* provide a sufficient reason for the actions which (when not speaking metaphorically) we call 'punishments'. A solution on similar lines has been suggested by Mr A. G. N. Flew,[12] and it seems to me to be a tenable view, so far as it goes. But, for the following reason, I do not think it goes to the root of the matter. Unless the utilitarian is prepared to adopt the kind of deterrent theory on which punishment is treated as a kind of arbitrary coercion, as a device for making others conform to one's will irrespective of their own preferences or principles, the good effects of punishment to which the utilitarian appeals depend upon the punishments being regarded by the offenders and by others as just, i.e. as deserved for morally wrong actions. This being so, there is an important sense in which retributive considerations are fundamental and utilitarian considerations derivative.

POSTSCRIPT (1968)

There are many statements in this paper at which students should look critically, especially the last. What I offered as an analysis of *the* concept of moral desert I should now describe as an account of *one* conception thereof; one which originates from certain forms of Christian belief in which divine retribution plays an important role. I no longer have any inclination to side with any retributive theory which claims that the fact that a person has committed a moral offence is a *sufficient* reason for his being made to suffer, meaning a reason which is independent of the value of the foreseeable results of the individual act of punishment or of the enforcement of the laws or rules in question. Nor, I think, should Christians, who emphasise the benevolence of the deity, think of divine punishment as justifiable except as a means of promoting the future good of those who are punished. What remains of my former position scarcely deserves to be called 'a retributive theory'. It is important not to lose sight of the fact that punishment, by definition, is 'of an offender' and 'for an offence'. And I still think that the principle of proportion – between degrees of guilt or blameworthiness and severity

---

[12] At a symposium of the Scots Philosophical Club at Aberdeen on 16 May 1953. Printed in *Philosophy*, Oct 1954, and reprinted pp. 83–102 below.

of penalties – is an important element in our conception of justice. (Here 'our' refers to most people in countries influenced by the Christian religion.) Admittedly this principle is somewhat vague. It is concerned with justice *for the individual offender*, and this is a consideration distinct from those stressed by the deterrent and reformative theories; which are, therefore, incomplete, even if we grant, as I should, that the primary function of legal punishment is to deter and thereby protect the law-abiding. The question which now interests me most is whether the principle of proportion can be derived from utilitarian principles. The arguments I used in 1954 to support a negative answer are *much* too cursory. Bentham seems to be trying to answer my question, when he offers rules to guide legislators concerning 'the proportion between punishments and offences' (*Introduction to the Principles of Morals and Legislation*, ch. xiv). But he did not sufficiently distinguish the legislator's problems from those of the judge. It is the judge who has to try to ensure just treatment of the individual offender. Bentham's first rule is: 'The value of the punishment must not be less in any case than what is sufficient to outweigh the profit of the offence'. (Does 'in any case' mean 'in framing any law' or 'in punishing any individual'?) Bentham drew the conclusion that 'there is no disputing' that 'the quantum of the punishment must rise with . . . the strength of the temptation'. Recognising the 'seeming harshness' of this conclusion, he adds that 'the stronger the temptation, the less conclusive is the indication . . . of the depravity of the offender's disposition,' and that 'the strength of the temptation may offer ground for abatement of the demand for punishment' (section 9). If a utilitarian develops Bentham's hint, distinguishes the problems of the legislator and the judge, and does not treat the Greatest Happiness Principle as applying *only* to rules or laws or *only* to individual actions, can he not accommodate the principle of proportion?

5 ◊ The Justification of Punishment

ANTONY FLEW

I

I want to discuss philosophically, to examine the logic of, the three parts of this expression 'the justification of punishment', and then to draw from this discussion one or two morals for discussions of the justification of punishment. This paper is based on one originally given to the Scots Philosophy Club at its Aberdeen meeting in 1953, as the third part of a symposium on *The Justification of Punishment*.

II

(*a*) *Punishment*. (i) This term is both vague and 'open-textured' (Waismann).[1] It is vague, in as much as in several directions there is no sharp line drawn at which we must stop using it: when does punishment of the innocent or illegal punishment cease to be properly called punishment at all? (Here we must beware the scholasticism which F. P. Ramsey attacked in Wittgenstein, when the latter insisted that we *cannot* think illogically. For though there does come a point at which 'thinking' is so illogical, 'punishment' so wayward, that we should refuse to call them thinking or punishment at all, there is nevertheless a wide margin of toleration. And of course, as usual when we say there comes *a point at which*, what we really mean is that there comes *a twilight zone after which*.) It is open-textured, in as much as many questions of its applicability could arise over which even full knowledge of current correct usage might leave us at a loss. We might be at a loss not because this case fell within a more or less recognised No-Man's-Land of vagueness across which no sharp line had been drawn, but because it was of a sort which had simply not been envisaged at all: would it be punishment if no effort was made or even pretended to allocate

[1] *Logic and Language*, ed. Antony Flew, vol. 1 (1951), pp. 119–20.

the 'punishments' to the actual offenders, but only to ensure that the total of hangings, say, balanced the total of murders; irrespective of who was hung? (See Ernest Bramah[2] on thus 'preserving the equipoise within the Sacred Empire'.) A third feature, which partly overlaps both the other two, is that several logically independent criteria are involved. Ideally these are all simultaneously satisfied, but there is no strict unanimity rule here to paralyse action: so the word may be applied, and correctly, where one criterion is definitely not satisfied (and not merely where, through its vagueness, there is no doubt as to whether it is or is not satisfied).

Once these features, which this concept shares with so many others, are recognised it becomes clear that it would be well as a prelude to possible discussions of the ethics of punishment to list the criteria. This usually useful preliminary is in this case exceptionally important. It is exceptionally important, first, because there is – since ideas here have certainly developed and are still changing and controversial – every reason to expect there are minority users of the word 'punishment', that some people will insist that certain elements are essential which others will not so regard. It is exceptionally important, second, because in ethical controversy the temptation to produce from up one's sleeve at later stages in the argument apparently decisive definitional jokers is very strong, and can only be removed by making clear from the start what is and what is not to be involved in the central notions.

In listing the criteria satisfied by what, without honorific[3] intentions, we may call a standard case of punishment, in the primary sense of the word, we have to realise: both – as we have already mentioned – that there are some non-standard users with their private variations on this primary use; and that there are secondary uses of the word (with which those intending to discuss the ethics of punishment are not directly concerned); and that it is correctly applied even by standard users in its primary sense to non-standard cases of punishment, i.e. cases in which not all the criteria are satisfied, but which because of its vagueness the word can cover.

I am going to present my remarks here as *proposals*. This is not because I regard them as arbitrary. On the contrary, they are based

---

[2] *The Wallet of Kai Lung* (1900), *Kai Lung's Golden Hours* (1922), and *Kai Lung Unrolls His Mat* (1928).

[3] There is for instance nothing honorific in saying that this car is a standard model, not 'custom-built'.

on what I take to be the general or at least the dominant tendencies in current usage; though I shall not give as many illustrations as would otherwise be necessary because Mabbott has already done a large part of this work, in his 'Punishment', which is quite the most valuable article I know on this subject. I am presenting my remarks as proposals because it needs sometimes to be emphasised that no philosophical analysis of the meaning of any term worth so analysing, however conservative the intentions and protestations of its protagonists, can ever leave things exactly as they were. For it must necessarily tend to change the meaning for us and our usage of the terms it analyses – ideally by summarising it and making clear its implications.

(ii) I *propose*, therefore, that we take as parts of the meaning of 'punishment', in the primary sense, at least five elements. *First*, it must be an evil, an unpleasantness, to the victim. By saying 'evil' – following Hobbes – or 'unpleasantness' and not 'pain', the suggestion of floggings and other forms of physical torture is avoided. Perhaps this was once an essential part of the meaning of the word, but for most people now its employment is less restricted. Note in this connection the development of an historically secondary use of the word, as applied first perhaps to a battering in boxing, and then extended to similar situations in other sports where there is no element of physical pain (e.g. as an equivalent to 'trouncing', of bowling in cricket).

Second, it must (at least be supposed to) be for an offence. A term in an old-fashioned public school, though doubtless far less agreeable than a spell in a modern prison, cannot be called a punishment, unless it was for an offence. (Perhaps the victim was despatched there for disobedience at home.) Conversely, as Mabbott most usefully stresses, if a victim forgives an offender for an injury which was also an offence against some law or rule, this will not necessarily be allowed as relevant to questions about his punishment by the institution whose law or rule it is. For this we can offer a mnemonic in the 'material mode of speech': 'Injuries can be forgiven; crimes can only be pardoned.'

Third, it must (at least be supposed to) be of the offender. The insistence on these first three elements can be supported by straightforward appeal to the *Concise Oxford Dictionary*, which defines 'punish' as 'cause (offender) to suffer for an offence'.

Notice here that though it would be pedantic to insist *in single cases* that people (logically) cannot be punished for what they have not done; still a *system* of inflicting unpleasantness on scapegoats – even if they are pretended to be offenders – could scarcely be called a system of punishment at all. Or rather – to put it more practically and more tolerantly – if the word 'punishment' is used in this way, as it constantly is especially by anthropologists and psycho-analysts,[4] we and they should be alert to the fact that it is then used in a metaphorical, secondary or non-standard sense in which it necessarily has appropriately shifted logical syntax (that is: the word in this case carries different implications from those it carries in a standard case of its primary sense). A likely source of trouble and confusion.

Fourth, it must be the work of personal agencies. Evils occurring to people as the result of misbehaviour, but not by human agency, may be called penalties but not punishments: thus unwanted children and venereal disease may be the (frequently avoided) penalties of, but not the punishments for, sexual promiscuity. To the extent that anyone believes in a personal God with strong views against such sexual behaviour, to that extent he may speak of these as divinely instituted punishments though, allowing the linguistic propriety of this, the fact that so often the punishments fall on the innocent and can be escaped by the guilty should still give pause.

(Note here: first, that there is a distinction often and usefully made – but rarely noticed even by those making it – between the 'natural' penalties *of* and the prescribed penalties *for* such and such conduct (gout *of* port-bibbing: free kicks *for* fouls); and, second, that the expression 'to the extent that' is peculiarly appropriate to beliefs about God and a quasi-personally sustained moral order in the universe, since with most people these meander somewhere between complete conviction and complete disbelief. Also to offer the present distinctions between the uses of 'punishment', 'penalty of' and 'penalty for' as if these were already completely given in present (correct) usage would be seriously to misdescribe the confused situation which actually confronts us.)

Fifth, in a standard case punishment has to (be at least supposed

---

[4] Cf. e.g. J. C. Flügel, *Population, Psychology, and Peace* (1947), pp. 70-1. 'Another germane example is the stigma of "illegitimacy", and this example illustrates the important fact that the punishment of suffering in question need not necessarily be endured by the culprit' and 'There is such a thing as vicarious punishment'.

to) be imposed by virtue of some special authority, conferred through or by the institutions against the laws or rules of which the offence has been committed. Mabbott brought this out clearly. A parent, a Dean of a College, a Court of Law, even perhaps an umpire or a referee, acting as such, can be said to impose a punishment: but direct action by an aggrieved person with no pretensions to special authority is not properly called punishment, but revenge. (Vendetta is a form of institutionalised revenge between families regarded as individuals.) Direct action by an unauthorised busybody who takes it upon himself to punish might be called punishment, since there is no unanimity rule about the simultaneous satisfaction of all the criteria. But, if so, it would be a non-standard case of punishment. Or it might equally well be called pretending (i.e. claiming falsely) to punish. The insistence on these fourth and fifth criteria can be supported by appeal to the *Oxford English Dictionary*, which prefaces the same definition as that given in the *COD* with 'As an act of superior or public authority.'

Besides these five positive criteria I *propose* negatively that we should not insist: *either* that it is confined to either legal or moral offences, but instead allow the use of the word in connection with any system of rules or laws – state, school, trades union, trade association, etc.; *or* that it cannot properly be applied to morally or legally questionable cases to which it would otherwise seem applicable, but instead allow that punishments – say – under retrospective or immoral laws may be called punishments, however improper or undesirable the proceedings may be in other respects. Laxity in both these directions conforms with normal usage; while in the second it has the merit of separating ethical from verbal issues.

I shall say nothing about 'collective punishment' except that, while no doubt the original unit on which punishment was inflicted was not the individual but the family, tribe, village, clan, or some other group, nevertheless for most of us today 'collective punishment' is somehow metaphorical or secondary: it is a matter of regarding a group as an individual, for certain purposes.[5]

[5] Compare here (a) K. R. Popper's examination of the appropriateness and limitations of the metaphor involved in regarding rogue states as criminals: *Open Society*, vol. 1 (1945), pp. 242 ff.; (b) the Nuremberg Trials: a colossal effort to discover what the guilt of the Nazi regime amounted to in terms of the particular guilt of particular Germans. This point I owe, like so much else, to Mabbott: first privately, and later to his *The State and the Citizen* (1967).

(b) *Justification*. This term is multiply relational. A justification has to be of A, rather than B, against C, and to or by reference to D; where A is the thing justified, B the possible alternative(s), C the charge(s) against A, and D the person(s) and/or principle(s) to whom and/or by reference to which the justification is made. The variables may have more than one value even in one context: there may, for instance, be more than one charge. But they do not all have to be given *definite* values *explicitly*. Indeed the point of saying all this lies precisely in the fact that in most cases of justification the values of some of the variables are given only implicitly by the context, and perhaps rather indefinitely too. Hence, just as in the notorious case of motion, it is possible to overlook (some of the implications of) the relational nature of the concept. The alternative(s) for instance, may be unstated and even conceived only very hazily: but that there must be at least one alternative is brought out by considering that 'There is no alternative' is always either a sufficient justification or a sufficient reason for saying that the question of justification does not arise. Finally, and most important – again compare the case of motion – the reference point, the fourth variable [the person(s) or principle(s) by reference to which justification is made], has the same rather indefinite value implicit in most actual contexts: the value 'whom I consider reasonable people, and what (fundamentally) they agree on.'

Presumably this has contributed to the use of 'justification' as a near synonym for 'reason for', which in turn has been a very minor determinant of the modern fashion – for which there is much to be said – of presenting moral philosophy as an enquiry into what are and are not *good reasons* in ethics. But note here, first, that the word 'justification' may, even in contexts where all the variables have the same values, be used in two relevantly different ways: either as implying that the proposed justification is, or as not implying that it is, morally or otherwise acceptable to the user. In the latter case if it is *very* unacceptable the word may be put in protest quotes. (*Mutatis mutandis* the same is true of 'reason'.) Second, that this mode of presentation tends to conceal the existence of really radical ethical disagreements. This point has been pressed in a critical notice of S. E. Toulmin's *The Place of Reason in Ethics* by J. Mackie (*Australasian Journal of Philosophy*, 1951). Presumably Toulmin would answer, on Kantian lines, that he was elucidating *the nature of ethics as such*: from which the fact that certain reasons were relevant and good, and others irrelevant and bad, followed necessarily. This would imply that those who seem to be doing ethics but admit different reasons to that extent cannot be doing ethics at all, or at least are very unreasonable people: by definition. Which is perhaps fair enough: providing that steps are taken to bring out just what must be involved in rejecting the definitions implicitly accepted by Toulmin, and that many would reject some of the implications of these definitions, and that their position in so doing is monstrous. To say this last is abandoning pure analysis to take sides, as all men must, in a struggle. It is making a normative, participant's utterance and not a purely analytic neutral's observation.

(c) *The.* The assumption behind the use of the definite article is that there is one and only one (unless the whole expression is interpreted, as it rarely is, as strictly equivalent to 'justifying punishment'). This is questionable twice over, at two levels: first, because the variables admit of various values – what would serve as justification against one charge and for a Roman Catholic could be simply irrelevant against another and for an atheist humanist; and, second, because in any one context (i.e. where the same values are given to all the variables) there may be two logically separate acceptable justifications both independently sufficient. And surely this is not merely possible but likely. For the fields of human causation, motivation, and justification are precisely those in which overdetermination is most common. (An action is said to be *overdetermined* when at least two motives were at work to produce it, either of which alone would have been sufficiently strong to do so separately. The concept, *mutatis mutandis*, obviously can and should also be applied to matters of causation and justification.)

III

We come now to some applications of ideas suggested in our outline examination of the parts of the expression 'the justification of punishment' to ethical discussions of the justification of punishment. We shall do this mainly by reference to Mabbott's paper, mentioned above. But we shall have an eye to other contributions, especially those made to the Aberdeen symposium, also mentioned above.

(a) *Theorising and justifying*. Traditionally, views about the circumstances, the severity, and the forms in which punishment is justified – and why – have been presented as *theories* of punishment. Sometimes the metaphor has been developed by speaking of justification as providing 'a theory to square with the facts (our moral convictions)'.[6]

This idiom seems to me radically misguided. It is misguided, first, because it conceals the essentially relational character of justification, which makes it an entirely different sort of thing from theorising in the positive sciences [see II (b) above]. It suggests, for instance, that the work of justification *could* be completed finally, for ever, and for everyone.

Second, it is misguided because it misrepresents questions of value as questions of fact or philosophy: and in so far as these 'theories' are intended as justifications it is wrong to present them as enquiries into why we do, or what are our reasons for doing, what we do. Mabbott begins: 'I propose . . . to defend a retributive theory and to reject absolutely all utilitarian considerations from its justification' (p. 39 above). In supporting this he writes: 'The view that a judge upholds a bad law in order that law in general should not suffer is indefensible' (p. 44 above). This piece of judicial psychology is irrelevant. Surely not 'upholds' but 'should uphold' is meant. It is quite difficult enough to disentangle factual, ethical, and philosophical questions without adopting an idiom which obscures the differences between these, and encourages such confusing slips as this one.

Third, it is misguided because it conceals the dynamic character of fruitful ethical discussion about justification. It suggests that two men embarking on such a discussion must start from a static, given, unalterable set of 'facts' (their moral principles or convictions) and go on thrashing out together the implications in this field of these principles. Whereas in fact these 'facts' (convictions) are often modified in the course of the discussion itself: just because that brings out unacceptable implications of, or reveals unnoticed inconsistencies between, these 'facts' (convictions). [Compare the mistake made by Aristotle in *Nicomachean Ethics* III iii 3. 1112^a 18 ff.], where his account of deliberation is similarly static and over-formal. Except at § 13 (1112^b 25–7) it overlooks that men, being imperfect seers of implications and not omniscient, are often

[6] One of the Aberdeen symposiants.

led to modify their objectives in the course of, and in the light of deliberation about, the means to reach these.]

Fourth, it is misguided because it embodies and hides certain questionable assumptions: that 'our moral convictions' are in agreement, and that they are unchanging. Both are false. Though in both cases, of course, it depends a lot on whom 'our' is referring to. But with the former assumption, even taking British professional philosophers as the us-group, it is difficult to believe that debate about the ethics of contraception, abortion, homosexuality, and suicide, would not reveal differences both in the weight given to different admitted prima facie obligations, and even perhaps in what were admitted as obligations at all. For instance, if I may follow one bit of unconventionality, the mention of such subjects in connection with philosophical ethics, by another, the mention of religious gulfs – the Roman Catholics among us are surely committed to the (at least almost) unconditional repudiation of all these as always morally wrong; and this not as purely religious tabus but as a matter of natural (as opposed to revealed) obligation. In the case of the latter assumption, one would hope that some of the moral convictions of us especially are open to alteration by argument.

Both assumptions are peculiarly questionable in connection with punishment. Not merely do the ethical views of different people differ pretty considerably, as we can see from the continuing arguments about the proper purpose, justification and reform of punishment; but the same person often holds inconsistent views at different times or even at the same time. Who of us can manage to be consistent about the relative weight of retributive and utilitarian considerations? and this not merely because we are always being tempted whenever we are emotionally involved against the offender to give more weight to the former than we should in a cool hour adjudge proper; but also because even in cool hours it is so hard to be sure and steady about difficult particular concrete problems of conduct.

(b) *Punishment as necessarily retributive.* The question 'Why should *he* be punished?' asks about the punishment of a particular person on a particular occasion. This is the type of question with which Mabbott was concerned. He formulated his problem as: 'Under what circumstances is the punishment of some particular person justified, and why?' (p. 39 above). He gave the answer:

'The only justification for punishing any man is that he has broken a law' (p. 45 above). This is supposed to be a retributive view and to be an ethical matter: as is made clear in the sentence already quoted: 'I propose to defend a *retributive* theory, and to reject absolutely all utilitarian considerations from its *justification*' (my italics). This would lead us to expect arguments, or at least assertions, to the effect that the vicious (or the criminal) deserve, and ought to be made, to suffer for their wickedness (crimes): without regard to the public advantage of such a system. But – to my mind fortunately – this is not at all what we are given. Roughly: in so far as Mabbott's view can be called retributive it is not a justification (satisfactory or otherwise)[7]; and in so far as any sort of justification is offered it is that of an ideal (not hedonistic) utilitarian.

(i) Unfortunately, Mabbott never makes clear how far he is appealing to the meanings of words and how far to 'our moral convictions'. The confusion is easy, for the latter are often encapsulated in the former, and expressions like 'what we should say' are ambiguous as between moral and linguistic propriety. But it does seem as if his answer to his main question is intended to depend upon the very meaning of the word 'punishment'. Yet in so far as this is so he is not really offering a justification, based on retributive ethical claims, but a necessary truth drawn from, and elucidating the meaning of, the word 'punishment'.

It is interesting to compare here the position of F. H. Bradley: 'Punishment is punishment only where it is deserved. We pay the penalty because we owe it, and for no other reason. If punishment is inflicted for any other reason whatever than because it is merited by a wrong, it is a gross immorality, a crying injustice, an abominable crime.' (*Ethical Studies*, pp. 26–7.) This is similar to but not the same as Mabbott's position. Not the same; because Mabbott 'dissents from most upholders of the retributive theory – from Hegel, from Bradley, and from Dr Ross' (p. 41 above) on the grounds that the essential link is between crime and punishment and not between doing wrong and punishment. Similar; because both are confusing necessary truths with ethical claims. If Bradley's first and second sentences express necessary truths, then the ethical claims made in the third are out of place; for if this is so then how-

[7] Significantly, C. W. K. Mundle at Aberdeen and in a revised version of his paper (see Paper 4) was unable to recognise Mabbott as a fellow retributionist.

ever gross the immorality, crying the injustice and abominable the crime it *cannot* be punishment at all if it is not both deserved and paid because owed.

Furthermore, not only is Mabbott's 'retributive justification' – in so far as it rests on an appeal to the meaning of the word 'punishment' – not what it pretends to be, but this appeal itself cannot be made out completely. First, because while a *system* of 'punishing' people who had broken no laws could not be called a system of punishment, the term 'punishment' is sufficiently vague to permit us to speak *in single cases and providing these do not become too numerous* (if they do become too numerous then *ipso facto* the use, the meaning, of 'punishment' has changed) of punishing a man who had broken no law (or even done no wrong). This objection might be met by saying that the term already is more precise than we have allowed, or by now deciding to make it so. The effect of adopting the latter alternative – like that of all such manœuvres with meanings – would be of course to shift and not to solve the *ethical problems*. (Consider the Rousseauian dialogue: Q. I know how to recognise the General Will: but is it always morally sound? A. The General Will is always upright – by definition. Q. But now how do I recognise it – so defined?) Second, because Mabbott wrote that 'the *only justification* for punishing any man is that he has broken a law' (my italics): and it is surely impossible to draw the italicised point out of the present meaning of 'punishment'. One can only say that the question 'Did he do it?' is always relevant to the question 'Ought he to be punished?', or even that it is the only question which is always, because *necessarily*, relevant: appealing for this to the meaning of 'punishment' as 'an evil inflicted on an offender for an offence'. But we cannot maintain that there is a contradiction involved in attempting to justify a single punishment for any reason other than that the victim has broken a law. Of course, this objection too could be met by a suitable adjustment of the meaning of 'punishment'. However, this adjustment would be both greater and harder to defend than that required to meet the former objection, and it would likewise involve a (not necessarily undesirable) shifting of any *ethical* problems, which cannot be dealt with by any manœuvres with definitions.

(ii) In so far as Mabbott's solution to his problem is intended as an ethical claim it is open to grave objections. Taken in this way it is a claim that, while it does make sense to speak both of punishing those who have broken no law and of doing so for other reasons than this (with other justifications than this); the *sole* and *always requisite true* justification is that the victim has committed an offence. (Mabbott did not add 'sufficient': presumably in order to allow for the possible justifiability of pardons and for the unjustifiability of enforcing certain laws.)

The objections both depend on what might be canonised as The Principle of the Multiplicity of Ethical Claims. Everyone who is not a one-track fanatic – which Mabbott emphatically is not – recognises as prima facie valid grounds of obligation several ethical rules or claims: (indeed it might be said that a creature recognising one and only one was not doing ethics at all, even fanatically). But to recognise several rules or claims which are logically independent is to open the way to both overdetermination and conflict. For it is to concede that it is at least logically possible that there can be circumstances both such that in them one claim reinforces another; and such that obeying one claim means disobeying another, satisfying one involves overriding another. And, fortunately in the former case, notoriously in the latter, with the sets of claims which people actually do recognise, such circumstances do occur. The objection to saying that the *sole* justification for punishing someone is that he has committed an offence is that Mabbott and almost everyone else would in fact allow that a punishment in certain circumstances was overdetermined in its justification – was justified at least twice over. Certainly: because, though Mabbott claims to 'reject absolutely all utilitarian considerations from its justification', he is prepared to appeal to these to justify *systems* of punishment. But if a *system* is to be justified even partly on such grounds, some cases within that system must be partly justifiable on the same grounds: the system surely could not have effects to which no case within it contributed. (See III (c) below.)

The objection to saying that this justification is *always* requisite is that, if you allow any moral claims other than that only offenders ought to be punished, then in certain circumstances one of these might be conceded to have overriding force; and hence to justify the punishment of an innocent man; and hence to show that this retributive justification is not always requisite. Unless, of course, you are prepared to insist that no one who has not committed an offence ought ever to be 'punished' for it: though the heavens fall. And though it is probably true that the evil effects of such injustice will almost always outweigh the good; still, unless we can believe in some Providential guarantee that this is *always* so we cannot accept such a claim, and at the same time accept other claims which logically might sometimes override it – for instance, the claim to do what one can to prevent the fall of the heavens or some similar catastrophe.

We shall not argue further for these objections or provide illustrations: because Mabbott would no doubt be willing to admit them; and because this paper is in any case primarily concerned only with the prolegomena to ethical discussion. Nevertheless one easy but mistaken assumption does call for notice. To show that something is just (or unjust) is not always and necessarily to show that it is justified (or unjustified); in spite of the common root and similar appearance of the words 'just' and 'justification'. The sentence before 'The only justification for punishing any man is that he has broken a law' was 'Any criminal punished for any one of these reasons [*pour encourager les autres* etc. – A.F.] is certainly unjustly punished.' But the former is no sort of restatement of the latter: something may be just but open to all sorts of (moral or legal) objections; (and of course something may be just and it may be possible to justify it on further grounds). Again (on p. 41 above) Mabbott seems to be making the same assumption, where he argues that even the most excellent consequences cannot 'prove the punishment was just'. For though this is true, they may nevertheless be conceded to *justify* the injustice.

(iii) A third interpretation of Mabbott's solution, which is perhaps nearest to what he actually had in mind when he wrote (as opposed to what he perhaps, or really, or ought to have, meant) is that 'The only justification for punishing any man is that he has broken a law' amounts to an assertion that, if we are considering the punishment of a particular person on a particular occasion *and are accepting that the penal system is generally all right*, the sole consideration relevant to the question 'Would it be justified or not?' is 'Did he commit an offence for which this is the penalty prescribed?' (We here neglect for the sake of simplicity, and with Mabbott, questions of extenuation and excuse.) Whereas if we are considering the merits of a particular law, or the advantages of having a system of laws, or of a penal enforcement of those laws (as opposed perhaps to psychiatric enforcement by the compulsory treatment of offenders); then other and – particularly – utilitarian considerations are relevant.

This interpretation involves the most important distinction, which it is one of the chief merits of Mabbott's paper to underline, between systems and particular cases within those systems.[8] He criticises, for instance, a writer who 'confuses injustice within a penal system with the wrongfulness of a penal system' (p. 47 above) and later maintains that 'it is essential to a legal system that the infliction of a particular punishment should *not* be determined by the good *that particular punishment* will do either to the criminal or 'society'. . . . One may consider the merits of a legal system or of a credit system but the acceptance of either involves the surrender of utilitarian considerations in particular cases as they arise' (p. 50 above).

The first objection to the position thus interpreted is that what Mabbott is saying in the passage just quoted is only *necessarily* true in the great majority, not in all, particular cases: for there is no *contradiction* involved in saying that you accept a system but propose nevertheless to allow an occasional exception. This notion of 'necessary truth in a great majority of cases' sounds scandalous and contradictory. It is perhaps a stumbling-block; but it is not contradictory. It is just what is often needed in and appropriate to the 'informal logic'[9] of the vague, elastic, concepts of everyday discourse (as opposed to the strict rigid 'p' and 'q' and 'triangle' of the formal disciplines of mathematics and symbolic logic). It might have been used in II (a) above to make the point that, in the present meaning of 'punishment' it is not incorrect to speak of punishment where one or other criterion for what we called a standard case of punishment is not satisfied, so long as these exceptional cases remain exceptional: we might have said that it is necessarily true in the great majority of cases that a punishment satisfies each (and all) of the criteria listed.

This being so, it is not possible to say that anyone accepting that there ought to be a system has committed himself to saying that

---

[8] Compare Hume in the second *Inquiry*, app. iii, p. 256: 'The result of the individual acts is here, in many instances, directly opposite to that of the whole system of actions; and the former may be extremely hurtful while the latter is to the highest degree advantageous.'

[9] This phrase is borrowed from G. Ryle 'Ordinary Language' in *The Philosophical Review* (1953), reprinted in *Ordinary Language*, ed. V. C. Chappell. This article is an invaluable exposition of the actual views and assumptions of those philosophers who 'care what dustmen say'.

utilitarian considerations are *necessarily* irrelevant to this or that particular case. The most that can be said – and this is very well worth saying – is that such a person is thereby committed to the surrender of utilitarian considerations in particular cases *as a rule*, a rule to which there can be exceptions. But, unfortunately, exceptional cases do not arrive labelled as such. So it is always open to someone to say that *this* is the case where an exception ought to be made.

Mabbott's short way with misplaced utilitarianism therefore will not work. His mistake here can be seen as yet one more example of our perennial and pervasive failure to realise that the concepts of everyday discourse have not, and, if they are to do the sort of jobs they are needed to do, cannot have, the sharp outlines and rigidity of the concepts of the calculi of mathematics. Since this short way will not work perhaps it would be wise to re-examine, in a parallel excursus of our own, the sort of move which he handles so toughly in his *Excursus on Indirect Utilitarianism*.

Excursus on Indirect Utilitarianism. 'When I am in funds and consider whether I should pay my debts or give the same amount to charity, I must choose the former because repayment not only benefits my creditor . . . but also upholds the general credit system' (pp. 42–3 above). 'The view that a judge upholds [sc. *ought* to uphold? – A. F.] a bad law in order that law in general should not suffer is indefensible' (p. 44 above). Mabbott has two arguments against these appeals to the *indirectly* utilitarian (ethical) advantages of keeping promises, enforcing laws, repaying debts, in cases either where the *direct* results seem unlikely to be the best from a utilitarian point of view or where the *indirect* benefits may increase the balance of *direct* advantage. First, with Ross, he claims that the indirect consequences of single breaches of rules have been exaggerated. Second, emphatically as supposedly decisive, he claims that the indirect disadvantages of breaches are the consequences of people getting to know of the breaches, not of the breaches as such: 'It follows that indirect utilitarianism is wrong in all such cases. For the argument can always be met by "Keep it dark"' (p. 44 above).

But this is too short a way with dissenters. The first claim is perhaps all very well. But, of course, a series of exceptions in single cases can add up to the effective abandonment of a general rule.

And Mabbott himself is emphatic about the possible utilitarian advantages of having even a bad system of laws rather than no system at all. A beach is made up of single grains of sand. The second claim too is sound enough. But again the 'indirect utilitarian' could argue that while the occurrence of single exceptions can, as a matter of fact, be kept dark (although it is almost impossible in any particular case to be sure that we shall succeed in suppression) it is, as a matter of fact, impossible to hush up the occurrence of a large number of exceptions. And, once again, large numbers are made up by the accumulation of units.

Of course such indirect utilitarian arguments[10] – depending as they do on *contingent* facts, about the actual effects upon the maintenance of a system of particular breaches of the prescriptions of that system, and about the possibilities of hushing up the occurrence of such breaches, cannot show that it is never and *necessarily* impossible to justify, upon utilitarian principles, the making of an exception by a breach of the prescriptions of a system, which can itself be justified upon utilitarian principles. To adapt one of Mabbott's own examples: suppose someone, having willed his property to be disposed of by a friend in accordance with private oral instructions, makes that friend promise to devote the money to a futile purpose; then, especially if the friend were the only witness of the making of that promise, even when all possible weight had been given to indirect utilitarian considerations of the importance of maintaining the system of promise-keeping and confidence in promises made, still it might be that the balance of good, on utilitarian principles, was overwhelmingly on the side of breaking this particular promise, diverting the money to a beneficent purpose, and keeping the matter dark. Mabbott takes this as the *reductio ad absurdum* of any utilitarianism (ideal or hedonistic or what have you). Perhaps it is paradoxical, and perhaps it is repugnant to the present moral convictions of many or even most of us. Nevertheless a utilitarian might very well accept and even glory in the paradox, insisting that this was precisely the sort of case in which 'our moral convictions' ought to be reformed.

[10] It is the possibility of such indirect utilitarian arguments which ensures that properly thought out utilitarianisms are self-regulating doctrines. Compare I. M. Crombie's 'Social Clockwork' in *Christian Faith and Communist Faith*, ed. D. M. Mackinnon (1953), especially pp. 109 ff.

'Reform' is surely a key word here. For at any rate the classical utilitarians were concerned not merely with the reform of institutions but with the reform of ethical ideas and ethical reasoning. Mill's *Utilitarianism* is devoted to deciding 'the controversy respecting the criterion of right and wrong' (Everyman edition, p. 1): and phrases like 'a test of right and wrong' (p. 2) 'the moral standard set up by the theory' (p. 6), and 'the utilitarian standard' significantly recur again and again. 'Though the application of the standard may be difficult, it is better than none at all: while in other systems, the moral laws all claiming independent authority, there is no common umpire entitled to interfere between them' (p. 24). Mill refuses 'to enquire how far the bad effects of this deficiency have been mitigated in practice, or to what extent the moral beliefs of mankind have been vitiated or made uncertain by the absence of any distinct recognition of an ultimate standard' (p. 8). But his phrasing makes clear his belief that there was a need for reform which he was hoping to meet. The burden of his charge against 'the intuitive school of ethics' and of the corresponding claim for its 'inductive' rival rests on the failure of the one and the success of the other in producing the test or standard required. And the acceptance of this alone makes possible a corresponding reform in ethical reasoning: 'Whether happiness be or be not the end to which morality should be referred – that it should be referred to an *end* of some sort, and not left in the dominion of vague feeling or inexplicable internal conviction, that it be made a matter of reason and calculation, and not merely of sentiment, is essential to the very idea of moral philosophy; is, in fact, what renders argument or discussion of moral questions possible' (*Essay on Bentham*).[11]

[11] Perhaps we should emphasise here that, of course, Mill (though not Bentham) was very insistent indeed about the great importance of 'secondary principles'. The proposed reform did not consist in or include anything so monstrous as the suggestion that we should 'endeavour to test each individual action directly by the first principle' (*Utilitarianism*, Everyman ed., p. 22). There is no need to expatiate here in view of J. O. Urmson's recent powerful attack on these and other popular misconceptions of Mill (*Philosophical Quarterly*, 1953). But for a grim warning of the results of accepting this suggestion which Mill was not making see Arthur Koestler's *Darkness at Noon* (1940) on the Party 'travelling without ethical ballast', where the self-regulator – see footnote 10 above, p. 98 – is not in use.

Let us now return to the objections to Mabbott's solution in its third interpretation. The second objection is that on examination this resolves itself into one or the other of, or a confusion of, the other two. For, on the one hand, it may amount to saying that punishment is necessarily 'retributive', in the sense in which this thesis has already been examined and explained (in III (b) (i) above). In this sense it is the assertion that the sole consideration relevant to the question 'Would it be justifiable to punish him' is 'Did he commit an offence for which this is the penalty prescribed?', and that this is so because of the very meaning of 'punishment'. Or, on the other hand, it amounts to the same thing as the ethical claim, [examined in III (b) (ii), above] that the sole and always requisite true justification for punishing a man is that he has committed the appropriate offence. [See II (b), above, on *good reasons* in ethics.] Decisions as to what is and is not to be allowed to be relevant in ethical discussions can – when the consideration concerned is not *necessarily relevant* [compare III (b) (i) *ad fin*] – themselves be value decisions. Consider how my (really ethical) refusal to take into account the effects on, say, Egyptians or Negroes of my actions could be given a logical look by saying that these are *irrelevant*: by refusing to admit as any sort of *reason* in any discussion about the right thing to do any statement of the form 'That would harm E, an Egyptian, or N, a Negro'.[12]

(*Summary of Section III* (b)). The upshot is that in general there must be a 'retributive' element in punishment, in as much as punishments to be punishments must be of an offender for an offence; though this is not a matter of universal logical necessity but only of 'necessary truth in the great majority of cases', since there can be occasional exceptions. Mabbott's main mistakes were, I think: first, to insist that punishment is *necessarily and always* 'retributive' in this (non-ethical) sense; second, to think that such a supposedly necessary truth about punishment (or anything else) could constitute a retributive or any other sort of moral justification of it (or anything else). To attempt to justify from the concept alone is like trying to prove existence from the concept alone – the Ontological Argument. There is this at least to be said for it, that if 'our moral convictions' are to be accepted as the arbiter, then the attempt to

[12] 'Mr Lyttelton has helped to force through a federation based on the admitted policy of regarding African political opinions as irrelevant' (*Observer*, 23 Aug 1953).

justify from the concept alone will amount to an appeal to the popular moral convictions encapsulated in ordinary language.

(c) *Overdetermination.* Sometimes it seems to be assumed that there must be an inconsistency in justifying the adoption and enforcement of a law or a system of laws by *both* utilitarian *and* retributive appeals. (To which party do you belong?) But there is no necessary inconsistency in this, any more than there is in having advocated the nationalisation of coal but now opposing the nationalisation of chemicals or cement: though of course the people making these appeals or combining these policies may say other things, or offer supporting reasons, which do involve them in inconsistency. Thus having a law against murder, or against any other sort of behaviour which is reckoned to be wrong whether it is made illegal or not, can be defended: both on the grounds that this makes for commodious living and against lives nasty, brutish, and short; and on the grounds that it makes for wicked men getting their deserts. (I suspect that not only would most people resort to both sorts of arguments but that Mill too would have done so – though he would have said that any 'secondary principle' of retri bution for ill-desert had *ultimately* to be justified by reference to the 'first principle', the 'Greatest Happiness Principle'. I cannot hope to make good the historical claim here. But I refer again to Urmson's most excellent paper, cited above, and to the fact that Mill made 'the turning point of the distinction between morality and simple expediency' that for wrong doing 'a person ought to be punished' (*Utilitarianism*, Everyman ed., p. 45)).

Perhaps philosophers have been misled into this assumption by undertaking to find a single unitary and comprehensive justification for all justified punishments, what is deceptively described as 'a theory of punishment'. This must commit them to producing: either an ethical claim which is to be insisted on in every case, and to which no exceptions whatever will be admitted; or a necessary truth which obtains the universality required only at the cost of ceasing to be any sort of ethical justification.

IV

We have tried in this paper to bring out the main features of the logic of the expression 'the justification of punishment'; and to apply the lessons to one outstanding paper about the justification of punishment. We have not attempted, except in so far as was absolutely necessary, incidentally, to do any actual justification on our own account. Indeed the entire paper might be considered as prolegomena only, except that they are prolegomena of the sort which suggest that the later enterprise – in the form of a comprehensive and universal enquiry as opposed to either a series of piecemeal jobs done in particular contexts or the attempt to find generally useful principles to which there will be occasional exceptions – was misconceived.

POSTSCRIPT (1967)

I am grateful to the Editor of the present book for giving me this opportunity to indicate that and where I have profited from the discussion appearing in the journals during the thirteen years since the first publication of my own contribution.

1. Professor Kurt Baier (see his article, reprinted below as Paper 8) quoted me: 'The term "punishment" is sufficiently vague to permit us to speak *in single cases and provided these do not become too numerous* (if they do become too numerous, then *ipso facto* the use, the meaning, of "punishment" has changed) of punishing a man who has broken no law (or even done no wrong)' (p. 132 below). Baier objects – and rightly – 'that Flew has got the analysis wrong'. After a further quotation from my paper he continues: 'It is not pedantic, but plain wrong, to insist in single cases that people (logically) cannot be punished for what they have not done. But this is not a statistical matter at all. True, a system of inflicting unpleasantness on scapegoats *as such* is not a system of punishment, but then a single case of inflicting unpleasantness on a scapegoat *as such* is not a case of punishment either' (pp. 132–3 below: italics in original).

By all this I am persuaded. But to bring out the precise nature of my mistake, and thereby to show precisely what the truth here really is, we need to refer also to section 4 of Mr Anthony Quinton's 'On Punishment', which appeared first in *Analysis* 1954–5 (reprinted above as Paper 3) and which was presumably being written at the same time as my own paper. The crux surely is that punishment has necessarily (to be at least pretended) to be for an offence.

Quinton proceeds to defend this insight by urging – the line of argument is his while the words and examples are mine – that the expression 'I am punishing you although I know that you are innocent of any crime' is as improper logically as 'I promise that I will although I do not intend to'. This is so notwithstanding that it would be as proper to say, in the third person, that Stalin had many people punished although he himself knew them to be innocent as it would be to say, equally truly, and again in the third person, that he promised to have free elections in the countries occupied by the Red Army although he never had the slightest intention of permitting anything of the sort.

It is, therefore, perfectly conceivable – and here the example is borrowed from Baier – always granted the notorious incompetence of the Ruritanian police and judiciary, that all those punished in that unhappy land might in fact be innocent. In that case it would become entirely proper and correct to say that all the victims of the Ruritanian penal system were being unjustly punished – always provided, that is, that those responsible believed (or at least pretended to believe) that the sufferers were suffering for their (supposed) offences.

Baier objects against Quinton, and in this again I think that he is clearly right, that to say '"I am punishing you for what you have not done" . . . need not be absurd at all. The executioner may whisper it to the man who has been sentenced to death.' The two cases which Quinton has taken to be analogous would be parallel 'only if to *say* "I am punishing you . . ." *were* to punish you, just as [to say] "I promise you . . ." *is* to promise you. In other words, the verb "to promise" is a performatory word, "to punish" is not' (p. 135 above: italics in original).

Certainly the executioner may without any logical impropriety whisper these words of unconsoling consolation. Nor would the fact that in this one case (or even the fact that in all cases) his victim (or victims) was (or were) indeed innocent be sufficient to disqualify this case (or the whole system) as a genuine case (or system) of punishment. What would disqualify would be if the executioner did not whisper but shouted, and if no one said him nay. For the execution of one of a tyrant's innocent victims to become not just plain old-fashioned murder but unjust capital punishment there has to have been at least a pretence of a trial, a pretence of legality.

2. In 'It Serves You Right', in *Philosophy*, 1962, Mr A. R. Manser writes: 'For example, Mr Quinton says "The retributivist thesis, therefore, is not a moral doctrine, but an account of the meaning of the word 'punishment'". Other writers have agreed with Mr Quinton, e.g. Professor Flew, and Mr Benn' (p. 295).

Here the fault of which I have to repent is not that with which Manser charges me, but another. For I had believed: both, in general, that I was putting great emphasis upon this fundamental distinction between questions about the meaning of the word 'punishment', and questions about the possible justification of the ongoings and systems of ongoings to which that word may properly be applied; and, in particular, that I had made it clear how, although 'there must be a "retributive" element in punishment, in as much as punishments to be punishments must be of an offender for an offence', nevertheless it is completely wrong to think that any 'necessary truth about punishment (or anything else) could constitute a retributive or any other sort of moral justification of it (or anything else).' I even added: 'To attempt to justify from the concept alone is like trying to prove existence from the concept alone – the Ontological Argument' (p. 100).

It is, therefore, a mistake to side me with Quinton on this issue. I should never at any time have dissented from Manser's insistence that it is erroneous to the point of perversity to suggest, as Quinton does, that 'retributivism, properly understood, is not a moral but a logical doctrine, and that it does not provide a moral justification of the infliction of punishment but an elucidation of the use of the word' (p. 55 above). Furthermore I should always have been ready, not to say eager, to offer as the ideal example of retributivism as a moral (or immoral) doctrine precisely the supposed eternal punishments of Hell, so aptly yet so unfashionably cited by Manser: 'In fact this might be described as the archetypal instance of retributive punishment, for eternal damnation cannot be regarded as having any reformative function, and the degree of punishment usually said to be inflicted in Hell seems sufficient deterrence without the addition of eternity. . . . The damned in Hell were there because they deserved it, and were not worthy of pity. St Thomas says, "Therefore the blessed in glory will have no pity on the damned" ' (p. 297).

3. Having thus seen how Manser was misled, presumably by the inadequacies of my exposition, to see a disagreement between us where in fact there was – and is – only strong concurrence I have no call to be surprised to find that Mr K. G. Armstrong's 'The Retributivist Hits Back' in *Mind* 1961 (reprinted as Paper 9 below) accuses me of confusing questions about the justification of the infliction of particular penalties in particular cases with questions about the justification of whole systems of punishment; and that too in a passage in which I had thought I was employing this very distinction. This passage quoted by Armstrong (p. 149 below) is one about which I now feel uneasy on other grounds: 'though Mabbott claims to "reject absolutely all utilitarian considerations from its justification", he is prepared to appeal to these to justify *systems* of punishment. But if a *system* is to be justified even partly on such grounds, some cases within that system must be partly justifiable on the same grounds: the system surely could not have effects to which no case within it contributed' (p. 94 above).

From these two cases of – as it seems to me – misapprehension, and from Mr D. Locke's generous tribute to the achievement represented by Armstrong's conjunction of the two fundamental distinctions involved therein [see Locke's 'The Many Faces of Punishment' in *Mind* (1963), p. 568] there surely is only one moral proper for me to draw. It is, yet once more, to take to heart an observation attributed to the rhetorician Quintilian: 'One ought to write not just so that the reader may, but so that he must, understand.'

6 ৯ *Two Concepts of Rules**

JOHN RAWLS

In this paper I want to show the importance of the distinction between justifying a practice[1] and justifying a particular action falling under it, and I want to explain the logical basis of this distinction and how it is possible to miss its significance. While the distinction has frequently been made,[2] and is now becoming commonplace, there remains the task of explaining the tendency either to overlook it altogether, or to fail to appreciate its importance.

---

* This is a revision of a paper given at the Harvard Philosophy Club on 30 Apr 1954.

[1] I use the word 'practice' throughout as a sort of technical term meaning any form of activity specified by a system of rules which defines offices, roles, moves, penalties, defences, and so on, and which gives the activity its structure. As examples one may think of games and rituals, trials and parliaments.

[2] The distinction is central to Hume's discussion of justice in *A Treatise of Human Nature*, bk III, pt ii, esp. secs. 2–4. It is clearly stated by John Austin in the second lecture of *Lectures on Jurisprudence* (vol. I, 4th ed., 1873, 116 ff.; 1st ed., 1832). Also it may be argued that J. S. Mill took it for granted in *Utilitarianism*; on this point cf. J. O. Urmson, 'The Interpretation of the Moral Philosophy of J. S. Mill', in *Philosophical Quarterly*, vol. III (1953). In addition to the arguments given by Urmson there are several clear statements of the distinction in *A System of Logic*, 8th ed. (1872), bk VI, ch. xii, pars. 2, 3, 7. The distinction is fundamental to J. D. Mabbott's important paper, 'Punishment' (see Paper 2). More recently the distinction has been stated with particular emphasis by S. E. Toulmin in *The Place of Reason in Ethics* (Cambridge, 1950), see esp. ch. xi, where it plays a major part in his account of moral reasoning. Toulmin doesn't explain the basis of the distinction, nor how one might overlook its importance, as I try to in this paper, and in my review of his book [*Philosophical Review*, vol. LX (Oct 1951)], as some of my criticisms show, I failed to understand the force of it. See also H. D. Aiken, 'The Levels of Moral Discourse', *Ethics*, vol. LXII (1952), A. M. Quinton, 'On Punishment' (Paper 3), and P. H. Nowell-Smith, *Ethics* (1954) pp. 236–9, 271–3.

To show the importance of the distinction I am going to defend utilitarianism against those objections which have traditionally been made against it in connection with punishment and the obligation to keep promises. I hope to show that if one uses the distinction in question then one can state utilitarianism in a way which makes it a much better explication of our considered moral judgments than these traditional objections would seem to admit.[3] Thus the importance of the distinction is shown by the way it strengthens the utilitarian view regardless of whether that view is completely defensible or not.

To explain how the significance of the distinction may be overlooked, I am going to discuss two conceptions of rules. One of these conceptions conceals the importance of distinguishing between the justification of a rule or practice and the justification of a particular action falling under it. The other conception makes it clear why this distinction must be made and what is its logical basis.

I

The subject of punishment, in the sense of attaching legal penalties to the violation of legal rules, has always been a troubling moral question.[4] The trouble about it has not been that people disagree as to whether or not punishment is justifiable. Most people have held that, freed from certain abuses, it is an acceptable institution. Only a few have rejected punishment entirely, which is rather surprising when one considers all that can be said against it. The difficulty is with the justification of punishment: various arguments for it have been given by moral philosophers, but so far none of them has won any sort of general acceptance; no justification is without those who detest it. I hope to show that the use of the aforementioned distinction enables one to state the utilitarian view in a way which allows for the sound points of its critics.

For our purposes we may say that there are two justifications of

[3] On the concept of explication see the author's paper *Philosophical Review*, vol. LX (Apr 1951).

[4] While this paper was being revised, Quinton's appeared in *Analysis*; footnote 2 above. There are several respects in which my remarks are similar to his. Yet as I consider some further questions and rely on somewhat different arguments, I have retained the discussion of punishment and promises together as two test cases for utilitarianism.

punishment. What we may call the retributive view is that punishment is justified on the grounds that wrong-doing merits punishment. It is morally fitting that a person who does wrong should suffer in proportion to his wrong-doing. That a criminal should be punished follows from his guilt, and the severity of the appropriate punishment depends on the depravity of his act. The state of affairs where a wrong-doer suffers punishment is morally better than the state of affairs where he does not; and it is better irrespective of any of the consequences of punishing him.

What we may call the utilitarian view holds that on the principle that bygones are bygones and that only future consequences are material to present decisions, punishment is justifiable only by reference to the probable consequences of maintaining it as one of the devices of the social order. Wrongs committed in the past are, as such, not relevant considerations for deciding what to do. If punishment can be shown to promote effectively the interest of society it is justifiable, otherwise it is not.

I have stated these two competing views very roughly to make one feel the conflict between them: one feels the force of *both* arguments and one wonders how they can be reconciled. From my introductory remarks it is obvious that the resolution which I am going to propose is that in this case one must distinguish between justifying a practice as a system of rules to be applied and enforced, and justifying a particular action which falls under these rules; utilitarian arguments are appropriate with regard to questions about practices, while retributive arguments fit the application of particular rules to particular cases.

We might try to get clear about this distinction by imagining how a father might answer the question of his son. Suppose the son asks, 'Why was *J* put in jail yesterday?' The father answers, 'Because he robbed the bank at *B*. He was duly tried and found guilty. That's why he was put in jail yesterday.' But suppose the son had asked a different question, namely, 'Why do people put other people in jail?' Then the father might answer, 'To protect good people from bad people' or 'To stop people from doing things that would make it uneasy for all of us; for otherwise we wouldn't be able to go to bed at night and sleep in peace.' There are two very different questions here. One question emphasizes the proper name: it asks why *J* was punished rather than someone else, or it asks what he was punished for. The other question asks why we have the institution of punishment: why do people punish one another rather than, say, always forgiving one another?

Thus the father says in effect that a particular man is punished, rather than some other man, because he is guilty, and he is guilty because he broke the law (past tense). In his case the law looks back, the judge looks back, the jury looks back, and a penalty is visited upon him for something he did. That a man is to be punished, and what his punishment is to be, is settled by its being shown that he broke the law and that the law assigns that penalty for the violation of it.

On the other hand we have the institution of punishment itself, and recommend and accept various changes in it, because it is thought by the (ideal) legislator and by those to whom the law applies that, as a part of a system of law impartially applied from case to case arising under it, it will have the consequence, in the long run, of furthering the interests of society.

One can say, then, that the judge and the legislator stand in different positions and look in different directions: one to the past, the other to the future. The justification of what the judge does, *qua* judge, sounds like the retributive view; the justification of what the (ideal) legislator does, *qua* legislator, sounds like the utilitarian view. Thus both views have a point (this is as it should be since intelligent and sensitive persons have been on both sides of the argument); and one's initial confusion disappears once one sees that these views apply to persons holding different offices with different duties, and situated differently with respect to the system of rules that make up the criminal law.[5]

One might say, however, that the utilitarian view is more fundamental since it applies to a more fundamental office, for the judge carries out the legislator's will so far as he can determine it. Once the legislator decides to have laws and to assign penalties for their violation (as things are there must be both the law and the penalty) an institution is set up which involves a retributive conception of particular cases. It is part of the concept of the criminal law as a system of rules that the application and enforcement of these rules in particular cases should be justifiable by arguments of a retributive character. The decision whether or not to use law rather

[5] Note the fact that different sorts of arguments are suited to different offices. One way of taking the differences between ethical theories is to regard them as accounts of the reasons expected in different offices.

than some other mechanism of social control, and the decision as to what laws to have and what penalties to assign, may be settled by utilitarian arguments; but if one decides to have laws then one has decided on something whose working in particular cases is retributive in form.[6]

The answer, then, to the confusion engendered by the two views of punishment is quite simple: one distinguishes two offices, that of the judge and that of the legislator, and one distinguishes their different stations with respect to the system of rules which make up the law; and then one notes that the different sorts of considerations which would usually be offered as reasons for what is done under the cover of these offices can be paired off with the competing justifications of punishment. One reconciles the two views by the time-honoured device of making them apply to different situations.

But can it really be this simple? Well, this answer allows for the apparent intent of each side. Does a person who advocates the retributive view necessarily advocate, as an *institution*, legal machinery whose essential purpose is to set up and preserve a correspondence between moral turpitude and suffering? Surely not.[7] What retributionists have rightly insisted upon is that no man can be punished unless he is guilty, that is, unless he has broken the law. Their fundamental criticism of the utilitarian account is that, as they interpret it, it sanctions an innocent person's being punished (if one may call it that) for the benefit of society.

On the other hand, utilitarians agree that punishment is to be inflicted only for the violation of law. They regard this much as understood from the concept of punishment itself.[8] The point of

---

[6] In this connection see Mabbott (Paper 2 above), p. 57.

[7] On this point see Sir David Ross, *The Right and the Good* (Oxford, 1930), pp. 57–60.

[8] See Hobbes's definition of punishment in *Leviathan*, ch. xxviii; and Bentham's definition in *The Principles of Morals and Legislation*, ch. xii, par. 36, ch. xv, par. 28, and in *The Rationale of Punishment* (1830) bk. 1, ch. i. They could agree with Bradley that: 'Punishment is punishment only when it is deserved. We pay the penalty, because we owe it, and for no other reason; and if punishment is inflicted for any other reason whatever than because it is merited by wrong, it is a gross immorality, a crying injustice, an abominable crime, and not what it pretends to be.' *Ethical Studies*, 2nd ed. (Oxford, 1927), pp. 26–7. Certainly by definition it isn't what it pretends to be. The innocent can only be punished by mistake; deliberate 'punishment' of the innocent necessarily involves fraud.

the utilitarian account concerns the institution as a system of rules: utilitarianism seeks to limit its use by declaring it justifiable only if it can be shown to foster effectively the good of society. Historically it is a protest against the indiscriminate and ineffective use of the criminal law.[9] It seeks to dissuade us from assigning to penal institutions the improper, if not sacrilegious, task of matching suffering with moral turpitude. Like others, utilitarians want penal institutions designed so that, as far as humanly possible, only those who break the law run afoul of it. They hold that no official should have discretionary power to inflict penalties whenever he thinks it for the benefit of society; for on utilitarian grounds an institution granting such power could not be justified.[10]

The suggested way of reconciling the retributive and the utilitarian justifications of punishment seems to account for what both sides have wanted to say. There are, however, two further questions which arise, and I shall devote the remainder of this section to them.

First, will not a difference of opinion as to the proper criterion of just law make the proposed reconciliation unacceptable to retributionists? Will they not question whether, if the utilitarian principle is used as the criterion, it follows that those who have broken the law are guilty in a way which satisfies their demand that those punished deserve to be punished? To answer this difficulty, suppose that the rules of the criminal law are justified on utilitarian grounds (it is only for laws that meet his criterion that the utilitarian can be held responsible). Then it follows that the actions which the criminal law specifies as offences are such that, if they were tolerated, terror and alarm would spread in society. Consequently,

---

[9] Cf. Leon Radzinowicz, *A History of English Criminal Law: The Movement for Reform 1750–1833* (1948), esp. ch. xi on Bentham.

[10] Bentham discusses how corresponding to a punitory provision of a criminal law there is another provision which stands to it as an antagonist and which needs a name as much as the punitory. He calls it, as one might expect, the *anaetiosostic*, and of it he says: 'The punishment of guilt is the object of the former one: the preservation of innocence that of the latter.' In the same connection he asserts that it is never thought fit to give the judge the option of deciding whether a thief (that is, a person whom he believes to be a thief, for the judge's belief is what the question must always turn upon) should hang or not, and so the law writes the provision: 'The judge shall not cause a thief to be hanged unless he have been duly convicted and sentenced in course of law' [*The Limits of Jurisprudence Defined*, ed. C. W. Everett (New York, 1945), pp. 238–9].

retributionists can only deny that those who are punished deserve to be punished if they deny that such actions are wrong. This they will not want to do.

The second question is whether utilitarianism doesn't justify too much. One pictures it as an engine of justification which, if consistently adopted, could be used to justify cruel and arbitrary institutions. Retributionists may be supposed to concede that utilitarians *intend* to reform the law and to make it more humane; that utilitarians do not *wish* to justify any such thing as punishment of the innocent; and that utilitarians may appeal to the fact that punishment presupposes guilt in the sense that by punishment one understands an institution attaching penalties to the infraction of legal rules, and therefore that it is logically absurd to suppose that utilitarians in justifying *punishment* might also have justified punishment (if we may call it that) of the innocent. The real question, however, is whether the utilitarian, in justifying punishment, hasn't used arguments which commit him to accepting the infliction of suffering on innocent persons if it is for the good of society (whether or not one calls this punishment). More generally, isn't the utilitarian committed in principle to accepting many practices which he, as a morally sensitive person, wouldn't want to accept? Retributionists are inclined to hold that there is no way to stop the utilitarian principle from justifying too much except by adding to it a principle which distributes certain rights to individuals. Then the amended criterion is not the greatest benefit of society *simpliciter*, but the greatest benefit of society subject to the constraint that no one's rights may be violated. Now while I think that the classical utilitarians proposed a criterion of this more complicated sort, I do not want to argue that point here.[11] What I want to show is that there is *another* way of preventing the utilitarian principle from justifying too much, or at least of making it much less likely to do so: namely, by stating utilitarianism in a way which accounts for the distinction between the justification of an institution and the justification of a particular action falling under it.

I begin by defining the institution of punishment as follows: a person is said to suffer punishment whenever he is legally deprived of some of the normal rights of a citizen on the ground that he has violated a rule of law, the violation having been established by trial

[11] By the classical utilitarians I understand Hobbes, Hume, Bentham, J. S. Mill, and Sidgwick.

according to the due process of law, provided that the deprivation is carried out by the recognised legal authorities of the State, that the rule of law clearly specifies both the offence and the attached penalty, that the courts construe statutes strictly, and that the statute was on the books prior to the time of the offence.[12] This definition specifies what I shall understand by punishment. The question is whether utilitarian arguments may be found to justify institutions widely different from this and such as one would find cruel and arbitrary.

This question is best answered, I think, by taking up a particular accusation. Consider the following from Carritt:

> the utilitarian must hold that we are justified in inflicting pain always and only to prevent worse pain or bring about greater happiness. This, then, is all we need to consider in so-called punishment, which must be purely preventive. But if some kind of very cruel crime becomes common, and none of the criminals can be caught, it might be highly expedient, as an example, to hang an innocent man, if a charge against him could be so framed that he were universally thought guilty; indeed this would only fail to be an ideal instance of utilitarian 'punishment' because the victim himself would not have been so likely as a real felon to commit such a crime in the future; in all other respects it would be perfectly deterrent and therefore felicific.[13]

Carritt is trying to show that there are occasions when a utilitarian argument would justify taking an action which would be generally condemned; and thus that utilitarianism justifies too much. But the failure of Carritt's argument lies in the fact that he makes no distinction between the justification of the general system of rules which constitutes penal institutions and the justification of particular applications of these rules to particular cases by the various officials whose job it is to administer them. This becomes perfectly clear when one asks who the 'we' are of whom Carritt speaks. Who is this who has a sort of absolute authority on particular occasions to decide that an innocent man shall be 'punished' if everyone can be convinced that he is guilty? Is this person the legislator, or the judge, or the body of private citizens, or what? It is utterly crucial to know who is to decide such matters, and by what authority, for

[12] All these measures of punishment are mentioned by Hobbes; cf. *Leviathan*, ch. xxviii.

[13] *Ethical and Political Thinking* (Oxford, 1947) p. 65.

all of this must be written into the rules of the institution. Until one knows these things one doesn't know what the institution is whose justification is being challenged; and as the utilitarian principle applies to the institution one doesn't know whether it is justifiable on utilitarian grounds or not.

Once this is understood it is clear what the counter-move to Carritt's argument is. One must describe more carefully what the *institution* is which his example suggests, and then ask oneself whether or not it is likely that having this institution would be for the benefit of society in the long run. One must not content oneself with the vague thought that, when it's a question of *this* case, it would be a good thing if *somebody* did something even if an innocent person were to suffer.

Try to imagine, then, an institution (which we may call 'telishment') which is such that the officials set up by it have authority to arrange a trial for the condemnation of an innocent man whenever they are of the opinion that doing so would be in the best interests of society. The discretion of officials is limited, however, by the rule that they may not condemn an innocent man to undergo such an ordeal unless there is, at the time, a wave of offences similar to that with which they charge him and telish him for. We may imagine that the officials having the discretionary authority are the judges of the higher courts in consultation with the chief of police, the minister of justice, and a committee of the legislature.

Once one realises that one is involved in setting up an *institution*, one sees that the hazards are very great. For example, what check is there on the officials? How is one to tell whether or not their actions are authorised? How is one to limit the risks involved in allowing such systematic deception? How is one to avoid giving anything short of complete discretion to the authorities to telish anyone they like? In addition to these considerations, it is obvious that people will come to have a very different attitude towards their penal system when telishment is adjoined to it. They will be uncertain as to whether a convicted man has been punished or telished. They will wonder whether or not they should feel sorry for him. They will wonder whether the same fate won't at any time fall on them. If one pictures how such an institution would actually work, and the enormous risks involved in it, it seems clear that it would serve no useful purpose. A utilitarian justification for this institution is most unlikely.

It happens in general that as one drops off the defining features of punishment one ends up with an institution whose utilitarian justification is highly doubtful. One reason for this is that punishment works like a kind of price system: by altering the prices one has to pay for the performance of actions it supplies a motive for avoiding some actions and doing others. The defining features are essential if punishment is to work in this way; so that an institution which lacks these features, e.g., an institution which is set up to 'punish' the innocent, is likely to have about as much point as a price system (if one may call it that) where the prices of things change at random from day to day and one learns the price of something after one has agreed to buy it.[14]

If one is careful to apply the utilitarian principle to the institution which is to authorise particular actions, then there is *less* danger of its justifying too much. Carritt's example gains plausibility by its indefiniteness and by its concentration on the particular case. His argument will only hold if it can be shown that there are utilitarian arguments which justify an institution whose publicly ascertainable offices and powers are such as to permit officials to exercise that kind of discretion in particular cases. But the requirement of having to build the arbitrary features of the particular decision into the institutional practice makes the justification much less likely to go through.

[14] The analogy with the price system suggests an answer to the question how utilitarian considerations insure that punishment is proportional to the offence. It is interesting to note that Sir David Ross, after making the distinction between justifying a penal law and justifying a particular application of it, and after stating that utilitarian considerations have a large place in determining the former, still holds back from accepting the utilitarian justification of punishment on the grounds that justice requires that punishment be proportional to the offence, and that utilitarianism is unable to account for this. Cf. *The Right and the Good*, pp. 61–2. I do not claim that utilitarianism can account for this requirement as Sir David might wish, but it happens, nevertheless, that if utilitarian considerations are followed penalties will be proportional to offences in this sense: the order of offences according to seriousness can be paired off with the order of penalties according to severity. Also the absolute level of penalties will be as low as possible. This follows from the assumption that people are rational (i.e., that they are able to take into account the 'prices' the state puts on actions), the utilitarian rule that a penal system should provide a motive for preferring the less serious offence, and the principle that punishment as such is an evil. All this was carefully worked out by Bentham in *The Principles of Morals and Legislation*, chs. xiii–xv.

7 ❧ Professor Flew on Punishment

J. D. MABBOTT

Professor Flew's vigorous and interesting paper, 'The Justification of Punishment' (Paper 5), discusses my article on 'Punishment' (Paper 2). It merits some rejoinder. Flew's paper ranges far beyond the particular issue of punishment, and much of what is most interesting in it has this wider relevance. I, too, therefore shall use punishment as a peg on which to hang some discussion of the wider problems of ethics.

I LANGUAGE

Flew begins his paper by pointing out that the word 'punishment' exhibits both vagueness and 'open texture'; and suggests that my argument suffers from neglect of these features. I agree about the linguistic facts. The word 'punishment' is used in a variety of ways and one cannot lay down rules to determine where its use becomes appropriate. Thus it is impossible to give a precise definition of the word as ordinarily used. This is the 'vagueness' point. It is also true that there are various different criteria for its use, and not all of these need be satisfied for the use to be natural and legitimate. This is the point about 'open texture'. We do find people talking of punishment of criminals (by the State), of blacklegs (by a union), of bad men (by God), of foolish men (gout for over-drinking), of villages or hostages (by an occupying power), of innocent men (as scapegoats), of children (by parents), of dogs (by their masters), of leaking boats (deodand), of toys (by children), of boxers (by Joe Louis), of bowling (by Don Bradman). I did not begin my 1939 article with a piece of dictionary-making of this sort, but it must be remembered that this fashionable practice was less fashionable then. I regard this interest in varieties of usage as relevant in philosophy only when the differences are logically important. Too much recent discussion of this type seems to me the magpie accumulation of usages without putting them to any philosophical purpose, except the purpose of showing that most ordinary words are vague or open-textured. Even when philosophical relevance is the aim, the search is often conducted by examining usage after usage in the hope that something logically interesting will emerge. This is like looking in every green field for mushrooms or in every oyster for a pearl. There seems, moreover, a tendency to suggest that if you go on talking long enough about how people talk, something of philosophical interest *must* emerge; as if hopeful meadow-walking was a way of making mushrooms grow, or as if opening enough oysters would in the end so irritate some oyster that it would produce a pearl. And there are even some who seem to think that this is the only method of mushroom-growing or pearl-culture – or philosophy.

Flew has walked over various linguistic meadows and opened various linguistic oysters, but I cannot see that this has enabled him to discover any mushrooms or pearls. Does he mean to suggest that no general answer can be given to any moral question about punishment, because the term is so vague and open-textured? His conclusion suggests this. Does he think that 'the justification of punishment' would have to mean the several justifications of punishment in each of its usages listed above? My article failed because it did not consider how gout could be justified as a punishment for the three-bottle man, how children are to be justified in punishing the toy that has tripped them, or how the punishing activities of Joe Louis and Don Bradman are to be defended. I do not feel very guilty on this score.

II THE STANDARD CASE

Fortunately, however, Flew does not surrender so easily as his own linguistic theory would require and as his conclusion suggests. He proceeds at once to formulate criteria for what he calls a strict and standard usage of 'punishment'. In deference to his own linguistic views, he calls these criteria 'proposals' of his own (rather than a definition of punishment in the strict sense). But he takes the sting out of this by adding that his selection of these criteria is not subjective or arbitrary, for they 'express the general dominant tendencies in usage'. Indeed he makes further admissions. Anyone would agree that the Louis-Bradman usages are metaphorical and secondary. But Flew admits that 'punishment' in connection with scapegoats or collective persons is metaphorical and secondary too, as is talk of gout as a punishment for intemperance (unless one believes that this suffering is inflicted by God for an offence against His laws). But this really means that all the examples in my list above except the first two (and perhaps punishment of children) are metaphorical and secondary uses. Therefore when I concentrated on punishment as defined by the strict criteria I was justified. A moralist who is considering the moral justification of promise-keeping does not invalidate his argument if he omits to discuss the moral implications (if any) of 'promise' in a 'young man of promise' or 'the clouds show promise of rain'.

With Flew's criteria for his standard case (pp. 84–7 above) I am in substantial agreement, but there are one or two points of detail I should wish to make. In his first criterion he uses 'evil' or 'unpleasantness' instead of 'pain' as essential to the meaning of 'punishment', on the grounds that 'pain' usually has physical implications. Few punishments in modern penology involve pain – flogging is the exception and it is on the way out. I think Flew takes 'evil' or 'unpleasantness' as wide terms to cover both physical pain and mental suffering. I have two quarrels with this. The word 'evil' is misleading because it carries too much moral flavour. When a man suffers apprehension in a doctor's waiting-room and pain in the surgery does this mean that there are two evil states of affairs on these two occasions? 'Disliked' would be a better word than 'evil' or 'unpleasant'. For even 'unpleasant' has its dangers. Most punishments nowadays are not afflictions of suffering, either physical or mental. They are the deprivation of a good. Rashdall alone among philosophic writers on punishment seems to me to recognise this (*Theory of Good and Evil*, vol. 1, p. 287, note 1). Imprisonment and fine are deprivations of liberty and property. The death sentence is deprivation of life; and in this extreme case every attempt is made to exclude suffering. Hanging is defended, as in the Royal Commission Report on Capital Punishment, as the most painless method of execution (paras. 726–31). It may be said that this does not affect the mental agony of awaiting the end. But again the aim of the punishment is not to cause this mental agony. If it were so, delay in execution would be desirable and the waiting period would be the punishment. But delay is defended on the ground that time must be given for an application for a reprieve (para. 763). And the Report insists that 'the preliminaries of the execution should be free from anything that unnecessarily sharpens the prisoner's apprehension' (para. 724). Flew's suggestion that we have progressed by substituting mental suffering for physical pain does not go far enough. We have taken the more important step of substituting the removal of something desired for the infliction of positive suffering. Plato first drew this distinction, in discussing ignorance. The absence or loss of knowledge is a deprivation of good. Ignorance is not essentially painful or unpleasant, though it may become so when one reflects on it (*Philebus*, 52a, b). I do not raise these points out of linguistic or lexicographical nicety. It is a standard objection to the retributive theory that retributive punishment simply adds evil to evil. By showing how, in these two ways, 'evil' is inappropriate, both because it is moral and because it is positive, I can weaken this standard objection. The world is a worse place the more evil there is in it and perhaps the more suffering there is in it. But it does not seem to me necessarily a worse place whenever men are deprived of something they would like to retain; and this is the essence of modern punishment.

Flew's second and third criteria (punishment must be *for* an offence and *of* an offender) seem to me correct, provided that 'offence' and 'offender' mean offence and offender against laws and not merely 'sin' and 'sinner'. It is to be noted (for future reference) that when it is not an offender but an innocent man who is punished, and this is done systematically, punishment is used in a secondary and metaphorical sense (pp. 85–6 above). Flew thinks it would be pedantic to deny that it is proper to speak of punishing an innocent man in single cases.

The fourth criterion is that punishment should be the work of personal agencies. Again I agree, and I thought Flew's analysis here most useful. My original article dismissed the whole problem of Divine punishment in a brief and cavalier sentence 'For a moral offence, God alone has the *status* necessary to punish the offender; and the theologians are becoming more and more doubtful whether even God must punish wrong-doing' (p. 41 above). But it is particularly interesting to notice here both the confusions of ordinary thinking and the difficulties of the theologian. I am sure many people still think of some suffering as visited on men for their sins. In Dostoievsky's *Crime and Punishment*, Raskolnikov found he was losing control of his thoughts after the murder and cried 'Can this be the punishment already beginning? Indeed! Indeed! it is.'

But men do not always see that this commits them, as Flew rightly says, to a belief in God and in a God of a particular kind – not necessarily of the Christian kind, where the necessary nexus of sin with Divine retribution is broken by conceptions of repentance, absolution and atonement.

The fifth criterion is that punishment must be by an authority whose rule has been broken. This excludes (as I argued in my article) punishment by men for immorality as such, or for anti-social action which breaks no rule laid down.

Flew adds two negative criteria. Punishment is not to be limited to the State. Any rule-making authority or its agents can rightly be said to punish. Penance and excommunication, expulsion from club or union, the chastisement of children by parents or teachers, the 'penalties' in games, are to be included as examples of the standard use of 'punishment'. I am not so sure about this, but I do not think anything serious depends on it. Finally Flew thinks that 'punishment' is strictly applicable to cases which are morally or legally questionable, e.g. to punishment under immoral or retrospective laws. As to punishment under bad laws, I agree. But to call retrospective penalties 'punishment' in the strict sense is to contradict the third and fourth criteria – that punishment must be of an offender and for an offence. It will not do for Flew to say that he was prepared to allow punishment of the innocent in single cases, for retrospective legislation is systematic and not single-case punishment of the innocent. Flew should therefore have treated it as a secondary and non-standard usage.

III THE JUSTIFICATION

Flew next raises some points about 'justification'. He notes that to ask for the 'justification' of anything is to assume that there is one and only one justification possible. But we may justify something as an alternative to something else or against a counter-charge, and these two justifications might well differ. Flew adds that we may also justify something by reference to principles and persons. This telescopes a number of different problems. Something may be justified by a number of different principles (as punishment both by deterrence and by reform). But if I myself so justify it then this is a case of the 'overdetermination' referred to later by Flew and discussed by me in Section V of this note. If, however, I justify it by one principle (retribution) and you justify it by another (deterrence), this is a case of reference to persons. If I talk of *the* justification when I am aware that I do not accept your principles and you do not accept mine, I am suggesting that there is one right answer to the question 'what justification?' and that others are wrong. Flew says this is to conceal the existence (and to misunderstand the nature) of ethical disagreement. Flew, of course, is implicitly making the opposite and now orthodox assumption that when two men differ on a moral (as distinct from a factual or empirical) issue it does not make sense to say one answer is correct and the other mistaken, or that their difference can be resolved by any rational process. We must conclude that, if I am asked for the justification of anything (punishment, or capital punishment), I must do one of three things. (*a*) I may list all the justifications (and presumably the reasons against) which anyone anywhere has advanced or could advance for (or against) it. (*b*) I may put forward my own justification, i.e. takes sides in a moral struggle, a struggle in which there are no awards for merit but only trophies for victory. (*c*) I may reply that the question is unanswerable and give up the claim to be *thinking* about it and, if I retain an interest in it, go in (more honestly) for preaching or prison reform. The last is the solution suggested by the conclusion of Flew's article.

All this is clear enough but it seems to me confused by Flew's references to Toulmin and others who have recently been discussing 'good reasons' in ethics. Flew seems to accuse these authors of *giving* 'good reasons' for certain lines of conduct; he says that Toulmin must maintain that those who give different reasons from his are 'not doing ethics at all'. Toulmin, it seems to me, would answer that if he himself gives a good reason for, e.g., abolishing capital punishment, he is not 'doing ethics' either. The thinking involved in moral decision is moral thinking, not ethical thinking. Or, if you prefer to say that anyone who is considering whether to punish his child and finding a good reason is 'doing ethics', then what Toulmin is doing is meta-ethics. He is asking what it is to be a 'good reason' – what are the general characteristics of moral (? ethical) thinking. I agree that this line is not an easy one to draw (and perhaps there is a third intermediate kind of thinking, of which our punishment discussion is an example). But Flew seems here not to realise that such a line is possible and is drawn by most recent writers on ethics (following Moore and Broad).

IV LOGICAL AND ETHICAL JUSTIFICATION

Flew's main attack on me lies in his view that I am never clear whether I am appealing to the meanings of words or to moral principles, whether I am trying to extract a moral justification out of linguistic usage by an appeal to what people *call* 'punishment', or whether I am really appealing to their views on right and wrong. Flew describes this elsewhere in his paper as the production from my sleeve of definitional jokers, as confusing necessary truths with ethical claims, as making a moral assertion masquerade as a piece of logic, and (most shocking of all) as an ethical ontological argument, attempting to prove existence (of a moral claim) from meaning (of a word).

I can now see that this misunderstanding of my paper was natural. It was also made by Miss Glover in her Note on my article in *Mind*, vol. XLVIII. She says that I have adduced no ethical arguments for retribution. My considerations are logical and legal. 'The logical point seems to be that the very definition of law involves punishment for its infringement . . . punishment is logically entailed (p. 498). And recently Mr Quinton in an article in *Analysis* (reprinted above as Paper 3) has urged that this logical point is the element of truth in the retributive theory. The meaning of 'punishment' includes a reference to past guilt. This implies that we cannot (logically cannot) punish the innocent, and that we can punish the guilty. But it does not imply that we ought to punish the guilty. The reasons for doing so are utilitarian – reform and deterrence – on Quinton's view.

I shall now try to make clear what I meant to say. I do think that a reference to past guilt is included in the meaning of punishment. I agree with Flew that the strict or standard or primary meaning of punishment is the infliction of an undesired state of affairs or the deprival of a desired state of affairs, imposed on a person for breaking a law by an agent of the authority whose law he has broken. I think secondary, loose, and metaphorical senses of punishment are interesting to dictionary-makers but not to philosophers. All of them anyhow make either obvious or impossible any answer to the question 'What justification?' I do not think (and never did, however incautiously I may have expressed myself) that this logical point has any ethical significance. I agree we must go on to ask 'ought persons to suffer injury or loss for breaking laws?' Similarly an accurate definition of 'revenge' or of 'forgiveness' or of 'suicide' would have to be supplemented by ethical judgements on these procedures also (and the first two *logically* include a reference to the past). What I was maintaining was that the officer of a society whose rule has been broken not only can (Quinton) but ought to punish the offender. The obligation is partly explained by his voluntary acceptance of the position of judge, and partly by his recognition of the value of a legal system which has rules with penalties. Quinton recognises that this is a possible account of one *kind* of legal system, a system in which *fixed* penalties are allocated to breaches of rules. [I take it he would admit its applicability to the cases in actual systems in which fixed penalties are laid down. An English judge not only can but *has a duty to* impose the death sentence on a person found guilty of murder. I assume in *this* case Quinton would not say that he (logically) can impose the death sentence but his moral duty is to impose whatever punishment will have (in this case) the best consequences.] But, Quinton points out, in our system in cases other than murder the penalty fixed is a maximum and the judge has discretion. The actual punishment given ought to be determined by considerations of utility. To which I would make two answers. The discretion is given by the law. Even if it would take more than forty shillings to deter or more than fourteen days to reform, the judge has no right to impose those sentences above the maxima. Second, I do not think the considerations which fix the penalty (within the maximum) are utilitarian. They concern not the *effect* on the criminal or others (in the future) but the degree of guilt (in the past) or the degree of responsibility (also in the past). One man knew his brakes were faulty, the other did not (though he could have and ought to have found out about this); one man was subjected to strong temptation, another was not; one man was the ring-leader, another was his tool. (It is to be noted that on utilitarian grounds the punishment for the tempted man and for the tool ought to be heavier than for the man less tempted or for the ring-leader, since it takes a stronger deterrent to make a man resist temptation or his gang-leader's wrath.) The Report of the Royal Commission on Capital Punishment, in noting that for offences other than murder the court has discretion, explains this by saying 'Offences of the same legal category differ greatly in gravity and turpitude, and the courts make full use of the wide range of penalties they have power to impose' (para. 20).

V CONTRADETERMINATION AND OVERDETERMINATION

Miss Glover quotes with telling effect the example of her great-great-uncle, who in defiance of my 'logic' refused to vote for a verdict of 'guilty' on a sheep-stealer (though it was clear he was guilty) because the punishment was death. Flew, however, sees that I was not maintaining an absolute obligation to punish a man who breaks a law. I do 'allow for the possible justifiability of pardons and the unjustifiability of enforcing certain laws' (p. 94 above). Punishment is, I think, a 'prima facie obligation' in the sense in which Ross uses this phrase, a claim on the agent of the authority whose law is broken. But there may be sufficient contra-determination to override this claim (e.g. the extreme badness of the particular law or the rottenness of the legal system). Sabotage from within a system may sometimes be a duty. In the same way a man to whom I have made a promise has a claim on me and a claim I recognise, but this claim may be overridden by sufficiently strong counter-claims; I may have to break a date to help at a smash.

Now precisely similar considerations apply in the case of over-determination, but here Flew seems to me greatly confused. It will bring out the difficulty best if we consider the case of truth. For Kant truth-telling was a claim which no counter-claim could over-ride. Most of us would hold that other claims can override this one. When it would cause great suffering to tell the truth there is contra-determination. But the counter-claim (to avert suffering) is of course not itself a truth claim. When I tell a tactful lie, the tact, the reason why I tell it, has obviously nothing to do with the justification of truth-telling. So I argue that sometimes men who have broken laws should be let off, for various possible reasons – first offenders, very bad law, rotten legal system. These other claims override the punishment claim. But the justification for them is of course not part of the justification for punishment. Now the crucial point is that over-determination must be explained in exactly the same way as contra-determination. Instead of a lie being tactful, the truth itself may be tactful and avert suffering. It may be my duty to tell a man the truth that he is *not* suffering from cancer. But there are then two good reasons for saying this – that it is true *and* that it is tactful. As before, the tact is not one of the reasons for the truth, any more than it is in the case of the tactful lie. While the morality of my statement is overdetermined its truth is not overdetermined. 'Why did you say that?' can be answered '(a) because it is true, (b) because it will make him happy.' But the question 'why do you say what is true?' cannot be answered, 'in order to make my hearer happy.' Flew's mistake in saying punishment may be overdetermined may be illustrated in the following dialogue. 'This is very hard to lift.' 'Yes, that is due to gravity.' 'But it seems much harder to lift than other similar chunks of metal.' 'That is because it is iron and is sitting on a magnet.' 'Ah, I see; one reason why bodies gravitate is magnetic attraction.' It is the fallacy of appealing to the principle of the multiplicity of ethical claims in order to explain the justification of one ethical claim.

I apply this to punishment. Punishment is an ethical claim. If I am an agent of a society (a judge or a juryman) and I have before me a man who has broken a law to which a penalty has been attached, I have a prima facie obligation or a responsibility to inflict punishment. There are other ethical claims which may contra-determine my decision (and justify me in letting the criminal off). There are also ethical claims which may overdetermine my decision. My sentence may reform the criminal or deter others. An act which has all the characteristics laid down in the definition of punishment (strict sense) will not necessarily reform the criminal (and indeed in itself is most unlikely to do this). If we want to achieve this extra aim, we must do a lot of other things besides simply giving him the punishment (the deprivation of liberty). We must send to him the prison chaplain or the string quartette. Similarly the punishment of the criminal will not in itself deter others. We must do other things – provide publicity. But neither the visit of the chaplain nor the publicity is part of the man's punishment; nor is reform or deterrence among the reasons for the decision to punish him. What is overdetermined is not punishment but the public sentencing of a man to imprisonment in a prison visited by prison chaplains and string quartettes. I completely agree that while punishing a man we ought to make every effort to use this opportunity in order to try *in addition* to reform him and to deter others.

Miss Glover was not alone in her surprise that the quotations with which I supported these distinctions in my original article were from books written by criminals. I make no apology for this. A penal system fails if it takes no account of the moral beliefs of those who suffer under it. But I can now quote in support of my view an authority more acceptable to these critics, indeed perhaps the best recent authority possible. Sir Alexander Paterson ('Alec Paterson') says 'The first duty of a prison as an institution of the State is to perform the function assigned to it by the law; and its administration must ensure that a sentence of imprisonment is a form of punishment. It must be clear, however, at the outset that it is the sentence of imprisonment which is the punishment and not the treatment accorded in prison. Men are sent to prison *as* a punishment and not *for* punishment. It is doubtful whether any of the amenities granted in some modern prisons can in any way compensate for the punishment involved in deprivation of liberty.' This is exactly what I said in my article. I would only add that the last sentence is characteristically cautious. It is absolutely certain not merely 'doubtful'. Let the most modern prison open its gates and how many of its inmates would stay on to enjoy its amenities? Granted that prison is primarily and necessarily an instrument of the law and that its first duty is to punish by depriving of liberty, Paterson goes on to say that there may be some useful by-products of any particular sentence of imprisonment. None of them, he makes clear, is a reason *for* punishment, nor is any of them produced *by* punishment. The world is safer when these men are locked up and 'it may be that others are deterred' (note, 'it may be'). 'But is the protection to society to be temporary (during the detention only) or lasting? If the latter, we must add reform – not in the moralist sense of soul-saving but reform as preventive.' (Note again, 'we must add reform' to punishment; for the imprisonment *is* the punishment and not the treatment accorded in prison.) My quotations are from *Paterson on Prisons* (1951) pp. 23–9.

Flew's confusion between the Multiple Claims Theory and a completely different one occurs on p. 100 above. Flew thinks that a moral rule is binding in most but not all cases and this leads him on to 'the scandalous logic' of 'necessary truth in a great majority of cases.' He thinks this loose logic is peculiarly appropriate to the vague and open-textured terms of moral discourse. But the Multiple Claims Theory holds a moral rule to be applicable to *all* cases, even those in which it may be overridden by a stronger claim. The 'scandalous logic' theory holds that, since moral terms are vague and open, any rule will apply only to a majority of cases. The difference is that between saying that the force of gravity operates on all bodies but (when iron filings fly up to a magnet or spaceships depart for the moon) it is overridden by a stronger force; and saying that gravity operates on most but not all bodies (not on the iron filings or the spaceship). The first answer of course is the appropriate one in this case. The filings do not defy the law of gravity: they exemplify it as much as Newton's apple. They are not exceptions. It is vitally important to decide which of these views we are to maintain in morals. The multiplicity view (Ross) maintains that, when I tell a lie to save a life, the obligation to truth-telling is not suspended or annulled or non-existent; it is overborne by a stronger claim. It is as forcible here as anywhere else. This is no exception to its operation. 'Exceptions' to a rule are examples of the operation of this rule and of another. They are fully intelligible. This view Flew endorses when he approves of the multiplicity theory. But it is completely different from his other view that the exceptions really *are* exceptions and arise because of the imprecision of *words*. The difference between the two methods is as great as that between Platonic and modern astronomy. Plato held that the heavenly bodies, being material objects, were bound to fail to exemplify precisely intelligible laws. Thus when a planet was observed to be off its circular track (to show an 'aberration') this is just what you would expect of a planet; and the aberration could not be intelligibly explained except by saying what the ideal or standard track is from which it diverges. For a modern astronomer aberrations are not failures to achieve intelligible motion but examples of it. Aberrations are signs of *other* equally intelligible factors. Plato's theory would kill scientific (or empirical) astronomy, as indeed it was meant to. So, too, Flew's linguistic imprecision theory would kill any attempt to render intelligible the exceptions to rules, as his conclusion shows it is meant to. The Multiple Claims Theory, like modern astronomy, makes 'exceptions' intelligible. Flew cannot have it both ways.

VI IDEAL UTILITARIANISM

Flew commends my article for drawing a distinction between systems and particular cases within systems (p. 96 above). This indeed is the distinction on which my whole theory turns. It is this vital distinction between saying:

(a) this action will have better results than any possible alternative action; and (*b*) this action is the following of a rule, which, if it were generally adopted, would have better results than any alternative rule, or system, would have.

In its application to punishment, it is the distinction between saying the punishment of a particular person on a particular occasion is right if that particular punishment will reform the criminal and/or deter others; and saying this punishment is right because it is the application of a rule whose general adoption would be in the public interest. Consequences are the primary concern of legislators, not of judges or juries. The question whether to make a law against murder with a penalty attached is a question of consequences – a utilitarian question; the question whether an individual criminal should be punished is not. Truth in such matters as this is not the monopoly of professional philosophers or even of professional lawyers. It may be looked for in the utterance of men of moral insight and penetrating intelligence. Dr Johnson was such a man (and I quote him in this capacity and not as a lexicographer). He said to Boswell on one occasion 'To punish fraud when it is detected is the proper art of vindictive justice; but to prevent frauds and make punishment unnecessary is the great employment of legislative wisdom.' Flew's discussion, however, seems to me constantly to blur this essential distinction. He telescopes adoption of a law into enforcement of it. He talks of the justification of having a law against murder as if this was the same as the justification of hanging a murderer (p. 101 above) – which is as if one should say the justification for making a promise is the same as the justification for keeping it. Flew says that my justification of punishment is 'ideal utilitarian' (p. 92 above). This is most misleading. I take ideal utilitarians to maintain, following G. E. Moore (whose view this term was devised to describe), that a particular act is right if it produces more good than any alternative act open to the agent. In agreement with Sir David Ross, I reject this view absolutely, not only over punishment but over all the other crucial cases Ross discusses. I agree with Ross that there are countless cases where the agent is under some obligation or claim or responsibility other than the responsibility to maximise good – cases therefore in which it is right to do an act which will produce *less* good than some alternative open to the agent. Where I differ from Ross is in being prepared to look for a justification of the *rules* which state these claims (such rules as those against stealing or promise-breaking or those imposing duties on parents or colleagues). I think they are justified by the good results which would follow *if* they were generally obeyed. This is not an ideal utilitarian theory, for two reasons. For an ideal utilitarian, it is the results of the particular act which make it right; for me the particular act is right (even if its results are bad) if it is the application of a rule whose general adoption would do good. For the ideal utilitarian it is actual consequences which make an act right; for me it is hypothetical consequences. (I defend this view more fully in *Moral Rules*, a lecture to the British Academy in 1953. It is attributed to Mill by J. O. Urmson in his article 'The Interpretation of the Philosophy of J. S. Mill', in the *Philosophical Quarterly* for January 1953.)

I pointed out in my 1939 article that when utilitarians are shown cases where it seems wrong to break a promise when more good will be done by breaking it, or to give money to charity rather than pay a debt, or to kill a wicked old moneylender (as in *Crime and Punishment*) they usually appeal to the indirect consequences of such infidelity, bilking, murder, to explain their wrongness. Even if more direct good would be done in each case by such actions, they could encourage similar breaches which would destroy the systems of confidence and security on which civilised life depends, I urged two arguments against this solution. First the harm done to a system by a single breach is slight. Flew replies (p. 97 above) that a 'series of exceptions can add up to the effective abandonment of a rule.' This of course is irrelevant, and is the old confusion between single act and systematical evasion. My second and main argument was that the system is not weakened unless the breach becomes known. Indirect utilitarian arguments can always be met by 'Break the rule and keep it dark.' Flew replies to this in three ways. (i) It is impossible to hush up a large number of exceptions. (ii) In some cases it is right to break the rule and keep it dark. (iii) While it is true that our moral convictions do revolt against breaking the rule and keeping it dark (and thus do urge us, e.g., to keep some promises when it would do more good to break them) these convictions should be reformed. A utilitarian should glory in the paradox this involves. To those arguments I reply as follows. (i) is again completely irrelevant and confuses the single breach with the systematic evasion. (ii) I entirely accept. Just as there are occasions on which public promises should be broken, so there are occasions on which secret promises should be broken. But there are also occasions on which they should be kept though their breaking would do more good. As for (iii) Flew here admits that we *believe* my assertion in the preceding sentence but says this belief should be reformed (p. 98 above). But a theory which can maintain itself only by reforming nine-tenths of the moral beliefs of men is not in a strong position. And is not the utilitarian principle itself a moral belief? If all the rest are invalid, why should it survive? Should not a good disciple of induction at this point give up ethics altogether, and say about ethics what Flew says about punishment – 'the enterprise of a comprehensive enquiry (as opposed to a number of piecemeal jobs done in particular contexts) or the attempt to find generally useful principles was misconceived' (p. 102 above)?

8 ⊠ *Is Punishment Retributive?*

K. E. BAIER

It would seem that punishment must of its nature be retributive, and also that it cannot be. It must be, for the infliction of hardship on someone is not punishment, unless it is as retribution *for* something he has done. It cannot be, for it makes sense to say that someone was punished for something he did not do. This seemingly simple, but actually quite intricate problem, has been discussed by Professor A. G. N. Flew in an article entitled 'The Justification of Punishment' and by Mr A. M. Quinton in a paper entitled 'On Punishment' (Papers 5 and 3 above). Both appear to me to misrepresent the nature of punishment. I shall begin by stating briefly what I hold to be the correct solution, and then point out where exactly they went wrong.

1. To say that someone has punished someone else is to say that someone entitled to administer the penalty for a certain offence has administered this penalty to the person who has been found guilty of this offence by someone with the authority to do so. The question whether or not someone has punished someone else could not even arise unless he belonged to a group which had the practice of punishing people. We could not say of a group that it had the practice of punishing people unless all the following conditions were satisfied. There must be someone, such as a father or legislator, whose job it is to prescribe or prohibit the doing of certain things or types of thing by certain people, in the form of commands or regulations, someone whose task it is to decree how a person disobeying these commands or regulations shall be treated, someone, such as a father or policeman, entrusted with the task of detecting cases of disobedience, someone, such as a father or judge, charged with meting out the penalty for such disobedience, and someone, such as a father or executioner, charged with administering it. Of course, all these different tasks may be entrusted to one and the same person, as in the case of punishment by a father or teacher.

It should be noticed that 'punishing' is the name of only a part-activity belonging to a complex procedure involving several stages. Giving orders or laying down laws, affixing penalties to them, ascertaining whether anyone has disobeyed the commands or laws, sentencing persons found guilty, are not themselves punishing or part of the activity of punishing. Yet these activities must be performed and must precede the infliction of hardship if we are to speak of punishment at all. Of course, these activities may take only rudimentary forms. A father does not legislate, but give orders; he does not necessarily affix penalties to breaches of these orders before the breaches occur, but determines the penalty after a breach or disobedience has occurred; he often does not take much trouble in finding out whether his child really is guilty, nor does he formally 'find him guilty' or pronounce sentence. All this is merely tacitly implied, but it is quite definitely implied. It would be just as odd for a father to send his son to bed without supper for being late, if he had found the son not guilty of this — either because the son was not told to be home by a certain time or because he was home by the time mentioned — as it would be for a judge to pronounce sentence on the accused when he has just been acquitted by the jury.

It follows from the nature of this whole 'game', consisting of rule-making, penalisation, finding guilty of a breach of a rule, pronouncing sentence, and finally administering punishment, that the last act cannot be performed unless things have gone according to the rules until then. It is one of the constitutive rules of this whole 'game' that the activity called punishing, or administering punishment, cannot be performed if, at a previous stage of the 'game', the person in question has been found 'not guilty'. The 'game' has to proceed differently after the verdict 'not guilty', from the way it must proceed after the verdict 'guilty'. It is only if the verdict is 'guilty' that there is any question of a sentence and its being carried out. And if, after the jury has found the accused 'not guilty', the judge continues as if the jury had found him guilty, then his 'I sentence you to three years' hard labour' is not the pronouncement of the sentence, but mere words. If, for some reason, the administration acts on these words, then what they do to the accused is not the infliction of punishment, but something for which (since it never happens) we do not even have a word.

A method of inflicting hardship on someone cannot be called

'punishment' unless at least the following condition is satisfied. It must be the case that when someone is found 'not guilty' it is not permissible to go on to pronounce sentence on him and carry it out. For 'punishment' is the name of a method, or system, of inflicting hardship, *the aim of which* is to hurt all and only those who are guilty of an offence. For this reason, a system of punishment requires a more or less elaborate apparatus for detecting those who are guilty and for allotting to them the hardship prescribed by the system. To say that it is of the very nature of punishment to be retributive, is to say that a system of inflicting hardship on someone could not be properly called 'punishment', unless it is the aim of this system to hurt all and only those guilty of an offence. Hence inflicting hardship on a person who has been found 'not guilty' (logically) cannot be punishing. This is a conceptual point about punishment.

The correct answer to our problem is that punishment is indeed of its very nature retributive, since the very aim of inflicting hardship *as punishment* would be destroyed, if it were inflicted on someone who had been found 'not guilty'. But at the same time, someone may be punished, i.e. have hardship inflicted on him *as punishment*, although he was guilty of no offence, since he may have been *found* guilty without *being* guilty. For all judges and jurymen are fallible and some are corrupt.

2. Flew holds a different view. He says (p. 100 above) that punishment is of its very nature retributive, but thinks that this applies only to the system of punishment as a whole, not to individual instances of punishing, because 'the term "punishment" is sufficiently vague to permit us to speak *in single cases and provided these do not become too numerous* (if they do become too numerous, then *ipso facto* the use, the meaning, of "punishment" has changed) of punishing a man who has broken no law (or even done no wrong)' (p. 93 above).

My first point is that Flew has got the analysis wrong. Punishment, whether a system or a single case, is of its nature retributive. Flew says it 'would be pedantic to insist *in single cases* that people (logically) cannot be punished for what they have not done' (pp. 85–86 above), but that '*a system* of inflicting unpleasantness on scapegoats ... could scarcely be called a system of punishment at all' (p. 86 above). These contrasts are misleading. It is not pedantic, but plain wrong, to insist in single cases that people (logically) cannot be punished for what they have not done. But this is not a statistical matter at all. True, a system of inflicting unpleasantness on scapegoats *as such* is not a system of punishment, but then a single case of inflicting unpleasantness on a scapegoat *as such* is not a case of punishment either. In Ruritania, everyone who has been punished during the last year or the last ten years may have been innocent, for in Ruritania the judges and jurymen and the police and prison authorities are very inefficient and very corrupt. A system of punishing people does not turn into a system of inflicting unpleasantness on scapegoats, simply in virtue of the fact that in this system innocent people happen frequently to get punished.

It is surely not true that, if under a certain system of punishment it happens that very many innocent people get punished, the meaning and use of 'punishment' has *ipso facto* changed. Let us envisage such a deterioration in our own legal system. It is not logically necessary that we should come to know about it. Even now many people claim to have been unjustly condemned. Every now and then we hear of a ghastly judicial error, and there may be many more than we hear of. Think of the many cases in which people accuse the police of having used third-degree methods for getting 'confessions'. For all I know, a very large percentage of people who are found guilty and are later punished, are really innocent. At least, this is conceivable. Yet, if it were true, the meaning and use of 'punishment' could not change *eo ipso*.

Or suppose we knew about it. What would we say? Simply that judges, police, and so on, were inefficient and/or corrupt, and that very many people got punished wrongly, i.e. unjustly, or by mistake.

Flew may have confused the unsound point he is making with another point which is sound. Suppose a group had what is properly called a system of punishment. It may then happen once in a while that a judge goes on to 'pronounce sentence' even after the jury has found the accused 'not guilty'. Or, to take a more probable case, that a teacher goes on to hit a pupil even after he has realised, perhaps even admitted, that the pupil is innocent. Now, it is true that we would still say that the group had a system of punishment even if such cases occurred, provided they were exceptional. We would not, however, say that they had a system of punishment, if these were not exceptions, but if the group had a system of doing just this sort of thing.

This is true, but again it is not a matter of statistics, not a matter of happening frequently or infrequently. It is a matter of being an exception rather than the rule, in the sense that it is understood to be *a breach of the rule*, rather than merely out of the ordinary. Not merely that judges usually, but not always, discharge the accused when he has been found 'not guilty', but that it is their *job* or *duty* to do so. If, after the jury has found the accused 'not guilty', the judge says 'I sentence you to three years' hard labour', this is not just an unusual case of punishing the man who is innocent, but not a case of punishment at all. And here it would not only not be pedantic, let alone wrong, but perfectly right to say that this case was not a case of punishment.

Flew, I suspect, may have been taken in by the word 'system'. He is, of course, right in saying that a system of inflicting unpleasantness on scapegoats, or a system of 'punishing' people who had broken no laws, cannot be called a system of punishment. This obvious truth, together with the obvious truth that men who have not broken any laws can be and sometimes are correctly said to have been punished, leads him to the view that the solution to the puzzle how one can say the one, but not the other, must be found in the difference between systems and single cases, which he takes to be the difference between the great majority of cases, and single cases (pp. 85–6 above).

But it is more complicated than that. The expression 'a system *of* "punishing" people who had broken no laws' means 'a system whose *declared and recognised nature* it is to "punish" those who had broken no laws'. Hence the importance of 'exception'. If it is still the declared and recognised nature of the group's infliction of hardship on people that it is to be directed to all and only those who are found guilty of an offence, then the cases of inefficient and corrupt judges, and judges guilty of flagrant breaches of the law, are clearly exceptions. And while these single cases are exceptions, the whole system can still be called a system *of* punishment, otherwise it is a system of something else.

3. Mr Quinton, on the other hand, does not think the solution of our problem lies in the distinction between systems and single cases of punishment, but he thinks it lies in the recognition 'that "punish" is a member of that now familiar class of verbs whose first-person-present use is significantly different from the rest' (p. 60 above). As soon as we recognise that while 'I am punishing you for

something you have not done' is as absurd as 'I promise to do something which is not in my power', we see that 'he punished him for something he had not done' is no more absurd than is 'he promised to do something that was not in his power'.

My first point is that it is simply not true that 'I am punishing you for something you have not done' is as absurd as 'I promise you to do something which is not in my power'. It need not be absurd at all. The executioner may whisper it to the man who has been sentenced to death. 'I am punishing you for something you have not done' would be analogous to 'I promise you to do this which is not in my power' only if to *say* 'I am punishing you . . .' *were* to punish you, just as 'I promise you . . .' *is* to promise you. In other words, the verb 'to promise' is a performatory word, 'to punish' is not. And if it were used performatorily in 'I hereby punish you . . .' (not, by the way, as Quinton has it, 'I am punishing you . . .'), then it would mean the same as 'I hereby sentence you . . .' and saying it would still not *be* punishing anyone, but merely sentencing him. Thus, Quinton's account is not true of punishing but at best of sentencing.

A similar mistake was made some time ago by Professor H. L. A. Hart in his important paper 'The Ascription of Responsibility and Rights'.[1] For the view he there expresses[2] is that judicial decisions are ascriptions of responsibility or rights and that these are 'performatory utterances', 'non-descriptive statements', statements not capable of being true or false. But while this is so of some judicial decisions such as pronouncing sentence, it is not true of others such as verdicts. When the jury says 'Guilty', the accused is 'guilty in law' and may have no further recourse against such a judicial decision, but that does not mean that he really is guilty. The verdict 'guilty' could be a performatory utterance only if uttering these words were making the accused guilty, as uttering the words 'I promise' is making a promise. It might be said that the jury uses the word in a technical legal sense, different from the ordinary. When the jury says 'Jury-Guilty', the accused is not indeed made guilty, but he is made jury-guilty. But this won't do, for what does jury-guilty come to? It simply means 'to be held guilty', 'to be regarded or treated as guilty'. But this is not what

[1] *Proc. Arist. Soc.* 1948–9. Reprinted in Flew, *Logic and Language*, vol. 1 (1953).
[2] *Logic and Language*, pp. 155, 157, 159, 161.

the jury is asked to decide or what it says. The jury is asked to give its opinion on whether the accused *is* guilty, not on whether he is to be *treated as* guilty, for different considerations might enter into the second question. For the purpose of the legal consequences, the jury's opinion about his guilt is authoritative. Thus, it is not true that the jury says 'Jury-Guilty', and thereby makes the accused jury-guilty. What is true is that the jury says 'Guilty' and thereby makes the accused jury-guilty that is to be held guilty. Hence the performatory model is out of place here, for when I say 'I promise', I am making a promise, not an 'uttered promise'.

It might be thought that Quinton had seen this point, for he says 'There is an interesting difference here between "forgive" and "punish" or "reward". . . . The three undertakings denoted by these verbs can be divided into the utterance of a more or less ritual formula and the consequences authorised by this utterance. With punishment and reward the consequences are more noticeable than the formula, so they come to be sufficient occasion for the use of the word *even if the formula is inapplicable and so improperly used*. But, since the consequences of forgiveness are negative, the absence of punishment, no such shift occurs' (pp. 60–1 above). At first sight, this distinction between the ritual formula and the consequences authorised by it might be taken to be the same distinction as the one I have drawn between sentencing and punishing. But on closer inspection, this turns out not to be so.

For while to say 'I forgive you' is indeed to use a formula, the use of this formula or ritual is not performatory in the way in which the use of 'I promise' or 'I hereby sentence you to . . .' is. For if I say the latter in the appropriate circumstances then I have promised or pronounced sentence. But when I say 'I forgive you' I may *merely say so*. It is moreover wrong to think that 'I forgive you' authorises the non-imposition of punishment. The assaulted girl, with her last words, may forgive her assailant, but this does not authorise 'the absence of punishment'. Nor is the infliction of punishment authorised by the formula 'I don't forgive you'. The former indicates the injured party's intention not to seek revenge, to resume friendly relations, and so on, the latter the opposite. On the other hand, the infliction of punishment is authorised by the formula 'guilty' or equivalent formulae, the non-infliction by the formula 'not guilty' and perhaps the Home Secretary's pardon. Thus, the difference Quinton has in mind is not the difference I have drawn between pronouncing sentence and punishing.

Lastly, it should be emphasised that it is not true to say that punishing is the utterance of a ritual formula involving certain palpable consequences whereas forgiving is merely the utterance of a ritual formula involving no palpable consequences, and that, therefore, 'punishing' sometimes refers merely to the palpable consequences even when the ritual formula is inappropriate, whereas this never happens in the case of forgiving. On the contrary, punishing and forgiving alike are certain kinds of doings, but they are doings which presuppose the correct completion of a certain more or less formal procedure culminating in the finding someone guilty of an offence. If and only if this procedure has been followed correctly to its very conclusion, can there be any question of someone's being or not being punished or forgiven or pardoned. One of the important differences between forgiving and punishing is that they presuppose different sorts of formalities. Forgiving is involved only where a man has been found guilty of an injury. Punishment is involved only where he has been found guilty of an offence. Many systems of crime and punishment make injuries offences, but not all offences are necessarily injuries. Vindictiveness and forgiveness, revenge and turning the other cheek are individual, punishment and reward are social ways of dealing with objectionable behaviour.

Although the infliction of hardship on an individual cannot be called punishment unless it is preceded by his having been found 'guilty' of an offence, the procedure leading up to this finding need only be formally and not materially correct. That is to say, as long as he was found 'guilty' in the proper way, even though he is not in fact guilty, the infliction of hardship which then follows will be punishment, provided no further slip occurs.

9 ⊠ *The Retributivist Hits Back*

K. G. ARMSTRONG

When Kingsley Amis, in his book *Lucky Jim*, wanted to sum up the intellectual outlook of Professor Welch's wife, whose actions throughout show her to be excessively conservative, stodgy, snobbish, authoritarian, and generally disagreeable, he spoke of 'Her opposition to social services because they made people lazy, her attitude to "so-called freedom in education", her advocacy of retributive punishment, her fondness for reading what English-women wrote about how Parisians thought and felt'. This is interesting, for nowhere else in the book was punishment so much as mentioned. Amis uses advocacy of the retributive theory purely as a symptom of a rather unpleasant, and certainly outdated, attitude, a symptom which his readers would surely recognise; and I think Amis was right – most of the people who read his book would understand the reference just as he intended it, would regard the theory as something which, if it is not dead already, certainly should be.

C. S. Lewis wrote an article defending retributivism. He is not a man whom one would normally expect to have any difficulty getting material published, yet the article appeared in an Australian periodical[1] because, he said, he could get no hearing for his view in England. He claimed it had become clear during the controversy over the death penalty that his fellow-countrymen almost universally adhered to a combination of the deterrent and reformatory theories of punishment. In the British philosophical world the position is apparently similar. J. D. Mabbott says: 'In the theory of punishment, retribution has been defended by no philosopher of note [for over fifty years] except Bradley. Reform and deterrence are

---

[1] 'The Humanitarian Theory of Punishment', in *Twentieth Century* (Mar 1949).

the theories accepted in principle and increasingly influential in practice.'[2]

'And', it may be said, 'this is just as it should be in an age that claims to be enlightened. Retributive punishment is only a polite name for revenge; it is vindictive, inhumane, barbarous, and immoral. Such an infliction of pain-for-pain's-sake harms the person who suffers the pain, the person who inflicts it, and the society which permits it; everybody loses, which brings out its essential pointlessness. The only humane motive, the only possible moral justification for punishment is to reform the criminal and/or to deter others from committing similar crimes. By making the punishment of wrongdoers a moral duty, the retributive theory removes the possibility of mercy. The only people who today defend the retributive theory are those who, whether they know it or not, get pleasure and a feeling of virtue from seeing others suffer, or those who have a hidden theological axe to grind. In any case, the theory is not only morally indefensible but completely inadequate in practice to determine what penalty the criminal should suffer in each case. Finally, the theory can be shown to be wrong by such simple facts of language usage as, for instance, that it makes sense to say "He was punished for something he did not do", because, *inter alia*, the theory demands that to say a man was punished for a crime logically necessitates that he committed it. Historically, morally, and logically, the theory is discredited.'

These, then, are some of the objections that have been urged against the retributive theory of punishment. In my view they are all mistaken – either because they are based on confusions about what the theory is, or else because they spring from erroneous moral judgments. One charge, that the proponents of the theory are sadists or have a vested religious interest in it, I shall not deal with. For all I know it could even be true, but it seems irrelevant to the present discussion; philosophers, of all people, should surely be above using the ploy of analysing a man's motives instead of meeting his arguments. As for the objection that the theory is out of date, i.e. unfashionable, this seems so ludicrous philosophically that I would not have mentioned it at all if it were not for the unfortunate fact that it is the most common objection of all. I shall certainly not bother with it any further, giving the reader credit for being free

[2] J. D. Mabbott in *Contemporary British Philosophy*, 3rd series, ed. H. D. Lewis (1956) p. 289.

from what Belloc called 'The degrading slavery of being a child of one's times.'

My aim is not to present, much less to establish as correct, a full-scale retributive theory, or set of theories, of punishment. I want firstly to sort out the issues in this confusing and confused area, and secondly to meet some of the attempts to discredit retributivism which are made either by painting it, as I myself did in summary fashion above, as a repulsive doctrine which could only be held by the morally insensitive, or else by reducing it to a harmless platitude which we all accept (so that the conflict between it and other theories of punishment turns out to have been no more than a foolish mistake). Let us start the process of clarification by deciding just what is meant by a 'Theory of Punishment', and what it would be for such a theory to be wrong.

I

It soon becomes clear when one studies the contexts in which the phrase appears that there is not just one type of theory being invariably referred to. Usually a theory sets out to resolve one or more of three main problems, although all too often the reader is not told which of them is being tackled. Indeed, one is often forced to the conclusion that the writers are not clear on the point themselves, which has led to a great deal of confusion and many false oppositions between theories which are not simply different but which are attempting to solve different problems.

PROBLEM I: DEFINITION

The first problem is over the meaning of the word 'punishment', and is thus a definitional or logical issue. We examine the way the word is used in ordinary language, the things to which it is applied, and try to produce some rule which covers all these cases and only these cases. Applying the same technique to many other words we would get a single unequivocal answer on which all users of the language would agree – in short, the definition of the term – but in the case of 'punishment' there is no such universally acceptable answer, and so we may speak of a 'theory of punishment' in the sense of a claim that a certain definition exactly marks out the correct use of the term.[3] For such a theory to be wrong would be for it to mark out some range of things or activities not in fact ordinarily referred to by the word 'punishment', or else to include only part of the proper range and/or more than the proper range. In this latter case we would probably say that the definition proposed was 'too narrow' or 'too wide', but the theory itself we would say was *wrong*, because it claims that the proposed definition exactly fits normal usage.

PROBLEM 2: MORAL JUSTIFICATION OF THE PRACTICE

The second problem that a theory of punishment may be trying to solve is 'What, if anything, is the moral justification of punishment as such?' Why should it be felt that this particular practice requires moral justification, when in the case of so many other practices – from warning to washing-up – we do not feel that the question even arises? Clearly because punishment involves the deliberate infliction of pain, i.e. distress of some sort, normally against the wishes of the recipient, and this is something to which there is a prima facie moral objection, the overriding of which requires justification.

It is important to notice that the moral justification of a practice is not the same thing as its general point or purpose, except in the eyes of those who have travelled so far down the utilitarian road that they never question the means if the end is desirable. Every human practice that is not utterly random or unconscious has some point, but not all have, and many do not need, a moral justification. An act or practice may have a very sound point indeed and still lack moral justification, e.g. torturing prisoners to get information, so that to say that the general aim of the practice of punishing criminals is, say, the protection of society is not *eo ipso* to produce a moral justification of the practice, unless we assume that Bentham was right all the way. There is an ambiguity in a phrase like 'The general justifying aim of punishment',[4] between *why* we do it, and why it is morally permissible – if it is – for us to do it.

[3] The claimed definition that has attracted most attention in recent years is that given by A. G. N. Flew in his article 'The Justification of Punishment' (see Paper 5 above).

[4] This is a key phrase in H. L. A. Hart's article, referred to below.

A theory dealing with the moral justification of punishment as such could be wrong in two ways: firstly the general moral theory on which it is based could be incorrect, and secondly the theory of punishment could be a misapplication of the general moral theory.

PROBLEM 3: PENALTY-FIXING

The third problem is this: which method or system of determining penalties for crimes is best? A theory of punishment dealing with this problem might better be called a theory of punishments, or a theory of penalties. The point of view from which the advocated method is said to be best varies; sometimes it is in the interest of society as a whole, sometimes of the criminal, sometimes of both. One thing these theories have in common is that they are not so much concerned with what is as with what should be the case. To be wrong, such a theory would have to be advocating a method of determining penalties which was actually *not* best, either because it was not best from the point of view considered, or because some other factor which ought, morally, to be primary had been overruled.

Of these three problems, then, one is definitional, one is concerned with ethics, and one is largely practical, but with important moral overtones. The last two are very commonly dealt with as one, but the distinction is important for reasons which will become apparent later in this article. Given this division of the problems of punishment, and the answering theories, into three categories, what of the attacks on retributivism?

II

It is generally considered that certain phrases which crop up fairly regularly in ordinary discourse, such as the troublesome 'He was punished for something he did not do', create at least a prima facie difficulty for retributive theories, and a number of different solutions have been offered in recent years.[5] Because it

[5] See especially A. M. Quinton, 'On Punishment' (Paper 3); A. G. N. Flew, 'The Justification of Punishment' (Paper 5); K. Baier, 'Is Punishment Retributive?' (Paper 8); and S. I. Benn, 'An Approach to the Problems of Punishment', in *Philosophy* (Oct 1958).

seems to me that all these solutions are more or less mistaken, I want to look again at this issue in the light of the above analysis.

In the case of which of the three problems could a fact of language usage help to establish or prove wrong a theory of punishment? For the definitional problem it would clearly be relevant, and I shall later examine the significance of a typical phrase. But can such a language fact prove anything about a theory which deals with the second or third problem, or, more specifically, can it prove such a theory wrong? I suggest that it can do so only indirectly.

Any attempt to solve the second or third problem must assume that the logically prior problem of defining the word 'punishment' has already been solved. Unless we know what punishment *is*, what it means to impose a penalty for a crime, we cannot even start to talk about what system of fixing penalties is best, no matter from what point of view we may be considering it. Similarly, we cannot decide what it is that morally justifies punishment until we know what it is we are trying to justify. If the definition of 'punishment' that these theories had worked with were shown not to be in line with usage then they would be wrong in the sense that they would have turned out not to be theories of punishment at all, but rather to be theories of something else. Incidentally, at this point we can already see where A. C. Ewing goes astray in his book *The Morality of Punishment*, for he starts with the assumption that, whatever it is, punishment is morally justified, and then rejects some definitions because he cannot agree that what they produce is morally justifiable (e.g. on p. 34). Clearly the logical order is first to decide what punishment is, *then* to decide whether this thing is morally justifiable or not.

But if the term 'punishment' *had* been correctly defined, is it still possible for a fact about usage to prove a theory dealing with the second or third problem wrong? I have already mentioned what it would be for such theories to be wrong in themselves; what, then, is the relevance of word usage?

Take the third problem. Setting what system of fixing penalties is best, no matter from whose point of view it may be considered, is essentially an exercise in practical reasoning. It is hard to see how the fact that the word 'punishment' is sometimes used in certain phrases could ever show that, say, the criminal was not in fact better off when his sentence had been fixed on such-and-such principles. Yet this is exactly what is required to demonstrate that a theory of punishment of the third type is wrong.

The position with theories of the second type is somewhat similar. The way ethical terms are used certainly can show that a general moral theory is incorrect, but this is not true of the way that non-ethical terms are used. Now 'punishment' is not in itself an ethical term: 'punishment', like all activity words, can occur in ethical propositions, but such propositions are not made ethical by virtue of *its* presence. Nor, if the general moral theory was correct, and, by hypothesis, the term 'punishment' had been correctly defined, could the theory of punishment be shown to be a misapplication of the general moral theory by some fact about word usage. But to establish the truth of this last assertion we will have to make a short excursion into the field of ethics.

When it has been settled what it is for an activity to be moral or good (general moral theory), we still have to decide whether each particular activity, in this case the activity of punishing, is a case of a moral or good activity. The method employed to decide this varies with the general moral theory, but it will turn out to be one of the following kinds of procedure:

(i) An appeal to intuition in the broadest sense. To decide whether a particular type of activity is good, a duty, what one ought to do, etc., one has simply to reflect (not ratiocinate) on it and one can just 'see' the answer. (Moore, Ross, in fact the majority of recent theories.)

(ii) A factual calculation of the total amounts of pleasure and pain that the action causes. (Hedonistic Utilitarianism.)

(iii) (*a*) A check on whether God has told us, by revelation, to do it. (The theory that good is that which God enjoins.)

(*b*) A check on whether the majority of the community approves of it. (The theory that Morality is social convention, i.e. Social Externalism.)

(*c*) A simple statement of whether the speaker himself likes or approves of it (Subjectivism) and wants others to do so too (Stevenson, Emotivists generally).

(iv) Settling whether it is in accordance with Human Nature and Man's Final End, both by examining our internal, intuitive attitude to it and by reasoning from what we already know of man's nature and destiny. (Thomist theory.)

(v) Checking it against a set of specific criteria of various sorts provided by the general theory for determining what is in

accordance with the Moral Law (Kant) or what are genuine
moral rules (Baier).

Now if we consider all these methods it can be seen that in no
case could the theory of punishment (moral justification) produced
by their use be upset by facts about the use of the word 'punishment'. Remember that the original data about what it is for an
activity to be good, moral, etc., and what punishment *is* are, in each
case, correct by hypothesis. In method (i) no further data at all are
introduced, so there is no possibility of error through false information. In method (ii) the additional information is scientific,
mainly psychological; it is about how men feel, not about how they
use words. In method (iii) there is room for error over (*a*) what God
has commanded, or (*b*) what the majority of the community *does*
approve of – it is very doubtful whether one could make an error
over (*c*) what oneself approves of or likes – but neither of these
could be *shown* to be erroneous by the way the word 'punishment'
is used in sentences not about revelation or approval. In method (iv)
an error could only come in through a false notion of Human
Nature or mistakes about Man's Final End; but our ideas about
Man's Nature and End are in no way dependent on the question of
which sentences using the word 'punishment' make sense and
which do not. In method (v) the possible sources of error will vary
with the criteria put up by the general moral theory for determining
whether an activity constitutes a breach of a genuine moral rule.
However, the only criterion which could be shown to have been
misapplied by our noting that it made sense to use the word
'punishment' in some given non-ethical sentence would be one
which specified that this must not be the case, e.g. 'An activity, to be
moral, must be such that the word signifying it cannot sensibly be
used in such-and-such sort of non-ethical sentences'. Now, of course,
no general theory of morals which would lead to the use of method
(v) has such a criterion, and it is hard to see what reason there could
ever be for introducing such a one.

We can see, then, that even if a theory of the moral justification
of punishment can be wrong in the sense of being a misapplication
of the correct general moral theory, whichever that may be, its
wrongness can never be proved by the fact that it makes sense to use
the word 'punishment' in some given non-ethical sentence. The
stage of appeal to language habits has already been passed.

So far, we have established that while a fact about how the word 'punishment' is used might well show that a theory of punishment in the definitional sense was wrong, such a fact could not show that a theory dealing with the moral-justification or penalty-fixing problems had done so incorrectly, except in the sense that they had dealt with something other than punishment. We must now turn back to definitional theories of punishment, to see what precisely is the effect on them of the fact, if it is a fact, that it makes sense to say, for example, 'He was punished for something he did not do.'

Irrespective of which problem or problems it sets out to solve, a theory of punishment can usually be put under one of three headings: Retributive, Deterrent, or Reformatory. When the problem is to define punishment these theories provide roughly the following answers:

1. *Retributive*: Punishment is the infliction of pain, by an appropriate authority, on a person because he is guilty of a crime, i.e. *for* a crime that he committed. I do not intend to go into the question of just what constitutes an appropriate authority, because the answer would appear in all three definitions, and it is the *differences* between them, concerning who suffers pain and why, that I wish to stress here. Also, I use the word 'crime' deliberately, as it is ambiguous between an offence against a rule, the law, morality, or someone else's rights.[6]

2. *Deterrent*: Punishment is the infliction of pain on a person in order to deter him from repeating a crime or to deter others from imitating a crime which they believe him to have committed. I am here subscribing to Benn's view that deterrence of the person punished is not reform. Reform means that the man intends to avoid repeating the crime, not from fear of punishment but because he sees that it was wrong. (Benn, 'An Approach to the Problems of Punishment'.)

3. *Reformatory*: Punishment is the infliction of pain on a person in order to reduce his tendency to want to commit crimes or to commit crimes of a particular sort.

I am not urging the acceptance of any one of these three definitions in preference to the others. I have set them out so that we may see what difficulties arise for retributivism in this area from the alleged

[6] For discussions of what the offence is against, see J. D. Mabbott (Papers 2 and 7) and C. H. Whiteley, in *Philosophy* (Apr 1956).

fact that it makes sense to say 'He was punished for something he did not do.'

What does it come to to say that X makes sense, where X is some sequence of words? If we take it loosely, in what I shall henceforth call the weak way, it comes to saying that when we hear X we can understand what is being asserted by the speaker, and this does not necessarily imply that he is using all the words contained in X in their exactly proper way, but only that what is said is, so to speak, 'near enough'. Thus, for instance, 'They half-killed him' makes sense in the weak way, even to someone not familiar with the phrase as an idiom, although killing, strictly speaking, is a deed that allows of no degrees – a man is either killed or he is not. But we can also take 'X makes sense' in a tighter way, which I shall henceforth call the strong way, as indicating that each word has been used quite correctly so that an analytical substitution can be made for any term involved without revealing any contradiction, inconsistency, or other logical impropriety.

If 'He was punished for something he did not do' makes sense in the weak way, how does this affect the retributive definition? It is fairly easy to see that it is not incompatible with the truth of the theory. The person who used the sentence could simply be asserting that someone who was not in fact the perpetrator of a particular crime had been treated as though he were, either because those in authority held sincerely though mistakenly that he *was* guilty of it or because they had deliberately tried to mislead the public.

If, however, the given sentence made sense in the strong way, it is equally obvious that the retributive theory (definition) *would* be proved wrong. Since, on the definition it proposes, to say that someone was punished for a crime involves saying that he committed it, the retributive definition would make 'He was punished for something he did not do' a self-contradictory proposition. Thus *either* the sentence does not make sense in this strong way *or* the retributive theory (definition) must be abandoned.

But any satisfaction which advocates of the deterrent or reformatory theories might feel over this incompatibility must be short lived, for if the sentence did make sense in the strong way this would be equally fatal to their own proposed definitions, although for a different reason. Here the difficulty lies not in ' . . that he did not do', but in '. . . *for* something . . .'. It is clear that the 'something' referred to is an act, a crime that somebody committed; but on neither the deterrent nor the reformatory theory is a man subjected to pain *for* a crime, but *to* deter him or others from committing crimes in the future or *to* rid him of the tendency to commit crime. The only theory with which the given sentence's making sense in the strong way would be compatible would be one which defined punishment as 'The infliction of pain on a person because a crime has been committed, whether by that person or not'. As far as I know, such a theory is not held by any philosopher in the Western World. That this should be so is, I suggest, strong prima facie evidence that the sentence does not in fact make sense in the strong way.

To recapitulate: Only theories of punishment of the definitional type could be affected by a fact of language not involving ethical terms. If it makes sense in the weak way to say 'He was punished for something he did not do' then the retributive theory (definition) is still tenable; if it makes sense in the strong way then not only the retributive, but also the deterrent and reformatory definitions are shown to be wrong. Thus the alleged difficulty is either no difficulty at all, or else it is an insuperable difficulty for all three definitional theories. In neither event are there grounds in word usage for dis- criminating against retributivism *vis-à-vis* its rivals.

In passing we may note an interesting asymmetry between the sentence we have been discussing and the sentence 'He was punished although he was innocent', where this is interpreted to mean not just that the man was innocent of the particular crime for which he was 'punished' but that he was 'punished' although he had not committed any crime at all. If 'He was punished although he was innocent', interpreted thus, makes sense in the strong way, then whilst the retributive theory (definition) is shown to be wrong the deterrent and reformatory theories (definition) are still viable.

The treatments of this question given by Flew and Quinton have already been effectively criticised by Baier (Paper 8); but Baier's own analysis differs from the one I have just set out. In his view, the fact that it makes sense to say 'He was punished for something he did not do' is *not* incompatible with the retributive theory, because the theory necessitates as a logical precondition of punish- ment not that the person who suffers the pain *in fact* committed the crime, but only that he was '*found* guilty' of committing it. This 'finding guilty' can either be informal and implicit (as in the case of a parent punishing a child) or formal and explicit (as in the case of a jury announcing its verdict). But the fault in this solution is that whilst the amended retributive definition it is based on includes everything that we would call punishment, it also includes things we would *not* call punishment. Merely to go through the moves of the 'game', as he puts it, is not enough to constitute a case of punishment. Take the case of a man who clearly did not commit a crime, and who is obviously not even believed to have committed a crime; if, despite his known innocence, a court went through the formal motions of a trial, including the moves of the jury uttering the word 'Guilty' at the appropriate time and the Judge sentencing him, and if he was duly executed – would it be proper to call this a case of punishment? Or consider a schoolmaster regularly beating one of his pupils after saying the words 'Bloggs! You were laughing!' (an informal declaration of guilt) although Bloggs never so much as cracks a smile and the teacher's eyesight is good – would we say Bloggs was being *punished* regularly? Would it not be more natural to say that these were cases of something other than punishment – victimisation perhaps?

III

Earlier, I claimed that a lot of contemporary writing on the subject of punishment is confused, much of the trouble springing from a failure to distinguish between the three separate problems involved. I can best support this claim by taking my examples from the two most quoted post-war articles on punishment.[7] Consider first this paragraph written by Flew[8] in criticism of J. D. Mabbott's article 'Punishment': 'The objection to saying that the *sole* justification for punishing someone is that he has committed an offence is that Mabbott and almost everyone else would allow that a punishment in certain circumstances was overdetermined in its justification – was justified twice over. Certainly: because, though Mabbott claims to "Reject absolutely all utilitarian considerations from its justification", he is prepared to appeal to these to justify *systems* of punishment. But if a *system* is to be justified even partly on such grounds, some cases within the system must be partly justifiable on the same grounds: the system surely could not have effects to which no case within it contributed' (p. 94 above).

[7] See Flew, Paper 5, and Quinton, Paper 3.
[8] Paper 5.

Here Flew is confusing Problems 2 and 3. The point is that justifying *systems* of punishment, i.e. which method or system of determining penalties for crimes is best (Problem 3), is quite distinct from justifying, morally, the practice of punishment as such (Problem 2). There is nothing inconsistent in Mabbott's view that, whilst the moral justification of inflicting pain on people who commit crimes lies solely in retributive considerations, one system of fixing *what* penalties are to be inflicted for *what* crimes may be better than another from the point of view of its consequences on a particular society, i.e. on 'utilitarian' grounds. Flew has failed to realise that the word 'justification' is used in two quite different ways in the context of discussions of punishment, depending on which problem a theory is trying to solve. When dealing with Problem 3 a *system* is 'justified' precisely by establishing that it *is* most in the interests of some stated person or group that penalties should be fixed on the lines it prescribes. Of course it is always possible that some system of determining penalties which has been 'justified' in this way may be objected to on *moral* grounds if it goes against a principle arising from the solution to Problem 2, e.g. if a system of fixing penalties, 'justified' by its deterrent effect alone, resulted in overruling the moral principle (derived from a retributive solution to Problem 2) that a very minor offence ought not to be punished more severely than a very serious one. But this is not surprising; if I say that punishment has a moral justification, I do not thereby resign my right to apply moral criticism to any system of fixing penalties. I might, for instance, hold that the practice of punishing is morally justifiable, yet at the same time say that the Nazi system of partly determining penalties according to the race of the criminal was immoral.

In his article 'On Punishment' Quinton recognises that theories of punishment may deal either with what punishment *is* or with the problem of morally justifying it as a practice (Problems 1 and 2). However, when he proceeds further he confuses the issue by misunderstanding retributivism in two ways. Firstly, he says that it is a logical and not a moral doctrine: 'It does not provide a moral justification of the infliction of punishment but an elucidation of the use of the word' (p. 55 above). We have seen that this is true of the retributive theory, as it is also true of the deterrent and reformatory theories, *but only when the theory deals with Problem 1*. If a particular retributive theory deals with Problem 2, as it well may, then it *is* a moral doctrine, albeit one that Quinton does not agree with, e.g. 'The moral justification of punishment is simply that the infliction of pain on those who have inflicted pain on others is a Good-in-itself, since it is a species of justice' would be a possible, though perhaps poor, retributive theory dealing with Problem 2. Of course it is true that retributive theories are very often concerned only with definition, but they can be, and sometimes are, concerned with moral justification or systems of penalty-fixing, e.g. Lewis's article 'The Humanitarian Theory of Punishment' argues for a retributive theory of penalty-fixing, and A. C. Ewing, *Morality of Punishment*, ch. 2, argues against such a theory, thus recognising its existence.[9] Secondly, Quinton misunderstands retributivism when he says that it regards punishment as trying to bring about 'A state of affairs in which it is as if the wrongful act had never happened' (p. 56 above). He criticises this doctrine as only applicable to a restricted class of cases: 'Theft and fraud can be compensated, but not murder' (p. 57 above). Here he is confusing *retribution* with *restitution*. If we recover stolen property, or if a confidence man repays the money he got by fraud, then although restitution has been made the retributivist would say that punishment was still due, i.e. the *loss* has been annulled but the *crime* has not. Only physically are things as they were before the crime. In the case of murder, restitution is clearly impossible – we cannot get back the life that was taken – but retributive punishment is still possible. Further, the *lex talionis* is not an *extension* of retributivism, as Quinton claims (p. 57 above), but a particular retributive theory dealing with Problem 3 (penalty-fixing), and in my view a poor retributive theory, as I shall explain later.

IV

What of the other charges against retributivism? Is it, as is so often said, inhumane? This charge, if correct, would count as a moral objection against a retributive theory of penalty-fixing (Problem 3). In the area of this problem it seems to me that

[9] In a note published after this article was written, A. S. Kaufman points out that F. H. Bradley, at least, was a retributivist who was not only concerned with the definition of 'punishment', but had a retributive view on the moral issue. ('Mr Quinton on Punishment', in *Analysis*, Oct 1959).

retributive theories stand up very well to comparison with purely deterrent or reformatory theories. If we penalise the criminal according to what he has done, we at least treat him like a man, like a responsible moral agent. If we fix the penalty on a deterrent principle (i.e. What penalty given to this criminal, or class of criminal, will effectively deter others from imitating his crime?) we are using him as a mere means to somebody else's end, and surely Kant was right when he objected to that! And why stop at the minimum, why not be on the safe side and penalise him in some pretty spectacular way – wouldn't that be more likely to deter others? Let him be whipped to death, publicly of course, for a parking offence; that would certainly deter *me* from parking on the spot reserved for the Vice-Chancellor! And of course a deterrent will deter as long as the person on whom the pain is inflicted is *believed* to be guilty by those we wish to deter. It really wouldn't matter, if deterrence is our aim in fixing penalties, whether he was in fact guilty or not; as long as we kept his innocence a secret we could make a very effective example of him. This conclusion has been acted on by more than one government in our own times.

If, on the other hand, our aim in fixing penalties is the reform of the criminal – his *cure*, some might say – then the logical pattern of penalties will be for each criminal to be given reformatory treatment until he is sufficiently changed for the experts to certify him as reformed. On this theory, every sentence ought to be indeterminate – 'To be detained at the psychologist's pleasure', perhaps – for there is no longer any basis for the principle of a definite limit to punishment. 'You stole a loaf of bread? Well, we'll have to reform you, even if it takes the rest of your life.' From the moment he is found guilty the criminal loses his rights as a human being quite as definitely as if he had been declared insane. This is not a form of humanitarianism I care for. Nor does it become any more humane if we drop the word 'punishment' – it is still just as compulsory. C. S. Lewis wrote a sentence on this point that is worth quoting, even if only as a masterly piece of propaganda: 'To be taken without consent from my home and friends, to lose my liberty, to undergo all those assaults on my personality which modern psychotherapy knows how to deliver, to be remade after some pattern of "normality" hatched in a Viennese laboratory to which I never professed allegiance, to know that this process will never end until either my captors have succeeded or I have grown wise enough to cheat them with apparent success – who cares whether this is called punishment or not.' (Lewis, 'Humanitarian Theory of Punishment'.) And, since prevention is better than cure, why wait until he commits a crime? On the Reformatory theory of penalty-fixing, it is the *tendency* to commit crimes that we want to eliminate, so if a man has the tendency let him be penalised before the damage is done. Let him be penalised for what he is, not for what he does, and let him be made over into what the authorities (or their experts) want him to be.

The usual riposte to the sort of charges I have been making against deterrent and reformatory theories of punishment (penalty-fixing) is to refer back to a retributive *definition* of punishment and rule out the charges as logically inadmissible.[10] 'The short answer to the critics of Utilitarian theories of punishment', writes S. I. Benn ('An Approach', p. 332), 'is that they are theories of *punishment*, not of any sort of technique involving suffering.' But to say, to those who ask why we shouldn't punish the innocent when it would be socially useful, that 'The infliction of pain on a person is only properly described as punishment if that person is guilty'[11] is to give an answer which is technically correct (for those who subscribe to a retributive definition of punishment) but which misses the point behind the question.

Suppose the questioner comes back as follows: 'All right then, if you want to quibble about terminological niceties when I'm trying to make a serious moral and practical enquiry, I'll rephrase my question. Why shouldn't we do to the innocent that which, when it's done to the guilty, is known as punishment?' At this point those theorists who offer a utilitarian moral justification for the practice of punishing (i.e. a deterrent and/or reformatory theory on Problem 2) are in a difficult position; for on their view what morally licenses us to inflict pain on a man is not that he is guilty – that is merely what gives us a *logical* licence to use the word 'punishment' to refer to the infliction of pain – but that there will be a socially useful result in terms of his reform and/or the deterrence of others,

[10] In an important and constructive paper, which did not appear until after this article was written, H. L. A. Hart has coined the name 'Definitional stop' for this sort of riposte. ('Prolegomenon to the Principles of Punishment', the Presidential Address to the Aristotelian Society, 1959–60, p. 5.)

[11] Quinton, Paper 3 (p. 59 above).

or, to put it more generally and in Mr Benn's terminology, that the decrease in mischief to the public will be greater than the increase in mischief to those who are subjected to the pain. The only objection these theorists could raise would be that inflicting pain on the innocent is not in fact an effective deterrent. This empirical hypothesis is of very doubtful validity – it is not hard to think of cases where a very great mischief to the public might be avoided by condemning and executing an innocent man under guise of punishing him, e.g. who knows but that Klaus Fuchs might have been deterred from passing information on the A-bomb to the Russians if the Government had previously 'framed' some innocent scientist on an espionage charge and executed him in a blaze of publicity? In any case, most people feel that there is more against 'punishing' the innocent than that it wouldn't effectively reduce crime. Nor does our sense of outrage arise solely from the lying imputation of guilt, as Quinton claims (p. 59 above), although this is undoubtedly a partial explanation. Surely our principal objection is to the deliberate infliction of *undeserved* pain, to the *injustice* of it, and this moral objection to taking deterrent and reformatory theories of penalty-fixing (Problem 3) to their logical conclusion can only be accounted for on a *retributive* theory of the moral justification of punishment as such (Problem 2), as I shall show in a moment.

But before we leave the question of penalty-fixing it is worth asking why it should be so often thought that retributive theories in this area are necessarily barbarous. The charge springs from the misconception, which I mentioned before, that there is only one such theory – the *lex talionis*. In fact, all that a retributive theory of penalty-fixing needs to say to deserve the name is that there should be a proportion between the severity of the crime and the severity of the punishment. It sets an upper limit to the punishment, suggests what is *due*. But the 'repayment' (so to speak) need not be in kind; indeed in some cases it *could not* be. What would the *lex talionis* prescribe for a blind man who blinded someone else? Even in those cases where repayment in kind of violent crime is possible there is no reason why we should not substitute a more civilised equivalent punishment; the scale of equivalent punishments will, of course, vary from society to society. There is also no reason, having got some idea of the permissible limits of a man's punishment from retributive considerations, why we should not be guided in our choice of the form of the penalty by deterrent and reformatory considerations.

In the area of the moral justification of the practice (Problem 2) a retributive theory is essential, because it is the only theory which connects punishment with desert, and so with justice, for only as a punishment is deserved or undeserved can it be just or unjust. What would a just *deterrent* be? The only sense we could give to it would be a punishment which was just from the retributive point of view and which also, as a matter of fact, deterred other people. 'But', it may be objected, 'you are only talking about *retributive* justice.' To this I can only reply: What other sort of justice is there?

A vital point here is that justice gives the appropriate authority the *right* to punish offenders up to some limit, but one is not necessarily and invariably *obliged* to punish to the limit of justice. Similarly, if I lend a man money I have a right, in justice, to have it returned; but if I choose not to take it back I have not done anything unjust. I cannot claim more than is owed to me but I am free to claim less, or even to claim nothing. For a variety of reasons (amongst them the hope of reforming the criminal) the appropriate authority may choose to punish a man less than it is entitled to, but it is never just to punish a man more than he deserves. It is a mistake to argue – as Ewing, for example, does in chapter ii of *The Morality of Punishment* – that, on the retributive theory, to punish a man less than the exact amount due is an injustice similar to punishing an innocent man. The retributive theory is not, therefore, incompatible with mercy. Quite the reverse is the case – it is only the retributive idea that makes mercy *possible*, because to be merciful is to let someone off all or part of a penalty which he is recognised as having deserved.

Retributive punishment is not revenge, although both are species of justice. Revenge is private and personal, it requires no authority of one person or institution over another; punishment requires a whole system of authorities given a right to secure justice. As members of the State, we surrender the right to secure justice ourselves to the authorities that the State appoints (though retaining, for example, our right to punish our own children). It is these state-appointed authorities, not ourselves, who must both punish malefactors and recover for us, by force where necessary, what a reluctant debtor owes us.

Finally, it is a distortion of the retributive theory to say that it involves the infliction of pain-for-pain's-sake. On my understanding of the theory, pain (which the appropriate authority is morally licensed to inflict because it is deserved) is inflicted for the sake of all or any of a number of different ends. Amongst these are the protection of society, the reform of the criminal – which punishment *may* achieve simply by making the criminal realise the full gravity of what he has done, as a child realises how serious his offence has been when he sees how angry it makes his father – and the deterrence of others. All these ends are in themselves both morally and socially desirable; where the infliction of pain is justified by desert, pain may be a morally permissible *means* to achieving them.

V

I do not claim to have demonstrated in this article that retributive theories are the correct solutions to each of the problems of punishment. My aim has been to make clear the distinction and interconnection between those problems and to show that, if we are to reject retributive theories, objections more powerful than those currently advanced and accepted will have to be found, since the current objections rest on confusions, or mis-statements of the problem, or mere prejudice.

Where the problem is to define punishment (Problem 1), some sort of retributive theory now seems to be fairly generally accepted, although whether the offence for which punishment is inflicted is against the law, some other set of explicit rules, or just the accepted moral standards of a community is still debated. Most of those who have examined the difficulty raised by the currency of the phrase 'He was punished for something he did not do' rightly conclude that the retributive definition is more or less immune, even if their reasons for so concluding are faulty. That able philosophers should accept such unsatisfactory solutions to the apparent problem bears witness to the strength of their conviction that a retributive definition is the right one.

The moral justification for the practice of punishment as such (Problem 2) is today sought almost invariably in reformatory or deterrent terms. For those who subscribe to simple utilitarian theories of morals of the total-pain-and-pleasure-to-society type, this is of course automatic, and short of refuting their moral theory as a whole one cannot hope to shift their position on punishment. But most of those philosophers for whom retributivism is not ruled out *a priori* by their general moral theory – i.e. most of that great majority who do not subscribe to hedonistic utilitarianism – also reject or, more commonly, ignore the retributive theory of the moral justification of punishment; and this despite the unique ability of that theory to connect punishment with the notions of desert and justice and, indeed, with the deep-seated general conviction we all have that to strike back and to strike first are two very different things, morally speaking, irrespective of the results they may produce or be intended to produce. This is surprising; for though I have not demonstrated that these considerations in favour of a retributive theory could never be outweighed by any conceivable arguments for deterrent and/or reformatory moral justification, I hope I *have* shown that they are too important to be altogether overlooked, or even to be summarily dismissed. It may be possible not to be moved by them, but they must at least be faced. I have referred to three factors which tend to account for the cavalier treatment of retributivism in the area of Problem 2. First, there is the mistaken belief that a retributive moral justification of punishment would make the infliction of pain on the guilty a positive, inescapable obligation, instead of merely creating a right to inflict pain which, like other rights, it may in some circumstances be foolish or mean to exercise. Second, there is the failure to distinguish between the moral justification of a practice on the one hand, and its 'general justifying aim' on the other. And third, there is the notion that if one concedes the definitional field to retributivism, there is no further area in which deterrent and reformatory theories can have a retributive rival, that one can 'dissolve' the traditional conflict between the theories by declaring that 'Retributivism is not a moral but a logical doctrine'.

When the problem is to find the best system of penalty-fixing there is no doubt that a purely retributive theory would have serious weaknesses, both practically, because it may be very difficult to decide which of two crimes is the more serious and thus deserving of severer punishment, and morally, because if deterrent and reformatory considerations are altogether ignored when the list of penalties is drawn up a great social good might be sacrificed in order to achieve a small improvement in the accuracy of a punishment from the retributive standpoint. But, on the other hand, I have pointed out that the charge that retributive theories of penalty-fixing are barbarous is based on the mistaken assumption that the only such theory is the *lex talionis*, and that a modified retributive theory is perfectly possible, one which only uses retributive considerations to fix some sort of upper limit to penalties and then looks to other factors to decide how much and what sort of pain shall be inflicted. Purely reformatory or deterrent theories of penalty-fixing, which lack that limit, run the risk of becoming far more inhumane than even a purely retributive theory.

Finally, I have been concerned to show that only if one subscribes to a retributive theory of the moral justification of punishment (Problem 2) has one grounds on which to object to taking the deterrent and reformatory theories of penalty-fixing (Problem 3) to their logical conclusion, i.e. to inflicting pain on the innocent as a deterrent to others and as a means to removing suspected criminal tendencies before they can be manifested in actual offences. Those who object that such action would not (logically) be punishment are not objecting to the action taking place but only to its being given a certain name. Yet surely most people feel that there is more difference between inflicting pain on the guilty and inflicting pain on the innocent than that one can and the other cannot be called punishment?

10 ⊠ Justice and Legal Punishment

JAMES F. DOYLE

In my approach to an acceptable theory for the justification of punishment, I begin by citing a few of Hegel's perceptive remarks on this subject. I do not appeal to Hegel in order to embrace or defend his theory of punishment, which is commonly described as retributive. Nor shall I make any pretence of adopting Hegel's idiom or philosophic principles – though I trust that the nature and extent of my obligation to him will be obvious. Rather I consider the following remarks, like the proposals of Professor Hart, to be a valuable prolegomenon to a perplexing topic. In a well-known passage Hegel wrote:

> If crime and its annulment...are treated as if they were unqualified evils, it must, of course, seem quite unreasonable to will an evil merely because 'another evil is already there'. To give punishment this superficial character of an evil is, amongst the various theories of punishment, the fundamental presupposition of those who regard it as a preventive, a deterrent, a threat, as reformative, &c. and what on these theories is supposed to result from punishment is characterised equally superficially as a good. But it is not merely a question of an evil or of this, that, or the other good; the precise point at issue is wrong and the righting of it.... In discussing this matter the only important things are, first, that crime is to be annulled, not because it is the producing of an evil, but because it is an infringement of the right as right, and secondly, the question of what that positive existence is which crime possesses and which must be annulled; it is this existence which is the real evil to be removed, and the essential point is the question of where it lies. So long as the concepts here at issue are not clearly apprehended, confusion must continue to reign in the theory of punishment.[1]

[1] T. M. Knox (trans.), *Hegel's Philosophy of Right* (Oxford, 1942), para. 99, pp. 69–70.

I have quoted these remarks at some length, because they effectively draw attention to conditions without which punishment cannot be viewed as fully intelligible or justifiable. Even if one objects that Hegel's statements are needlessly obscure and abstract, I believe he does point the way to a defensible theory of punishment.

First, Hegel warned that it is a mistake to conceive of punishment — for theoretical purposes, at least — as pain, suffering, loss, or some other unqualified evil. It is likewise a mistake to adopt this conception of criminal offences, though offences must always be in some meaningful sense examples of *legally* undesirable conduct. In any case such mistaken conceptions are the source of simplistic theories which account for punishment as retaliation or a 'returning of evil for evil'. The simplistic character of these theories is often masked by an alleged analogy between criminal and scientific laws — as if punishment follows offence, automatically, much as an effect is supposed to follow a cause. What is suppressed in these theories is the conscious decision to punish, this being the principal element needing guidance and justification.

These mistaken conceptions of crime and punishment have also lent plausibility to punitive theories based primarily or wholly on utilitarian considerations. According to utilitarian theories, what requires justification in punishment is its essential feature, namely pain or suffering.[2] From this claim it is only a short step to the conclusion that punishment can be justified only if the evil attending it is more than balanced by the achievement of some greater good, or the avoidance of some greater evil. The goods typically appealed to in this connection are the social utilities of legal conformity, reform of immoral habits, and satisfaction of the natural desire for vengeance; whereas the evils to be avoided are the opposite of these. However, as Hegel acutely observed, this mode of justification misses 'the precise point at issue'. That is, utilitarian reasoning yields neither an explanation nor a justification of punishment as the 'righting' of an offence or legally wrong act. No amount of theoretical ingenuity will alter the fact that, in the terms the utilitarian himself has adopted, the offence remains an evil and so does

[2] Benn, 'An Approach to the Problems of Punishment', in *Philosophy* (Oct 1958) p. 328, n., remarks that '"denunciation" does not imply the deliberate imposition of suffering, which is the feature of punishment usually felt to need justification.' Hart ('Prolegomenon', in *Punishment and Responsibility*, p. 2, n.), cites this claim with approval.

the punishment. Therefore punishment is still a matter of returning evil for evil, but now the deliberate practice of inflicting evil is guided and justified by considerations of gain and loss.[3] It is obvious that not every utilitarian theorist will be embarrassed by this conclusion. But according to Hegel they have not achieved what they set out to do: namely, provide a satisfactory rationale for legal punishment.

At this point it may be objected: Was Hegel warranted in demanding anything more from a philosophic justification of punishment than utilitarians have been able to provide? What can be meant by the claim that 'the precise point at issue is wrong and the righting of it'? How can punishment be conceived as annulling or righting a wrong?[4] In attempting to answer these questions, we should do well to follow the recommendations contained in Hegel's quoted remarks. We need, as a basis for argument, more adequate conceptions of a criminal offence and of legal punishment. The idea of an offence, in a minimally intelligible sense, is that of a violation of criminal law. This suggests that we ought to examine more fully the question of an adequate concept of law, this being

---

[3] Hart writes in 'Legal Responsibility', in *Punishment and Responsibility*, p. 44: 'I shall suggest a mercantile analogy. Consider the law not as a system of stimuli but as what might be termed a *choosing* system in which individuals can find out, in general terms at least, the costs they have to pay if they act in certain ways'. This view of the law is re-iterated in 'Prolegomenon', pp. 22-3.

[4] Hart as I recall does not mention the idea of annulment. Benn derides this idea, or considers it intelligible only as a disguised utilitarian principle. In 'An Approach', p. 328, he argues:

A veiled utilitarianism underlies Hegel's treatment of punishment, as annulling a wrong. For if punishment could annul the wrong, it would be justified by the betterment of the victim of the crime or of society in general. Not indeed that the argument is a good one; for the only way to annul a wrong is by restitution or compensation, and neither of these is punishment. . . . Similarly with the argument that punishment reaffirms the right. Why should a reaffirmation of right take precisely the form of punishment? Would not a formal declaration suffice? And even if the reaffirmation necessarily involved a need, right, or duty to punish, the justification would be utilitarian, for why should it be necessary to reaffirm the right, if not to uphold law for the general advantage?

As I shall subsequently try to show, this argument is both doctrinaire and alien to the idea of just law.

itself an underlying issue in the theory of punishment. In an effort to avoid, in our theoretical considerations, any possible limitations of actual legal systems, we should insist on adopting a concept of law which conforms as nearly as possible to recognised criteria of justice.[5] We need not engage in any detailed explication of a theoretical concept of law – a monumental task at best – in order to assent to certain minimal features of a just legal system.

Any system of criminal law which meets generally acknowledged requirements of justice would adhere to the principle of the absolute equality of worth of all members of the legal community, as persons. This entails that legal demands on personal conduct be imposed and enforced impartially and without sacrifice of personal dignity. That just law may impose no arbitrary restraint would be generally conceded. Nor can there be any doubt that just law may uphold and enforce the discharge of obligations which have been duly and deliberately undertaken. For our present purposes, one important requirement of law as a system of just demands is that these demands be, in some meaningful sense, self-imposed. Here self-imposition of legal obligations is considered to be a more deliberate and self-conscious process than mere acquiescence in, or consent to, these obligations. I interpret this principle as implying that everyone who is bound by the law ought to have meaningful access, at the same time, to participation in those institutions by which the law is legislated, adjudicated, and enforced.

Interpreted in the light of this minimal concept of law, what is important about a criminal offence is not its evil. (This is in any case a moral characterisation; and if it were a question of moral guilt, who could be said to be innocent?) What is most significant,

[5] In contrast with the view adopted here, Hart might be fairly described as a 'conventionalist' (in the Humean sense) in his view of a theoretical concept of law. He frequently adopts as a basis for discussion 'advanced' legal systems or enlightened legal practice. For example, his article, 'Legal Responsibility', begins with the statement, 'It is characteristic of our own and all advanced legal systems that the individual's liability to punishment . . . is made to depend on, among other things, certain mental conditions'. He thus interprets the primary task of legal philosophy to be the elucidation of prominent characteristics of such systems and practices. Unfortunately, being advanced or enlightened does not insure freedom from obscurantism or injustice. But compare H. L. A. Hart, *The Concept of Law* (Oxford, 1961), ch. ix, where he adopts a concept of law with a 'minimum content of natural law'.

for purposes of a theory of punishment, is that an offence is the violation of one or more legal obligations, performance of which is equally and justly demanded of the offender and of all other persons. As such, an offence is a challenge, in some degree, to the integrity and justice of a legal community – in Hegel's words, it is an 'infringement of the right as right'. Nothing could be more contrary to just law than simply to ignore such an act. But it is far from obvious that the appropriate or just response of a legal system to an offence is the infliction of evil. Indeed I contend that anyone will, after sufficient reflection, find it quite unreasonable to maintain that a system of law has rightful authority to inflict *evil* as such, on any person to whom the law properly applies – even if that person happens to be guilty of the most grievous legal offence. There can be no doubt that it is within the proper authority of law to preserve the integrity and justice of its system of mutual obligations. Yet where or whence within this authority is there a grant to inflict evil? To grant such authority to a system of law would be to empower this law with the very means which it is intended to oppose in the resolution of human conflict. Moreover, the authority to inflict evil as such would be incompatible with the idea of law as a system of mutual obligations, imposed above all else to preserve the equal worth of all persons. However (lest it be forgotten), what is primarily at issue in this discussion is the justification and rightful authority for the legal infliction of punishment. Once we eliminate the possibility of justifying the infliction of evil as such, we must either arrive at a more defensible concept of punishment, or else admit that theoretical justification is unattainable.

As Hegel suggested, the clue to an adequate concept of punishment lies in locating and identifying those aspects of a legal system which give positive significance to criminal offences. We might begin by comparing criminal offences with offences against civil law. These two kinds of offences are alike in several respects, one being that both give rise to claims. Rightful satisfaction of such claims in civil law is primarily a matter of compensation, whereas the claims arising from criminal offences are normally satisfied by punishment. Of course, not every claim engendered by criminal offences necessarily merits legal acknowledgment and satisfaction. Therefore we should describe justifiable punishment (if there be such) as the satisfaction of all the just claims invoked by the commission of criminal offences. Punishment interpreted in this way is obviously not an unqualified evil – though neither is it an unqualified good. If punishment is justifiable, it is not so primarily in virtue of the evil which may attend it. Nor is it justifiable as a moral good. Its justification depends, first, on the acknowledgment that criminal offences against a system of law invoke a variety of just claims, and secondly, on showing that punishment is an indispensable and just means for the satisfaction of these claims. Any criminal offence may be said to be *legally* annulled if all the just claims created by that offence are as nearly completely satisfied as possible. This is not to say that offences can be annulled or set aright in every sense – the poignant loss of a murdered man or an assaulted child can never be recovered. But an offence considered as a legal act – an act performed within a system of just demands – can be legally annulled under the aegis of rightfully inflicted punishment.

We now require further explication of the just claims created by criminal offences, and of the reasons why punishment is prescribed as an intelligible and a justifiable means of satisfying these claims. In general the claims initiated by offences can be characterised as issuing from these principal sources: first from the offender himself (since in practice his claims are the ones most likely to be overlooked), and further, from the immediate victim or victims of the offence, from the legal system, and from the society which the legal system serves and represents. Since the full enumeration of these claims would be onerous for both writer and reader, I shall here cite typical examples in order to shed further light on the idea of punishment.

To the offender we may reasonably ascribe as a just claim the preservation at all times of his worth and dignity as a person. This is the basis for further claims, such as the right to protection from arbitrary restraint and detention, and to satisfaction of all the requirements of impartial public hearing, trial, and sentencing. The offender may justly claim that all due care be exercised in judging the presence and degree of personal responsibility in the offence with which he is charged. Any punishment (here interpreted neutrally as some kind of legally imposed deprivation or coercion) must be based on reasonable conclusions regarding the nature and degree of his personal responsibility in the offence. The offender, no less than any other member of the legal community, has a just claim to at least the minimal conditions of self-development. As a person sufficiently responsible to answer and be punished for his conduct, the offender has the right to exercise every available opportunity to expiate and make reparation for his offence,[6] and to restore his reputation and status in the legal community.

In the past, claims of the victims of criminal offences have been emphasised, often to the point of excluding or neglecting other claims. However, the legal claims of victims need to be more objectively viewed from the perspective of a theory of just punishment. The immediate victim or victims (if any), as members of a legal community, have a right to demand efficient apprehension and just trial, sentencing, and punishment of offenders. For violations of personal trust, bodily health, life, and other legally recognised goods, victims may reasonably claim such reparation as is possible, commensurate with the loss. With other members of the legal community the immediate victims share a right to secure public censure of legal wrongs, as well as possible protection from the repetition of such wrongs. Such protection may entail legal detention or isolation of offenders. Under no circumstances, however, has the victim or anyone else a just claim to the imposition of retaliation, personal vengeance, malice, or cruelty on offenders. To make such a claim is to deny to offenders the essential – and fallible – humanity without which a just legal system would be unthinkable.

In the public response to criminal offences a legal system has the awesome role of adjudicating and enforcing the claims of all whom it represents. At the same time its own agents and authorities possess implicit claims which become overt with the commission of offences. The legal system as such has rightful authority to secure the necessary conditions for reasonable enforcement of law. This authority has been correctly interpreted as entailing the right to deter and prevent criminal conduct. Furthermore, there can be little doubt that any person, knowing his obligations under the law and therefore acknowledging his personal accountability for legally wrong conduct, may be deterred by the desire to avoid answering and being punished for such conduct. However, I hold that he is more reasonably deterred if he is prepared to accept this public response to illegal conduct as just and deserved, than if the prospect of this response is held up either as the threat of painful consequences, or

[6] The idea of expiation or, more generally, personal acknowledgment and fulfilment of responsibility for wrongs committed, is mentioned only in passing in Hart's discussion ('Prolegomenon', p. 9).

merely as a basis for calculating probable gain and loss.[7] Among other claims made in the name of a legal system as such, I would again mention the authority to deliver public censure and reprobation of legal wrongs. This aspect of punishment has been well expressed in a view attributed to Hegel: 'Punishment . . . is only crime made manifest'.[8] Occasionally this particular aim of public recognition and censure has even been cited as the primary justification for legal punishment.[9]

Beyond these and other rightful claims which we might associate especially with a legal system, society in the larger sense is a source of claims invoked by criminal offences. Involved in the idea of law itself is the social claim to satisfaction of reasonable expectations. Moreover, all members of society have a right to protection from violent or otherwise overtly dangerous offenders, through legal isolation or restraint. Somewhat less concretely, society may rightly look to law to uphold a standard of just and responsible conduct, especially in circumstances where such conduct is threatened. Plato once said that the noblest work of the law is to make men hate injustice. This educative role is not only desirable but is rightly claimed by all those whom a legal system represents.

Evaluation of the foregoing as claims which are just and legally authoritative, is based on criteria of entitlement, desert, and need, together with generally acknowledged principles of just laws. Satisfaction of such claims as I have described would obviously involve a variety of different legal responses. But since most of these claims ultimately devolve on criminal offenders themselves, their satisfaction would entail punishment in some form, or more likely in several different forms at once. The ideal of just punishment would be the complete satisfaction of all legally acknowledged claims without prejudice to any of them. There can be little doubt that any actual legal system would fall short of this ideal and would, moreover, be compelled to pursue policies based on utilitarian and pragmatic considerations. For this reason I do not deny that other criteria besides its justice may be offered in support of, or in opposi-

---

[7] Again I refer to Hart's economic analogy between the criminal law and a costing system.

[8] Knox, *Hegel's Philosophy of Right*, para. 101, 'Additions' 64, p. 247.

[9] For a brief recent summary of this tradition, see Joel Feinberg, 'Justice and Personal Desert', in Carl J. Friedrich and J. W. Chapman, eds, *Justice* (Nomos VI), (New York: Atherton Press, 1963) p. 82 n.

tion to, any actual practice of legal punishment. But where criteria other than its justice and authority are appealed to, either solely or primarily, there can be no meeting the obligation – as Hegel described it – to show that punishment is a righting of the legal wrong in criminal conduct.

Before concluding my defence with a brief reply to current doubts about the theory and practice of punishment, I should like to summarise this rejoinder to utilitarian theories. Like most utilitarian theorists, I have sought to answer the question, Why should we have the sort of criminal law which provides that those who commit offences against it are held legally accountable and subject to punishment? Those who adopt a utilitarian approach have replied, we should have such laws and therefore we should uphold the practice of punishment because punitive procedures will help secure the desirable objective of conformity to the law. Punishment serves this aim primarily because of its threatening, deterring, or preventive features. However, we prescribe limitations on the pursuit of this general utilitarian aim of punishment, by insisting first that suffering be inflicted only on those who qualify as legally responsible, and secondly that the severity of penalties not be excessive or discriminatory. These qualification confer on a system of law the additional advantage, that everyone subject to the law has a reliable basis for judging the desirable or undesirable consequences of his deliberate choices. Of course we consider it a desirable social aim to try to reform and rehabilitate criminal offenders as well as punish them. Our actual practice, in so far as it is based on utilitarian principles, is therefore an uneasy but tolerable compromise between punitive and reformative techniques.[10]

Like the utilitarians, I have also defended a system of criminal law, based on personal accountability and punishment, as something we ought to preserve. But in contrast with utilitarian reasoning, I have offered as the primary basis for this defence the argument that a system of law without provision for accountability and punishment could not be intelligible, just, or effective. There would be no point in legally proscribing certain types of conduct as criminal, unless such conduct were possible or even fairly common, and unless there were good reason to discourage its incidence. There would likewise be no point in having a system of criminal law,

[10] This paragraph is a radically simplified, though hopefully not unfair, summary of Hart's basic argument in defence of punishment.

unless performance of the legal obligations it creates could be reasonably and justly required of every person to whom the rules and sanctions of this system apply. I have inferred from this that legally responsible persons are presupposed by any system of criminal law, and that such persons ought to be held accountable for their conduct, where this conduct qualifies as criminal under the law. To hold qualified persons legally accountable is, in effect, to ascertain the nature and degree of the just response, on the part of the legal system, to the legal wrongs which have been committed. From the standpoint of the law these wrongs *are* wrong, not because of their undesirable effect on general conformity to the law, but because they are violations of legal obligations which have been rightfully imposed. Just response to these legal wrongs is primarily a matter of providing legal recognition, adjudication, and satisfaction of the variety of claims invoked by criminal violations.

I have argued that the practice of legal punishment derives its justification from these claims, so far as they merit legal recognition and satisfaction. However, these claims on a legal system do not establish rightful authority to inflict pain, suffering, hardship, or any other evil as such. Legal infliction of such evils is at best only indirectly justified, to the extent that they unavoidably accompany the exercise of rightful authority to punish. According to the theory defended here, the primary purposes of punishment are those of recognising, fulfilling, and restoring all rightfully imposed legal obligations which may be affected by criminal offences. Affirmation of these purposes, and therefore of the practice of legal punishment, is justifiable on the ground that pursuit of these purposes is a condition without which the justice and integrity of law could not be preserved. If I am now asked why we should prefer a system of law possessing these features, I can only reply with another question. By what other means may men reasonably hope to live together, both in harmony with one another and in full realisation of the dignity and value of each as a man?

These are the basic contentions of my rejoinder to utilitarian theories of punishment. They are also intended to meet the objections of those whose scepticism is directed against the justice of, or authority for, the practice of legal punishment. I have argued that such objections can be met, in principle, whatever may be the shortcomings of actual punitive practices. Two challenges in particular remain to be met. One of these concerns the justifiability of capital punishment, while the other has its basis in the vexed problems of personal responsibility.

Regarding the justifiability of capital punishment, I have already suggested implicitly that, according to the view adopted here, such practice is without foundation in a theory of just punishment. Indeed, one could go farther and assert that capital punishment is antithetical to the purposes and principles of punitive sanctions in the law. Requital, when properly understood in terms of a concept of just law, undoubtedly does have a legitimate role in punishment. However, as I have attempted to show, neither requital nor punishment in general is a returning of evil for evil, and therefore I see no support for the demand that a murder (or an act of treason, or some other serious offence) be paid for with a life. Of course we can imagine exceptional circumstances in which, for example, an offence brings about a justifiable demand for radical restraint and isolation of a dangerous offender, and yet no adequate means for this punitive procedure are available. In these circumstances is legal execution justifiable? A case such as this illustrates the relevance of utilitarian and other practical criteria, because in these circumstances the requirements of justice cannot be fully satisfied without probable sacrifice of other things on which we place great value. Since the case in question has already been defined as exceptional, there can be no theoretical solution to the issues which it raises. A theory of punishment is relevant to such cases, only to the extent that it elucidates what is at stake and what may have to be sacrificed. In any case the *institution* of capital punishment, according to the theory defended here, has no basis in the principles of just punishment.

Now I shall attempt, as briefly as possible, to reply to those critics who recommend that we abandon the attribution of personal responsibility to criminal offenders, and along with it the practice of punishing them. The consequence of acting on this recommendation would be to transform criminal law and punishment into a system of social hygiene, administered by a variety of specialists who are trained in the diagnosis and treatment of social ills. Clearly this recommendation goes to the very heart of our fundamental assumptions about human beings and their capacity to rule and be ruled by systems of law. On careful examination, however, the challenge is not so severe as one might at first suppose. The recommendation to abandon responsibility and punishment is based on faulty interpretation of the available evidence, and this faulty interpretation itself is traceable to a number of theoretical confusions.

As an example of these theoretical confusions, I would mention the belief – perhaps ultimately derived from Bentham – that the practical test of legal responsibility is whether or not a person can be effectively deterred by the threat of punishment.[11] This belief, together with the available evidence, supports the conclusion that a large proportion – perhaps the majority – of criminal offenders cannot be so deterred, at least by established punitive techniques. Hence it would seem that offenders should not be held responsible, and therefore should not be punished. Another example is the belief, based on retributive ideas of criminality, that legal punishment must be based on guilt, and that the proper measure of guilt is moral responsibility or wickedness. But since criteria of moral responsibility are so variable and apparently so subjective, it would appear to be more enlightened to dispense with considerations of guilt, and this in turn would make punishment superfluous. Finally, let us consider the type of offender portrayed by Lady Wootton. Offenders of this type appear not to be legally punishable, because they betray few if any of the normal signs of personal responsibility. Lacking such responsibility, they may have committed intolerable offences; yet they are treated as cases of mental disorder. Meanwhile much more promising individuals, whose offences may be far less grievous, must suffer punishment because they qualify as legally responsible persons. Many find this consequence paradoxical and repugnant, and on this basis recommend that we extend clinical treatment rather than punishment to all offenders.

I believe we can discern in all these examples of reasoning a failure to apprehend either the significance or the justification of legal punishment. First of all, legal punishment is appropriate and justifiable only as a response to criminal offences, not to socially undesirable conduct in general. Moreover, punishment is not imposed as an evil, but as a legal response to just claims, some of which derive from offenders themselves. That persons are not deterred by the threat of suffering does not necessarily make them any less responsible. Indeed to emphasise the criterion of the fear or

[11] This view of legal responsibility (to which Hart himself does not subscribe) and its basis in Bentham's philosophy, is critically discussed in 'Legal Responsibility', pp. 40–4, and in 'Prolegomenon', pp. 18–19.

the calculation of consequences is to adopt a misleading view of the basis of legal responsibility. On the other hand, moral guilt is equally misleading as a criterion in this context. What is most important in responsibility, from a legal standpoint, is acknowledgment of obligations as justly imposed and enforced. It is responsibility not only *for* one's conduct, but *to* others whom this conduct may affect. As a response to offences, legal punishment is a means of giving public recognition and encouragement to such responsibility. There is no reason to think that most persons do not possess such responsibility, or that they are incapable of striving toward the achievement of just law. Thus, where punishment is justly imposed, there is nothing paradoxical or repugnant in excusing or extending therapeutic treatment to one offender, because he does not qualify as punishable, and inflicting punishment on another, because he is in some degree legally responsible for his conduct.

Though I reject the recommendation of these critics, I would agree that legal punishment is not the only way to regulate anti-social conduct. It is in recognition of the likelihood and threat of such conduct that we establish criminal law. Law prescribes the vital obligations, and many of the typical ones,[12] to which everyone is equally expected to conform. In keeping with such law, punishment is the appropriate and just response to responsible failure to preserve this minimal and common conformity. But public efforts to diminish or prevent socially undesirable conduct ought to be directed against the conditions which promote such conduct, as well as against criminal offenders. As Dewey once urged, 'No amount of guilt on the part of the evil-doer absolves us from responsibility for the consequences upon him and others of our way of treating him, or for our continuing responsibility for the conditions under which persons develop perverse habits'.[13] To subscribe to a system of criminal law and just punishment, important as this is, is only one aspect of a defensible social response to undesirable conduct.

[12] I owe this language to the felicitous statement by Austin Farrer, *The Freedom of the Will* (Adam & Charles Black, 1958) p. 276: 'The legislator, we will say, is a rough schoolmaster to train us in a few typical responsibilities, and to enforce a few vital ones'.
[13] John Dewey, *Human Nature and Conduct* (New York: Modern Library, 1930) pp. 18–19.

11 ❧ *The Responsibility of Criminals*

WILLIAM KNEALE

I

Under the common law of England the defence of insanity is a complete answer to any criminal charge. But according to the rule laid down in McNaghten's case of 1843 the defence is established only if it is proved that the accused at the time of the offence was labouring under such a defect of reason from disease of the mind that he did not know the nature and quality of the act he was doing or, if he did know this, did not know that what he was doing was wrong. At the time the rule was formulated it was the last clause which attracted most attention. Peel, the Prime Minister of the day, when reporting McNaghten's acquittal to Queen Victoria, wrote: 'It is a lamentable reflection that a man may be at the same time so insane as to be reckless of his own life and the lives of others, and to be pronounced free from moral responsibility, and yet capable of preparing for the commission of murder with the utmost caution and deliberation and of taking every step which will enable him to commit it with certainty.' And Victoria in her reply protested with underlinings and exclamation marks against the absurdity of bringing in a verdict of 'not guilty on account of insanity' for a malefactor who was perfectly conscious and aware of what he did.[1] During the present century, however, many psychologists have argued that the relevant notion of insanity should be defined still more widely; and although this has not yet been done in England, the law has recently been altered to allow for a plea of diminished responsibility in murder trials. Since the phrase 'diminished responsibility' does not occur elsewhere in our law and has not received any special definition, it must be assumed that the word 'responsibility', as it occurs in this phrase, was intended by the legislature to bear an ordinary, non-legal sense appro-

[1] *Queen Victoria's Early Letters*, ed. J. Raymond (1963) p. 85.

priate to the context. Unfortunately no one has been able to explain satisfactorily what the phrase as a whole can mean; and when we try to think it out, we come on some very curious problems.

If, as the dictionary tells us, 'responsibility' means 'liability to be called to answer or account for one's acts', how can it possibly have degrees? Either one is to be called to account for a particular deed or one is not: there is no middle course. It might, no doubt, be said that a man in a certain mental condition was responsible for some things he did but not for others, and that in this way the range of occasions of responsibility was diminished for him. He might, for example, be responsible in certain circumstances for killing X but not for killing Y, because his constitution or his upbringing or both made him likely to have an over-mastering passion against Y in those circumstances, though not against X. But this cannot be the way in which the phrase 'diminished responsibility' is to be understood here, since the plea is not treated as a complete defence on any occasion but always as a partial excuse on the strength of which a jury may classify a killing as something less than murder. Does it then mean that a man who has killed someone may be responsible in the sense that he can be called to account and yet have diminished responsibility because he cannot be made to pay so big a penalty as others might whose responsibility was not diminished? This seems to be the most plausible interpretation of the phrase used by the legislature, but it is not at all easy to see how it should be applied in practice. If a man's responsibility can be diminished at all by his condition and circumstances, may it not perhaps be diminished in various degrees? And if so, what degree is to be required for acceptance of the plea of diminished responsibility? Is even the slightest emotional or volitional abnormality enough?

In a lecture to the Cambridge Institute of Criminology in 1960 Lady Wootton of Abinger described the recent change as an attempt to modify a system that was essentially punitive (I think she meant 'retributive') by smuggling into it humane ideas and aims which were totally incompatible with it. In her view the new ideas could never be expressed clearly in the language of responsibility, and it was therefore to be expected that lawyers and jurymen, who have to wrestle with them, would always be plagued with contradictions and unanswerable questions until the concept of responsibility was allowed to wither away. 'Forget responsibility', she said, 'and we can ask, not whether an offender ought to be punished, but whether he is likely to benefit from punishment.'[2] I do not remember any declaration by another writer against responsibility which is as outspoken and uncompromising as this, but there are undoubtedly many persons of intelligence who share Lady Wootton's dislike for talk of responsibility and think, as she does, that it is fated to disappear with the progress of scientific enlightenment. What attitude should we adopt towards their revolutionary suggestions?

If they are right, resistance to the change they want is not only stupid but inhumane. On the other hand, total abandonment of the concept of responsibility would involve such enormous changes in the pattern of human life that we cannot contemplate it seriously until the case for it has been stated much more carefully. It is certainly not impossible that words which have been used freely by millions of people for thousands of years should presently be found worthless for any but historical purposes: 'witchcraft' is an obvious example. But if there is a scientific mistake or a hopeless muddle in all ordinary talk of moral responsibility, it seems we must not only reform our penal system in the way Lady Wootton wishes but refrain from all moral praise or blame of our fellow men, since to say that a man is morally praiseworthy or blameworthy for an act is ordinarily held to imply that he is morally responsible for it. Indeed, the connexion is so close that the word 'responsible' and the phrase 'to blame' have come to be treated as interchangeable in that metaphorical usage in which we say that the bad weather was responsible, or to blame, for the poor harvest. Nor will it be enough to abstain from moral judgement on acts already performed, a course that might perhaps have something to be said in its favour. For on the supposition that men are never to be held responsible it will be both senseless and useless to remind men of their responsibilities, that is to say, futile to tell them that they will be blameworthy if they fail to do certain acts in the future. But can we imagine a characteristically human form of life in which all this is lacking?

In what follows I am going to suggest that we have various uses of the word 'responsible', and that, although these are closely connected, they are not inseparable. A few moments ago I gave an example of the use of the word to indicate a causal connexion.

[2] *The Times*, 13 Feb 1960. Other expressions of the same view are to be found in her *Social Science and Social Pathology* (1959) ch. viii.

Clearly this is derivative from talk about the responsibility of men for their deeds, but I do not suppose that Lady Wootton wants to ban it, any more than she would wish to ban metaphorical uses of the word 'witchcraft'. If this is so, may it not be possible for us to make important distinctions even between the uses in which men are said to be responsible for their deeds? I shall argue that we can distinguish at least three such cases, and that, while Lady Wootton is right in urging us to reject a certain kind of talk about responsibility, she is wrong in supposing that what she wants can only come about through the withering away of a single undifferentiated concept of responsibility hitherto used in all contexts by all plain men and legislators. In order to carry out this programme I must evidently deal first with the historical connexion between responsibility and retribution, since that is where Lady Wootton starts.

II

As the dictionary says, 'responsible' meant originally 'liable to be called to answer'[3] or, more shortly, 'accountable'. The corresponding word in ancient Greek is ὑπεύθυνος, which means literally 'subject to an audit or rectification (εὔθυνα)', and it was applied first to officers of state who had to render accounts and face a scrutiny at the end of their term of office. In modern times the most primitive of the surviving uses of 'responsible' is that in which we say that the Cabinet is constitutionally responsible to the House of Commons for its conduct of the national affairs or that the Domestic Bursar is statutorily responsible to the Governing Body for the management of the college catering. When we say shortly that the Bursar is responsible for the catering, we mean more generally that he is expected to look after it, and that if anyone has any criticism to make he should address it to the Bursar. If, however, some outsider who has no title to interfere sends a complaint to the Bursar, the latter, while admitting that he is responsible, may go back in irritation to the old sense and say 'That does not mean that I am answerable to you, Sir.' For the basic notion of responsibility is clearly that of being accountable under some rule to a determinate authority for a determinate sphere of action; and from

---

[3] It is interesting to note that 'answer', *respondere*, and ἀποκρίνεσθαι were all used first in the legal sense of 'answer a charge'. I owe this and a number of other valuable comments to Professor Herbert Hart.

this, it seems, all special uses are derived by analogy or metaphor or shift of emphasis. When, for example, we say that the bad weather was responsible for the poor harvest, we talk metaphorically of the non-human cause of a disaster in terms originally introduced for talking of certain causes. And when a business man says that an applicant for credit must be supported by a responsible backer, he does not mean that the backer must be one who may justly be called to account if the debtor defaults (though that, no doubt, is true), but rather that the backer must be a person who can in practice be called to account because he is not a fly-by-night but a solid citizen with a stake in the country. What, then, is the special point of talking about *moral* responsibility? How is this usage related to the original notion of responsibility?

I think it began with a belief that the moral law, or, as older writers would say, the natural law, requires an audit of all human behaviour and a settlement of moral accounts in which the wicked are made to pay for their misdeeds. And this belief in turn seems to be connected with an attempt to assimilate all moral obligations to the obligations undertaken by borrowers. If I am right, the development of our language for talking about these matters has had very important effects on human thought, and it is therefore proper to spend a little time in trying to establish the facts.

Consider first the word 'ought' and words of similar meaning in other languages. 'Ought' began life as a past tense of 'owe' but has come to be used exclusively in an extended sense to suggest that something can properly be claimed from a man. 'Should' has a similar relation to 'shall', which in old English had the sense of 'owe'. In German *sollen* can still be used in certain contexts with that sense, though it is most commonly used now with the general sense of 'ought'. In French *devoir* and in Italian *dovere* retain the two senses of 'owe' and 'ought' which they inherit from the Latin *debere*. Our English 'debt' is a derivative from *debitum*, the past participle of *debere*, but so too are our words 'due' and 'duty', which can still move back and forth between the special and the general. *Debere* itself seems to be a contraction of *dehibere* which meant originally 'keep' or 'retain' but came at a very early date to have the sense of 'keep what should be returned'. In Greek ὀφείλειν may mean either 'owe' or 'ought': and a little work with dictionaries will show that there are many similar words in other languages. There are, of course, other idioms for talking about what we ought to do, but some which at first sight seem independent of the notion of debt prove on closer examination to be connected with it. Thus the metaphor of being bound, which occurs in the moral vocabulary of many languages, seems to have been applied first in connexion with those obligations which arise, like debts, from promises. It came to be a maxim of Roman law that *obligationes* might arise also from *delicta*, or wrongful acts, but those arising from contracts were commonly treated as primary; and it is therefore no accident that in languages subject to the influence of Roman law derivatives of the word *obligatio* are still used, as 'bond' is used in English, with the special sense of 'instrument of debt'.

So far we have considered talk of duty in general as it might occur before the time for performance of the act or abstention which had been likened to discharge of a debt. But suppose a man has failed in performance. According to the way of thinking to which I have drawn attention he is still in debt, though it may be impossible now for him to pay in the way intended by the person who originally said that he had a debt. He must therefore pay in some other way, i.e. give compensation. There are lots of usages which bear witness to this way of thinking. In German the word for guilt, namely *Schuld*, is also the word for debt; and although 'guilt' in English seems to have a different origin, the phrase 'guilty of death' was at one time used in the sense of 'subject to the death penalty'. Furthermore, in all languages of which I have any knowledge the notion of punishment is closely connected with that of payments. In English we have the standard phrase 'pay the penalty' and the colloquial threat 'He shall pay for this'. In Latin we have *poenas solvere* and in Greek τίνειν. Sometimes, however, by a further extension of the commercial analogy punishment is considered as a negative wage earned by wrongdoing. This was the original point of the use of the word 'deserve'; and the metaphor is still very much alive in St Paul's *Epistle to the Romans* vi. 23, where he says 'The wages of sin is death'. When we talk of punishment as retribution we have a similar conception in mind. In this case payment is supposed to be made by the punishing authority, but it is payment of something undesirable, i.e. what I have called a negative wage, and the purpose of the payment is to settle the wrongdoer's moral account. So strong indeed is the association of account-keeping with punishment in our thought that the word 'atonement', which originally meant 'union' or 'reconciliation', has come to have the sense of 'expiation' or 'paying the penalty'. Presumably this happened because it was taken for granted that there could be no reconciliation until the moral account had been made to balance. Sometimes it is allowed that an aggrieved party can set the account straight by writing off what is due to him. That was the original sense of the English 'forgive' and of the low Latin *perdonare*, from which 'pardon' is derived. The idea is expressed very clearly in the Lord's Prayer: 'Forgive us our debts as we forgive our debtors.' Here the Greek word translated by 'debts' is ὀφειλήματα, derived from the verb ὀφείλειν which I mentioned earlier as capable of meaning either 'owe' or 'ought'. But in many religious systems it is thought there can be no remission, i.e. that it is impossible that the account should be squared except by actual payment of some kind. That is the doctrine of *karma* in Hinduism, and it seems to be assumed also in Anselm's version of the Christian doctrine of redemption, according to which even God could not save us without paying the price of our sins, though the debt was due to himself. Incidentally, the word 'redemption' was originally a commercial term which meant in general 'buying back' but could have the special sense of 'buying back what has been pledged as security for a loan'. Such terminology was more appropriate to the older theory, expounded by Origen and accepted by many Fathers of the Church, according to which Christ's salvation of man was payment of ransom to the devil in respect of rights which the latter had gained over man at the fall. It is a curious piece of evidence for the wide acceptance of an analogy between guilt and debt that the language of redemption has been used by Christians in the presentation of theological views which are so very different; and it is an extremely curious historical fact that there has never been an authoritative decision of the Church between those views.

In the earliest legal system of which we have record, that of Hammurabi, there is a lot about penalties, but these are considered as damages which a malefactor must pay to an aggrieved party, either human or divine. Thus there is a price to be paid to a man for the killing of a member of his household, just as for the killing of one of his animals, and the price varies according to the social status of the aggrieved party and the relationship which the dead man bore to him. The same was true in the earliest Roman law, in customary Norse law, and in primitive English law. It has been maintained, indeed, that there was at first no special criminal law, since all cases of wrongdoing were treated in the same way as those special cases which are called in modern legal parlance torts or civil wrongs, that is to say, cases where damages are payable. According to this account of the development of law, the only motive for active intervention in disputed cases by kings or other public officers was a wish to prevent the indefinite continuation of feuds that might disturb the peace of society. Their aim, it is said, was to get a settlement, and for this purpose it was important that they should be able to point to a set tariff of penalties such as that in the famous passage of *Exodus* xxi about an eye for an eye and a tooth for a tooth. I think it is a mistake to suggest that all primitive law is concerned with reparation for injuries. There are quite early codes which reveal a conviction that some kinds of wrongdoing, in particular homicide and certain sexual offences, should be punished apart from the demands of any plaintiffs. An example is the *Exodus* code to which I have just referred. But it is interesting to notice that penalties which cannot be regarded as damages to an injured man are often represented as satisfaction to an affronted god. In St Anselm's version of the atonement doctrine all human sin, being disobedience by a creature to its creator, is an offence for which divine honour requires infinite satisfaction.

At first sight it appears that believers in the doctrine of moral accounting have often applied their theory without any regard for the requirement of *mens rea*, or guilty intent, which is now regarded as fundamental in criminal law, unless expressly excluded in favour of so-called strict liability. In ancient Greek legend Oedipus had to pay a penalty for killing his father, although it was fated that he should do so and his act was unintentional in the sense that he did not know he was killing his father. Similarly many Christians have held that unbaptised children who die without having done anything intentionally will properly be made to pay infinitely in respect of a debt inherited from their ancestor Adam. At various periods men have been held liable to pay for things done accidentally, and sometimes even dumb animals or inanimate objects such as axes have been solemnly tried and found guilty of homicide. It is said, for example, that such trials took place in civilised Athens. If one started from consideration of these cases, one might be led to think that primitive men began with a notion of guilt which did not involve intention on the part of the agent and that the modern refinements of *mens rea* were introduced later. But I think that this would be a mistake, and that anyone who tried to develop such an hypothesis would find himself unable to give a plausible explanation of the course of history. It seems much wiser to start from the consideration that in the overwhelming majority of cases at all times guilt has been imputed to human beings who did what they did intentionally. Having assumed this, we can then try to explain the other cases by supposing that our ancestors some- times misinterpreted their own traditional formulae. Let us suppose, for example, that there is a law like that of *Exodus* xxi. 15 saying 'He that smiteth his father or his mother shall be surely put to death', and that a man has in fact smitten his father, though unin- tentionally. To us it seems clear that, even if the law were just, the man should not be made to pay the penalty, because it is appropriate only for disobedience to a generally accepted commandment 'Smite not thy father or thy mother', in which 'smite' must be understood to have the sense of 'smite intentionally'. But a judge who thinks himself bound to maintain the utmost rigour in his judgements may conceivably insist on taking the word in its widest sense and justify his interpretation by saying that, if the legislator had intended to exclude cases like this, he could have done so explicitly. Such misplaced rigorism is most likely to occur when the legislator is supposed to be divine. For it is not safe to assume that gods, whose ways are notoriously mysterious, share the commonsensical views of men, and so a judge who by lax interpretation fails to secure the satisfaction they demand may bring disaster on himself and his community. In any case, if I am right, the legal maxim which makes guilt depend on intention is primarily a principle of interpre- tation designed to preserve the ordinary standards of human legis- lation against perversely rigorous misunderstanding of penal laws.

When the doctrine of moral accounting is combined with a belief in divine creation of the world and God is supposed to be the creditor of all men, a special difficulty arises. How can it be just that a man who is dependent in everything on God should be required to pay a penalty to God in respect of anything he has done? He seems to be in a situation like that of a slave whose owner exacts extra labour from him because of a slip that is due to the slave's poor condition and so ultimately to the master's treatment of him. Such reflections were not unknown in pagan antiquity, but they were not so worrying then as they became later, because the pagan gods were not in general regarded as creators or supposed to be universally just. To Christian theologians these thoughts have always been disturbing, and even theologians who believe, like St Augustine, in the hereditary corruption of human nature have commonly insisted that Adam at least had freedom of choice, because they hope to justify the ways of God by speaking of human will as the first cause of sin and the root of evil. Those who, like Bradwardine and Jonathan Edwards, have declared openly that God's act in creation was the first cause of all our acts, including our sins, are exceptional, and what they have said has usually been met by strong opposition because it seems to clash with the doctrine of divine justice.

In recent times problems of this sort, which once bulked very large in the long and intricate debate about freedom of the will, have ceased to worry people as much as they used to do. Perhaps one reason is a general decline of religious belief. But another is certainly a loss of faith in the principle of moral accounting which underlay most of the older talk about moral responsibility, and this reason has influenced the religious no less than the irreligious. For many people of both groups now reject the retributivist theory of punishment, which is a form of the theory of moral accounting. Sometimes such rejection is based on an assumption that retribution is identical with revenge. This seems to me to be a mistake. For although people who seek revenge often use phrases of moral accounting, such as 'He shall pay for this', the hatred and anger that they show are not essential to the retributivist theory, and it is wrong to reject retribution merely because one dislikes hatred. There are versions of the doctrine in which retribution is simply a natural necessity independent of human passions. There is, however, a much better reason for rejecting the retributivist theory, namely, dissatisfaction with the whole web of metaphor to which it belongs.

III

When I began to present evidence for the existence of a widespread theory of moral accounting, you may perhaps have been inclined to say that I was confusing etymology with philosophical analysis. Although the word 'ought' started life as a variant of 'owe', that fact is of no philosophical interest if people in our time do not think that 'ought' has many of the same implications as 'owe'. And it must be admitted that some intelligent persons are surprised when they first hear of the historical connexion between these words. On the other hand, when I went on to speak of the use of accounting terms in connexion with punishment, you were probably inclined to allow that what I said had some relevance to modern practice. It seems, therefore, that the language of moral accounting, which began with an extended use of debt words to cover the whole range of duty, still has an influence on penal theory that it could scarcely retain if we understood our situation aright.

When applying a system of criminal law, we must, of course, consider very carefully what punishment it allows for each wrongdoing, and we may perhaps find the language of accounting useful for expression of some of the judgements we make in this connexion. We may speak, for example, of the different penalties that criminals of various kinds may be made to *pay* for their offences, and we may talk sensibly of the possibility of a prisoner's *earning* remission by good conduct. But it is a mistake to suppose that we can use the same language profitably when the question under discussion is the moral justice of the criminal law itself. For there are no penal provisions in the moral law, and it is not true that a wrong act gives rise to a moral debt, except in the important special case where it imposes on the agent an obligation to make such reparation as he can for a hurt to another person. In many cases of hurt it is already very difficult to decide what is appropriate reparation, because there can be no restoration of the situation as it was before the wrongdoing; but at least we know what considerations are relevant, namely the nature and amount of the suffering to be alleviated. When, however, we pass from compensation in a strict sense to the notion of expiating a sin or nullifying it by suffering, we have no standard by which to determine what suffering is appropriate to each sinner. For the old maxim of an eye for an eye is obviously inapplicable except in a very small range of cases. How, for example, can a childless youth who curses his mother have precisely the same done to him? In short, the whole theory of retribution seems to arise from a muddle-headed attempt to extend the notion of reparation beyond the limits within which it makes good sense. Such an attempt is sometimes favoured by the thought that all wrongdoing is an offence against God. But that is certainly not the only source of the belief in moral accounting, since the doctrine has been held by atheists.

If, as I have suggested, dropping of the doctrine of moral accounting has helped to free men from old theological perplexities about the responsibilities of creatures in relation to their creator, may it not perhaps also help to free them from more modern perplexities about the responsibility of persons who are psychologically abnormal? This is no doubt part of what Lady Wootton wants to maintain, and I for my part am prepared to accept it as correct. For if no one is responsible in the sense that he can justly be called to balance his moral account by expiation of his wrongdoings, as distinct from paying his debts in a properly limited interpretation of that phrase, it is useless to ask what difference mental abnormality makes to that kind of responsibility.

So much is clear, and yet some philosophers are inclined to say that we must retain the notion of moral desert as a limitation of what may be done to prisoners for the public good. That is what F. H. Bradley had in mind when he wrote:

> Punishment is punishment only when it is deserved. We pay the penalty because we owe it and for no other reason: and if punishment is inflicted for any other reason whatever than because it is merited by wrong, it is a gross immorality, a crying injustice, an abominable crime, and not what it pretends to be. We may have regard for whatever considerations we please – our own convenience, the good of society, the benefit of the offender; we are fools and worse if we fail to do so. Having once the right to punish, we may modify the punishment according to the useful and the pleasant, but these are external to the matter, they cannot give us the right to punish, and nothing can do that but criminal desert.[4]

I think Bradley has overstated his case by saying that punishment should not be inflicted for any other reason than because it is deserved. This formula suggests that punishment is to be inflicted for its own sake. But one may hold the opposite view, according to which punishment is a necessary evil, to be inflicted only for the public good, and still avoid the gross immorality of which Bradley speaks if one adopts the limiting principle that no one is to be punished beyond his deserts. For my own part I am prepared to

[4] 'The Vulgar Notion of Responsibility', in *Ethical Studies* (1927) pp. 26–7.

agree that punishment can never be justified in the wide sense of being shown to be morally desirable unless it can be justified in the narrow sense of being shown to be just to the person punished. But I do not now believe, as I once did, that acceptance of this thesis commits us to some form of the retributivist theory. In order for the punishment of a criminal to be just it is not necessary, or even possible, that it should be something deserved by him under a natural penal law. All penal law is positive law, and if we say, as no doubt we shall continue to do, that punishment is not in general just unless deserved, we should not read into the word 'deserved' anything inconsistent with this. Although the word started life as part of a vocabulary for expressing a theory of moral accounting which we now reject, it can still be retained, provided the statement that a criminal deserves his punishment is now taken to mean that he has brought it upon himself by an offence done of his own free will against a positive law that is itself just.

You will notice that in this explanation of a reasonable use of the word 'deserve' I have spoken of a law that is itself just. This is essential, because we certainly do not want to argue that whenever anyone is punished in accordance with some positive law he deserves what he gets. One point of continuing to talk about desert is precisely to allow for criticism of positive law, and this we can do if we recognise that words which were first introduced in connexion with a simple undifferentiated notion of law may take on new subtleties of meaning after the distinction of positive from natural or moral law. To suppose that because penal law is all positive there can be no sense in talking of the moral justice or injustice of any particular punishment would be as foolish as to suppose that because property law is all positive there can be no sense in talking of the moral justice or injustice of any particular distribution of property. What is needed is only the possibility of passing a moral judgement on the legislation as a whole. In the case of penal legislation such a judgement will involve a balancing of the evil of the suffering to be inflicted under the law against the evil that promulgation and enforcement of the law may be expected to prevent within a system which includes also suitably related provision against other types of crime.

All this is relevant to our problem about responsibility. When we decide that no one is to be held responsible in the sense of account-able for his wrongdoings under a natural law requiring expiation, we need not forswear all uses of the word 'responsible' if we can find a good sense for it in relation to our man-made penal system. And it seems that we can find such a sense. For when we say that an accused person is morally responsible in respect of an act with which he is charged, we may mean only that it is morally proper to hold him accountable in respect of that act under a penal law of the land, or in other words that he can rightly be made to pay the prescribed penalty if in fact he did the deed. Perhaps Lady Wootton would have us reject this use also, on the ground that it can only lead to the posing of unanswerable questions about the limits of responsibility. But it is important to notice that this use is quite independent of the retributivist theory of punishment to which she chiefly objects. Whether or not it is a profitable use, that is to say, a use free from confusion, must depend on the clarity or unclarity of the criterion for determining when it is morally proper to hold a man accountable for anything under a law of the land. That is the question to which we must now turn.

IV

When the notion of responsibility is connected with a scheme of moral accounting, it is commonly said that men are responsible only for what they do of their own free will, i.e. that they should not be called to account for what they do unintentionally or during insanity or under certain forms of duress. Since the development of meaning we have just considered is apparently no more than the substitution of accountability under just positive law for accountability under natural law, it may perhaps be supposed that it cannot involve any development of the criterion for responsibility. Whether we retain or reject the retributivist principle, we wish to say that no punishment is just unless the criminal has brought it on himself by an offence done of his own free will, and this formula seems to bring back again many of the difficulties of the old doctrine. I do not want to suggest that we can evade the problem of free will by abandoning the retributivist theory of punishment, but I think it worth noticing that the shift to a utilitarian or forward-looking theory does in fact enable us to find a new ground for using the phrase 'X may properly be called to account for Y'.

The point is made very clearly by Bentham in ch. xiii of his

Principles of Morals and Legislation, which has the title 'Cases Unmeet for Punishment'. According to his general theory the chief purpose of the legislator in making a code of criminal law should be to produce an artificial reconciliation of human interests by attaching to the various anti-social acts called crimes such unpleasant consequences for the agent as will be just sufficient to make them unattractive to potential criminals. He recognises that infliction of punishment may give satisfaction to aggrieved persons, and perhaps also to disinterested onlookers, and he is even prepared to allow that such satisfaction is unobjectionable if it comes as a free bonus from the operation of a rationally designed system of deterrents. But unlike some modern English judges, he is not prepared to allow that it should have any place in determining what penalties are to be imposed, and in the chapter to which I have referred he is especially concerned to show that utilitarianism imposes strict limits on the scope of criminal justice. In particular he argues that it provides a good explanation for the various defences recognised as valid in the criminal courts of civilised nations. According to his argument punishment is unfitting in four kinds of cases:

  (i) where it is groundless, because there is really no mischief to prevent,
 (ii) where it must be inefficacious,
(iii) where it is unprofitable, because it involves greater loss to the community than the mischief it is designed to prevent,
 (iv) where it is needless, because the mischief it is designed to prevent can be prevented in some other way, e.g. by simple instruction of the ignorant.

The second of these is the heading that interests us now. For it is said by Bentham to cover not only cases where the punishment serves no useful purpose (because it is under a penal law that has been made too late to be of any use, or because it is under no penal law at all, or because it is insufficiently publicised) but also all cases of infancy, insanity, intoxication, unintentionality, unconsciousness, missupposal, opposite superior force, physical danger, threatened mischief, duress, necessity, physical compulsion, restraint. What these latter cases are supposed by Bentham to have in common is that the persons concerned are all at the time of action in conditions that make them not susceptible to influence by threats. Thus, for example, a person who may in future be subject to physical compulsion cannot be deterred by fear of punishment from doing what he will then be compelled to do, and so infliction of punishment now on a person who has done something regrettable under physical compulsion is useless, even though it may be in accordance with a duly promulgated general provision of penal law.

Professor Hart has objected that Bentham's analysis proves at most the ineffectiveness of threats of punishment to persons who are themselves in any of the specified conditions. It is still conceivable, he thinks, that infliction of punishment on them might have the result of producing more conformity in others. For in a system of strict liability anyone who is at all susceptible to influence by threats knows that, if he is caught, he can have no hope of evading punishment by any excuse, and this consideration may perhaps make him more careful than he would be otherwise.[5] This criticism does not involve any attack on the fundamental assumption of utilitarianism, and I think Bentham could reply by saying, as Professor Hart himself has done on other occasions, that there is a strong moral presumption against a general system of strict liability because it deprives citizens of security against being made to suffer for what they do without *mens rea*. But behind Professor Hart's objection there may perhaps be the thought that Bentham's rationale of our customary limitation of responsibility by the requirement of *mens rea* cannot be on the right lines if it allows even the possibility of justifying strict liability by the collection of suitable evidence about its effect on human behaviour. I sympathise strongly with those who dislike strict liability, but I do not think we can assert *a priori* that it is wrong in all conceivable circumstances. If there is a mistake at this point in the Benthamite theory, it is not that the theory may perhaps allow a place for strict liability in exceptional circumstances, but rather that it takes no account of any evil except suffering as such and may for that reason admit strict liability too easily. There is, I believe, a special evil in the deliberate infliction of suffering on other human beings who cannot help themselves, and therefore a good reason why we should not ordinarily punish persons who have done all that is humanly possible to avoid breaking the law. Most often strict liability has been introduced because some offence whose consequences are thought to be very serious has

[5] 'Prolegomenon to the Principles of Punishment', *Aristotelian Society Proceedings*, 1959–60. I understand that there was in fact no strict liability in the English law of Bentham's day.

been found to be also one in respect of which there may be great difficulty in proving guilty intent. But to my mind it is least objectionable when the offence for which it is imposed is possible only for persons engaged in a special activity (e.g. sale of intoxicating drink) that may be avoided without hardship by anyone who is unwilling to face the special risks attached to it by the legislature.

Putting aside these special difficulties, we may say that according to Bentham's account of the requirement of *mens rea*, a man may be held responsible for an offence and so a fitting subject for punishment, as distinct from medical treatment or educational therapy of some kind, if he is a person who broke the law because of a character defect such as laziness or greed which is corrigible in general by threats of punishment under a morally admissible penal code. I put in the last phrase because we do not want to find ourselves driven to the conclusion that a man is responsible merely because he might be made law-abiding by some monstrous threat we are not prepared to use. And I have used the phrase 'corrigible in general' to allow for the obvious fact that convicted criminals have not been deterred from the particular offences of which they are found guilty. But it must be admitted there is a serious difficulty here. If Bentham is right, the mere fact that a man has committed a crime is some evidence to show that he is not responsible. For unless he is mentally defective in such a degree that he is obviously unfit to plead, he must be presumed to have known of the existence of penalties for acts of the kind he did, and yet it is clear he was not influenced by that knowledge when he acted.

It may perhaps be answered that we cannot decide whether or not a man is responsible until we have brought the legal penalties to his attention in a really vivid way by punishing him once or twice. But if we take this line, we shall be driven to say that any criminals who persist in repeating their offences are not responsible. That is to say, in many cases in which there is no obvious presumption against responsibility, we shall have to punish up to a certain point in an experimental way, hoping we may teach the criminals to take our threats seriously and govern themselves accordingly; but if after a certain number of punishments we find any of them reverting quickly to their crimes, we must conclude that we were mistaken in their case and treat them henceforth as persons who are not responsible. At first hearing this may sound strange and perhaps even shocking. For when we say that no one should be punished unless he deserves it, we ordinarily assume that the question of responsibility can be settled before the punishment is inflicted. From the point of view of the retributive theory there is indeed a monstrous paradox in the contention that criminals may be punished experimentally, and the paradox is not diminished by the suggestion that criminals are to be presumed responsible until the contrary is proved. For if responsibility is understood in the way required by Bentham's theory of punishment, it must be admitted that what we know of a convicted criminal before his punishment suggests already that he may perhaps be non-responsible, since he has broken the law in spite of his knowledge that there are penalties attached to the act.

Whatever the theoretical difficulties, it cannot be denied we often reason and act in this way when we are at our most humane. If, for example, a child breaks a family rule, we first warn him and then, if he repeats his offence, we punish him mildly. But if we find that he continues to break the rule in spite of punishment, we become worried and think that he ought perhaps to have different treatment. Perhaps this way of thinking is new, but it is certainly not confined to parents who have made themselves nervous by reading too much child psychology. For even in the criminal courts it is now recognised that persistent offenders may by the very fact of their persistence prove that they are not fit subjects for further punishment in the ordinary sense of that word. Unfortunately no one has yet found a dependable method of curing or reforming such persons. Those who are a serious danger to the public must obviously be kept in some form of preventive detention; but many persistent offenders are no more than a nuisance, and we cannot bring ourselves to imprison these for life nor yet to certify them as lunatics. We must hope that psychological advances will help us to cope with such problem criminals better than we have done so far; but I think it unlikely that we shall ever be able to detect them all before they start on careers of crime; and if we cannot do so, we shall have to punish them at the beginning in what I have called an experimental way, that is to say, on the hopeful assumption that they are responsible in the sense allowed by Bentham's theory.

These considerations go to show that we can make good use of the word 'responsible' within a utilitarian theory of punishment if we take it to mean 'suitable for punishment under a just law'. But I think that in practice we all expect more than this minimum from persons we call morally responsible, even though we are well aware of the defects of the retributivist theory and have no intention of returning to it. A paranoiac madman who believes he is the victim of a dastardly conspiracy may nevertheless hesitate to use violence against those whom he hates as persecutors, if he thinks that doing so will bring him straight into their hands and so lead to greater immediate suffering for himself. Genuine kleptomaniacs are not, as many persons think, unaffected by the fear of being found out and punished. What is peculiar about them is that they do not steal from ordinary motives of greed but rather to get the triumph of secret success in handling what is forbidden; and the answer to a question sometimes asked by magistrates is that they will not take things under the nose of a policeman unless they think that even in this situation they can escape detection. Again dogs and various other animals can be trained by threats, though not of course by threats attached to rules expressed in verbal form. In each of these cases the use of threats, made credible by occasional punishments, might perhaps be justified if there were great need for conformity and this could not be obtained by gentler methods; but most of us would refuse to agree that in these cases liability to punishment under a just law entailed full moral responsibility. And the reason is plain. Often when we say that a man is morally responsible for doing something wrong, we wish to convey nothing at all about punishment (which may perhaps be inappropriate for his particular wrongdoing, say verbal cruelty to a member of his family), but only that he is blameworthy. If therefore anyone asserts without qualification that we should get rid of the notion of responsibility, he commits himself to the view that no one should ever be blamed for anything. Perhaps Lady Wootton intends this, thinking of blame as a kind of penalty within the untenable theory of moral accounting. If so, I believe she is mistaken. In order to see why, let us consider what we mean by 'blame' and 'blameworthy'.

V

We often use the word 'blame' to mean the same as 'fix responsibility on'. But if we take 'responsibility' here in a moral sense, it looks as though we were going round in circles. For in this sense we say that to hold a man responsible is to consider him blameworthy and then that to blame him is to fix responsibility on him. It is easy, however, to escape from the circle. In its basic use 'blame' does not mean 'fix responsibility on', but rather 'speak ill of', 'censure', 'find fault with'. If the blame is expressed to the person blamed, it may also be called reproach, reproof, reprimand, chiding, or scolding according to the relation of the speaker to the person addressed and the manner he adopts. In all cases it is assumed that the person blamed could have chosen to act otherwise, but it is not esential that blame should be expressed to the person blamed for the purpose of influencing his behaviour in future, or indeed that it should be made known to anyone. We can blame dead men in our hearts.

At first sight the statement that a man is blameworthy, being equivalent to the statement that he deserves blame, may seem to presuppose acceptance of the theory of moral accounting; for clearly the desert of which we speak here is not desert under a positive law. But in practice an assertion of this kind is understood to mean primarily that it would be correct to say that the man did wrong in circumstances where he could have chosen to act otherwise. No doubt a man who has been blamed publicly for something he did not do or for something he could not avoid doing may say that he has been treated unfairly, since publication of incorrect blame is a kind of hurt. Similarly blame that is correct may be described as just. All this is suggested in a very natural way by talk of desert in connexion with blame. But justice in our judgements of the acts and characters of men depends simply on truth, not on satisfaction of an independent requirement for the squaring of moral accounts, and we may therefore hold a man blameworthy without holding that publication of our blame would be a good act. Even when we have decided that a man is blameworthy in the strict sense, we have still to decide whether it would be morally right to publish our blame, either to the man himself or to others, since the over-all rightness, or moral expediency, of a social act of censure is not to be identified with its justice in that special usage in which justice is here equated with truth. In certain cases, for example, we may consider that censure will inflict useless suffering, or even that it may lead to some undesirable development in the character of the person censured.

Why, indeed, should we ever blame a man to his face? Is publication of blame simply expression of resentment? It has often been remarked that when we are hurt or threatened by supposedly free agents we may feel resentment which we should not feel against automata or madmen who behaved in a superficially similar way. Perhaps verbal expression or such resentment sometimes serves a useful purpose by producing in a quicker and more economical way the results that might have been produced by a good hiding. That is the sort of explanation that is suggested by biological consideration of the place of resentment in animal life. But it is wrong to think of blame as essentially the expression of resentment, whether personal or impersonal. For it is possible to blame a man without being in any way resentful towards him, and it is also possible to be influenced by blame from another in a way quite different from that in which one would be influenced by his expression of resentment. When they are rational, that is to say, in good working order as beings with minds, men have a peculiar ability of being moved in their choices by a desire to rectify their shortcomings and in particular their defects of character. But to blame a man to his face is to tell him he has some such defect, and so, if the blame is based on a convincing analysis, it *may* sometimes be effective in producing a change for the better. Human nature is so complex, however, that it is by no means certain that blame will always have this effect, even on a generally rational hearer; and the prospects are least favourable when the blame is accompanied by marks of resentment, since hostility breeds hostility. But there is at least the possibility that censure may lead to reform, and we cannot conceive a characteristically human form of life in which no account is taken of this.

Now I want to suggest that one basic element in our modern concept of moral responsibility is that of susceptibility to influence by moral considerations, in particular by thought of the need to rectify one's own shortcomings, and that the non-responsibility of psychopaths consists precisely in their unresponsiveness to these considerations. I have spoken especially of the need to rectify our shortcomings, which is a second-order moral consideration, because we talk of responsibility most often in connexion with faults. If, as is very unlikely, there were a man who responded without fail to all first-order moral considerations and so was entirely free from moral faults, we should certainly not say that he was lacking in moral responsibility; but it is also difficult to conceive any circumstances in which we should want to speak of him as responsible. Throughout its history the word 'responsible' has retained its original meaning of 'subject to audit', but in the usage which now interests us the audit is one imposed neither by nature, as in the retributivist theory, nor by political society, as in the utilitarian theory, but by conscience, and the adjustment which it is intended to achieve is not a squaring of accounts by payment of any kind but the correction of character faults.

If a man is of such a sort that he cannot be altered by self-censure, he is not morally responsible, i.e. not a fit person to be called to an audit of conscience. I think Aristotle was thinking of such persons when he said in his *Nicomachean Ethics* that some men are incorrigible and gave it as a mark of their peculiar defect that they are not subject to remorse. But he seems to have believed that all persons in this condition could have been reformed by suitable censure at an earlier age, whereas we have recently come to recognise that men may be non-responsible in my third sense without having gone through a stage of being responsible. Indeed we are now inclined to think that the condition is always pathological. The difference is interesting and important. Aristotle's teaching corresponds to the ordinary untutored assumptions we make in dealing with each other. We always treat men as morally responsible until the contrary is proved, and we find it difficult to know what to think of an otherwise normal man who does evil deeds deliberately and shows no sign of remorse. If we can convince ourselves that he came to this condition through a gradual blunting of his susceptibility to moral considerations, we may perhaps say, as Aristotle did, that he is very wicked indeed and think of him as incorrigible only because he requires a stiffer dose of censure than we have ever been able to give him. But a close study of unusual cases, which is not possible for judges and jurymen, seems to show that there is a sort of moral deafness which can never be penetrated by any amount of moral shouting; and when it appears that we have to do with a man who suffers from this, the sensible course is not to work ourselves up to still greater heights of indignation, but rather to try other means of producing a change for the better, if we can think of any which are morally permissible.

You will notice that this third account of moral responsibility is like that I have attributed to Bentham, except that it refers to blame where he spoke of punishment. The difference is important, but it may easily be overlooked because punishment is commonly accompanied by blame and the two may be confused together under such phrases as 'expression of disapproval'. What is essential to the new account is that a morally responsible person can be moved by recognition of his own moral defects; and censure by others is relevant only as a method by which a man's moral defects may be brought to his notice. Conceivably the desirable effect might be produced in a man in some other way, e.g. by his discovery, either in real life or in fiction, of persons who criticised themselves by higher standards than those he applied to himself. But our new definition, like Bentham's, implies that we must in general deal with our fellow men, including those who are criminals, in an experimental fashion, starting with the assumption that they can be moved by considerations of the kind we call moral, provided these are presented in a way which does not arouse an unfavourable attitude such as resentment. Similarly we must be prepared to face the possibility of total failure.

VI

What practical conclusions may we draw from all this? I think there are two.

First, it is quite unrealistic to suggest that we should dispense entirely with the notion of responsibility, since the attempt to do so would involve rejection of much more than an outworn metaphor. In the context of penal justice, which especially interests Lady Wootton, it would mean abandonment of the requirement of *mens rea* and introduction of a general system of strict liability. For we have seen that one important use of the word 'responsible' is to distinguish persons who may properly be punished, or at any rate detained against their will, from those who should be left in full liberty. It is true that Lady Wootton's main concern is to withdraw from the courts all questions about the sanity of prisoners, except perhaps the preliminary question whether they are fit to plead, and it may be that if she were asked to produce a new code she would be content with an alteration of practice whereby the word 'guilty' would not be taken to exclude psychopathic abnormality but would be understood always in an extended sense like that it had in the now obsolete verdict of 'Guilty but insane', which is said to have been introduced on the suggestion of Queen Victoria. Sometimes, however, her pronouncements are so sweeping that it seems she would abolish all the ordinary defences of accident, mistake, etc., by which an accused person may at present disclaim responsibility and would require a criminal court in every case to consider only whether the person brought before it had done the action alleged against him in the broadest possible interpretation of the charge, i.e. without any requirement of intentionality, before handing him over to reform commissioners for treatment in whatever way they thought best. If this is indeed her proposal, it seems to me extraordinary and by no means progressive. Possibly she thinks that in practice her reform commissioners would separate out cases of accident, mistake, and the rest for treatment similar to that they get now under the principle of *mens rea*, namely immediate release. But if so, why not provide for this in advance, as we do at present by use of the legal concept of responsibility? What men need in society before all else is security from arbitrary interference, and it seems to me that it is the first task of the courts to provide this.

Secondly, Lady Wootton is right in thinking that courts of criminal justice should not be asked to decide whether an accused person has *full* moral responsibility. The reason, however, is not, as she suggests, that it is impossible to make any good sense of the question, but rather that judges and juries have neither the evidence nor the training required for answering it. If, as I have said, full moral responsibility involves ability to respond to moral considerations, the question whether an offender has such responsibility must be left to be settled, if at all, after conviction, when he can be studied with much greater care and treated, as Lady Wootton wishes, in the way most likely to improve him. In the past, when hanging was the penalty for murder, it seemed necessary to find an answer in the court room, because it was thought that no one should be executed who was not fully responsible. But since the abolition of the death penalty the situation has changed radically, and for the better. If a person is found to be of a pathologically selfish character and not easily to be restrained, either by moral considerations or by fear of punishment, it is unlikely he will now get treatment which seems to him less disagreeable than that given to offenders who are thought fully responsible. On the contrary, since he is a greater danger to society, he may well be detained for a longer period. In practice the defence of insanity as defined by the McNaghten rules has rarely been offered in any but murder cases, because the prospect of detention in a criminal lunatic asylum for an indefinite period is more disagreeable to most people than the prospect of any legal punishment except death; and for similar reasons it seems that no criminal now has any incentive to pretend that he suffers from a serious mental disorder of the volitional kind. Why then should we continue to think of the defects of this kind as excuses of the same order as accident or mistake which must obviously be investigated before conviction and sentence? And if there is to be detention in either case, why should we try to settle the nature of the appropriate treatment once and for all at the time of sentence before any persons with real experience of criminals have had any opportunity to collect evidence by patient examination? No doubt distinctions must be made among convicted persons, but this can be done much better at a later stage.

The change in legal procedure which I think desirable might conceivably be achieved, as I suggested a moment ago, by withdrawing from criminal courts all debatable questions about the sanity of accused persons and using the word 'guilty' in the wide sense advocated by Queen Victoria. But in view of the associations which that word has gathered it would be much better if magistrates and juries were no longer asked to decide on the guilt of the persons brought before them but only to say whether they convicted those persons of wilfully (i.e. intentionally) doing acts that are forbidden by law.

To make such a system work satisfactorily there must, of course, be a greatly improved service for the individual care of convicted persons and a new code of continuing legal safeguards to prevent any injustice to them, in particular by unnecessarily long detention. I have not attempted to work out the details, and I realise that what I have said is no more than a bare beginning. But I am sure that the first step towards reform of the penal law must be an effort to get rid of confused thinking. So long as we are muddled and uncertain about our aims it is always possible that we may fall into injustice or inefficiency – or, what is more likely, both at once.

12 ✣ *The Struggle against Crime*[1]

GIORGIO DEL VECCHIO

Disease, poverty and crime are scourges which have always afflicted the life of man. The progress of science and of civilisation has found some remedy for the first two but no great advance has been made against the third. Crime in various forms still rages in all states, not excluding those which boast of being the more civilised. If some types of crime are less frequent, others have increased. It has been remarked that every modern invention, while marking an advance in art and industry, has given rise to new forms of crime. New sanctions have been devised, prisons have been improved and more prisons built, but in vain. Even the death penalty, where it is still applied, does not restrain murderers, and experience shows that all other threats are equally useless.

Theorists continue to discuss the purposes of punishment. Is it retribution? expiation? reform? deterrence? social defence? There is no agreement. Often several purposes are put forward together, while the facts prove that none of them is achieved.

The most widespread idea is that the basis of punishment is the reciprocation of evil with evil (*malum passionis propter malum actionis*). But, although at first sight this may appear incontrovertible, it is open to grave objections. Morality requires us to do good always and to all men. If a man has done evil, that is no reason why we should do the same. St Thomas justly wrote: 'Non enim debet homo in aliquem peccare propter hoc quod ille peccarit prius in ipsum.' Not even a supposed public interest authorises us to violate the universal precept of charity. Therefore the public interest can and must be protected by some other means, without the disgraceful aim of causing suffering.

The barbaric system of *talio* in its most cruel forms has now been abandoned by all civilised people, but there still prevails a notion which is substantially similar, namely, that it is permissible to inflict

[1] Translated from the Italian by Professor A. H. Campbell, Professor of Public Law in the University of Edinburgh.

pain on those who have committed crimes, not to obtain reparation (which in fact is not obtained thereby), but because the suffering of another causes a certain satisfaction. This is a reason repugnant to every correct conscience.

The alleged absolute justice of repaying evil with evil (maintained by Kant and many other writers) is really an empty sophism. If we go back to the great Christian moralists, we find explicit assertions of the contrary principle, namely, that evil is to be put right only by doing good. Thus St Paul: 'Be not overcome of evil, but overcome evil with good' and St Peter: 'Not rendering evil for evil, or railing for railing: but contrariwise blessing.'

In theology, the ultimate justice, the supreme condemnation and the supreme reward, belong to God and not to men, because they presuppose infallibility. 'Vengeance is mine; I will repay, saith the Lord.' Our judgments are fallible and hence we must be cautious in pronouncing condemnation. The Gospel warns us: 'Condemn not, and ye shall not be condemned: forgive, and ye shall be for-given.'

This, however, does not solve the problem of defence against crime and the human necessity of this defence cannot be denied. Opposition to wrong lies in the nature of right and law; he who violates the legal order should, according to the legal order, be restrained. Hence the universally admitted rule of legitimate defence, which the Romans rightly attributed to *naturalis ratio*. It is true that the protection of rights belongs, as a rule, to the State and only when recourse to the organs of the State is impossible can it be undertaken by the private individual, but that does not impair the universality of the principle.

Restraint is, however, a theoretical concept subject in practice to a serious limitation. Crime, in many cases, produces a result which cannot be undone. *Quod factum est infectum fieri nequit.* The legitimate claim for compensation for the harm done is at the present day almost always merely theoretical and is not effectively satisfied. Moreover, compensation, as it is commonly understood, namely, applying only to the victims of the crime, does not fully satisfy the principle of justice, because crimes disturb and offend not only those who are directly their victim but also the whole social order. Hence, according to the common opinion, the necessity for the infliction of an evil. This inference, however, is both morally reprovable and logically inaccurate. Logic would require that the duty of compensation should be extended to cover the whole of the damage done, and this duty should be fulfilled by doing honest work, under proper control; but this should not be imposed for the sake of causing suffering. To this point we shall return.

Our present penal systems are not conducive to the improvement of our criminals. In most cases, they embitter them and cause them to feel a grudge against society. Provident and salutary as a work of moral re-education might be, it is an illusion to think that it can be carried out in prison. It more often happens that the more artful criminals find opportunity to instruct the less expert, as is shown by the crimes often committed after, sometimes immediately after, release from prison.

It is said that the punishments inflicted on criminals deter others from following their example. The weakness of this is clearly demonstrated by statistics, which prove, in general, the permanence of the phenomenon of crime. Further, it must be remembered that the human person always bears in himself something sacred, and it is therefore not permissible to treat him merely as a means towards an end outside of himself.

The history of criminal law is in large part a history of abolitions. Cruel procedures, like torture, once thought indispensable, and punishments no less cruel, such as amputation, have been progressively abolished, not only because they were repugnant to a more enlightened moral conscience but also because their utter uselessness had been learned by experience. It has been observed that, as a rule, the atrocity of crime matches the atrocity of the penalty; ruthless punishments, far from mollifying men's ways, corrupt them and stir them to vengeance. 'The useless prodigality of punishments', wrote Beccaria, 'has never made men better'. Yet can it be said that cruelty has entirely disappeared from our modern penal systems?

The modern legislation of civilised countries has introduced certain notions which in part correct the mistaken ideas on which the legislation is still based. These include the conditional suspension of sentence, the institution of open prisons, special courts for juveniles, and so on. They are significant indications which may presage the more extensive and fundamental reforms which are still a *desideratum*. Almost all modern penal establishments are still so ordered as to inflict suffering on the prisoners and to deprive them of the possibility of working; they are a kingdom of idleness and of consequent degradation.

Furthermore, men who are condemned to imprisonment are deprived of the power to fulfil the duty to maintain their families which is imposed on them by the civil law. It is inconsistent to cast on the innocent the effect of the fault of the guilty. It is deplorable and unjust, not only economically but also, and above all, morally, that our present-day punishments, especially long-term or life imprisonment, cause suffering not only to the guilty man but to his innocent family.

The foregoing considerations may suffice to show the grave defects of our present penal systems. Are we then to conclude that the struggle against crime should be abandoned? Far otherwise; it should be intensified but conducted with other methods more effective and better fitted to achieve the end.

The principle of legitimate defence, that is, of the immediate repulse of attack, remains unimpaired. This obviously has nothing to do with punishment. It establishes an exemption from liability when one has been compelled to do something, which in itself would be criminal, 'by the necessity of defending a right of one's own or of another person against a present danger of wrongful attack' (to use the words of the Italian Penal Code). The Code adds 'provided that the defence is proportionate to the attack', but to observe an exact proportion in such a case is not always practically possible, so the threat of punishment for abuse of the right of defence could properly be applied only when the disproportion is great and manifest. (It might be better if this point were made clear, either by legislation or by juridical decision.)

There is another preliminary observation to be made which is in a broad sense connected with the same concept of legitimate defence. It is obviously reasonable, and it has never been doubted, that persons mentally abnormal, if they are dangerous to themselves or to others, should be rendered harmless, even if this involves restriction of their personal liberty. Similarly, it must be allowed that the man who by his conduct proves his will to commit serious crimes should be restrained by similar safety measures. But these measures, like the restrictions imposed on dangerous lunatics, have and should have it as their sole purpose to make these persons harmless, to restrain them in their deviant intentions, not to make them suffer. This distinction is important and must be kept in mind if we are to set the problem of penal justice in its proper terms. Our problem is, in short, to ask what treatment should be imposed on wrongdoers over and above this 'moderate defence' which is necessary to prevent the accomplishment of the crimes they have threatened or embarked on.

It is a fundamental maxim of justice that everyone should bear the consequences of his acts; hence comes the duty to repair the harm which one has caused to another and the correlative right to claim such reparation in the most adequate form. In some cases the harm done and consequently the duty of reparation affect only the individuals concerned, as in the non-payment of money due under a contract; in these cases there is obviously sufficient reparation in a civil judgment for payment or compensation. But if the wrongful act is done with criminal intent or with such a degree of fault as is equivalent to criminal intent, the resultant harm commonly is the concern not only of the individual who has suffered it but also of all fellow-members of the society, whence comes a need for reparation of a public nature, going beyond private compensation.

The inveterate prejudice that for a man who has committed a crime to spend a certain period in prison amounts to 'reparation' still underlies our modern penal systems, even when it is clearly apparent that the damage done by the criminal is thereby not 'put right' but is increased by the cost of his maintenance in prison. Penal codes do, admittedly, attach to the commission of a crime further obligations of 'restitution' and 'compensation', but this rule is scarcely ever applied, whether because it does not in law extend to the harm caused to public order or because in fact most condemned criminals lack means to pay.

We may admit that an exact calculation of the damage done, in its full extension, is very difficult; but the difficulty of a correct assessment does not preclude the obligation to make the attempt and to achieve, if not absolute accuracy, a certain approximation. Moreover, the courts have gone some distance with regard to private interests, in framing an 'equitable assessment' even of such damage as is not immediately translatable into terms of pounds, shillings and pence. The same line should be followed in the matter of damage caused to public order, that is, to society as a whole, and, even if here the valuation had to be much reduced and even become purely symbolic, this would represent a greater regard for and a closer approximation to the requirements of justice than the quite arbitrary determination for the various types of crime of a number of years, months or days to be spent in prison, just as in former days a certain number of lashes with the whip.

Here we must ask: How are we to obtain the effective fulfilment of the duty of compensation, which must be more impelling and more weighty when it has to satisfy the requirements both of civil and of penal justice? What I would propose is in effect to reduce penal justice to civil justice, in short, to unify the two types of justice. Clearly this would require a radical reformation of our present institutions, which are inadequate and ill-suited for such a purpose.

At present the delinquent who has served, or been in some way excused from, his sentence can pass his time in ample indolent ease without having made compensation for the harm he has done, or, in other words, without having paid his debt. Is this just?

In my opinion there should be established a special office or department to maintain surveillance over the way of life of those who have not satisfied their legally admitted debts, so as to prevent at least the worst cases of offence against good faith and morals. When the source of the debt is a criminal act, there should be imposed on the debtor a duty of labour according to his capacity, having regard to all the circumstances and always in humane and civil form. The surveillance should not be attended by any compulsion, so long as the debtor voluntarily applied his activity to the payment of the debt; but if, and only if, he did not do so, there would be justified the compulsory imposition of prescribed tasks with a corresponding diminution, greater or less, of his liberty. Thus there would be a series of degrees, and of forms of surveillance more or less strict both over his mode of life and over his obligation to work, and there would be no place, even in the most serious cases, for the useless cruelties of ancient penal systems and the not so much lesser cruelties of modern systems. And, obviously, the produce of his labour should be applied to the satisfaction, even if it be but partial, of the claim of whoever – society or individual – has suffered wrongful harm.

The duty to work, we know, is, as a general rule, moral rather than legal and could not be altogether made a matter of law without imperilling the first and fundamental right of human personality, which is the right of liberty. The duty to work can, however, become a true juridical duty, that is to say, can be the object of a claim by another, when its non-observance indicates the breach of duties undertaken to others, and particularly when these arise from crime or tort. We must not forget that rights are essentially *bilateral* and that excessive indulgence towards one party necessarily becomes unfairness to the other.

One last consideration must be added. Crime is not only an individual act for which the individual delinquent must answer; it is also a social fact, which, particularly in its most widespread and constant forms, indicates something defective and unbalanced in the structure of society. It is therefore vain to think that the struggle against crime should be carried on and can be won solely by imposing legal sanctions on those who transgress. We must also examine the roots of the evil, which often lie deep in ignorance and poverty; we must take all heed for the education and the moral training of the whole people, with special attention to those most in need; we must correct and try to eradicate, with timely and courageous reforms, always inspired by the principles of charity and justice, the faults, the abuses, the iniquities and the oppressions which infect the social organism, in whatever form and whatever place they show themselves. This is an immense task, which calls for the co-operation of all human virtues and all human powers; perhaps it will never be completely accomplished, but it indicates the goal towards which our efforts should be directed.

Only in this way can we hope to diminish the scourge of crime which has been attacked in vain with the gallows and the prison. This scourge is for all men an admonition and, in a sense, an expiation. The admonition should be more deeply felt when it is not possible to make the guilty person directly repair the harm done. It is not out of place to imagine a duty of reparation, even if but partial, which in such case would be made incumbent on society towards the victim, by way of recognition of the share of blame which the fact of the crime imposes upon the whole of society.

13 ⊠ *Blame*

J. E. R. SQUIRES

I

'Blame is a kind of punishment. People are blamed and punished for breaking rules and doing what they shouldn't. They commonly fear both and try to avoid them. Similar excuses shield them from both. Blame is the opposite of praise, which is a kind of reward. Blaming is something men do and can only be understood on the assumption that they do it for a purpose and use means adapted to their purpose. This purpose is to encourage people to keep certain rules and to refrain from anti-social behaviour. Blame is justified, then, if a person has done what he should not have done and the blame would have a reforming or deterring effect.'

(1) Punishment involves various types and degrees of penalty, but blame involves no obvious material disadvantage or discomfort. There is no flogging, imprisonment or fine.

'This is because blame involves only words, not sticks and stones. It is verbally mediated punishment.'

(2) Blame, unlike punishment, doesn't require properly constituted authorities or formal procedure of any kind. Anyone can blame anyone else. For instance, a man may blame his neighbours and a child its parents, but only in special circumstances can a man punish his neighbours or a child punish its parents. They are in no position of authority.

'Suppose Tommy is not allowed to go to the fair. He becomes deliberately awkward, rejecting meals, refusing to go to bed and being rude to visitors. He is punishing his parents, although he has no position of responsibility over them.'

At best this is an extended use of the word 'punishment', comparable to that adopted when we say boxers are giving or taking a lot of punishment. Just as this latter description blurs the clear distinction between punishing someone and merely inflicting discomfort on him, so the former extension blurs the distinction between punishing someone and retaliating or taking revenge on him;

between acting from a position of recognised authority and simply getting one's own back. The requirement that the person who administers the punishment should be in a position of authority holds good in standard cases of punishment, though there is no such requirement in the case of blame.

'This begs the question unless a method for distinguishing standard from extended uses is provided. However, blame is informal verbal punishment.'

(3) It is perfectly possible for a person to have broken the law, to be found guilty and yet to escape punishment, but it doesn't seem possible for people to decide that someone has done something wrong and yet for that person to escape blame. Similarly, it is possible that we should find someone guilty of a punishable offence and yet not punish him because the point of doing so would be thwarted or overweighted by other considerations. It may be cruel or inexpedient to punish certain people. However, there is no corresponding way in which people withhold blame, having decided that someone is responsible for a blameworthy act.

'Possibly there are many offenders who should escape blame. For example, a sick man may be to blame for many things, but we ought not to blame him if this would worsen his condition. Again, a cantankerous or drunk person may be highly blameworthy, but it may not be wise to blame him, lest he become violent.'

(4) Suppose the owner of an orchard marches into his neighbour's house and declares: 'You have taken my apples, in breach of our moral code. You were wrong to have done it. You ought to have known better and have no excuse.' It would be completely bewildering if he were to add, 'But never mind, I won't blame you for it'. This would be a stultifying addition in the circumstances. Either he didn't really believe the neighbour took the apples or was wrong to do so, or else he was disingenuous in saying he didn't blame him. But if the judge says in court, 'You have taken the apples and in so doing have broken the law. We have found you guilty according to proper procedure. Nevertheless, I am not going to punish you', then his statement may be misguided, but not unintelligible or disingenuous. The man in the dock would probably brighten up when he heard it, but it is doubtful if the neighbour would cheer up in the former case after the accusation. When told he was not blamed, he would scarcely know what to think.

'This difference can be explained without retracting the view that blaming is punishing. It is indeed disingenuous or contradictory to express one's opinions as to the wrongness of a person's acts to that person and at the same time claim that one is not blaming him, because the very expression of the opinion to him constitutes blaming him. That's just what blaming is, a punitive lashing of the tongue. But in other respects it is analogous to non-verbal punishment, such as fines and incarceration.'

(5) You can blame someone when he isn't there, but you can't hang him when he isn't there. Not only does blame involve no authorities, procedures or penalties, but it is possible to blame someone quite beyond our control or influence. Thus, we blame, but cannot punish, Nero and Caligula, as well as contemporary tyrants, when we have unfortunately no prospect of changing their conduct. It is noteworthy that superficially similar things, such as reprehending, reproving, reprimanding and reproaching, follow punishment rather than blame in requiring someone to face the music. You may fulminate against the Prime Minister in your bath, but you haven't reproved, reproached or told him off. That would demand more courage. Still less have you reprehended him, for these, like punishment, require that you should be in an official or superior position with special power or responsibility over the subject in some relevant respect. So if you want verbal punishment then reprimanding or reprehending are better candidates than blame. And if you want informal lashings of the tongue, reproving and telling off are probably more apt. But it is questionable whether blame is any kind of punishment.

'It is unnecessary that unfavourable opinions should be expressed to the person himself for the expression to count as blame. Perhaps to tell anyone that someone has committed an offence counts as blaming the supposed offender, whether he hears about it or not. But this expressing of an opinion is something that we do and will still need to be justified in terms of our purposes in doing it.'

(6) Suppose you express an unfavourable opinion about Hooper's conduct to Brown, but not to Jones. If blaming is the expressing of such opinions we ought to say that you blamed Hooper to Brown but not to Jones. But we wouldn't say such a thing – or, rather, if someone who had obviously mastered the language said such a thing, it would probably be taken as a mildly amusing accusation of insincerity, comparable to 'He believes in God on Sundays but not for the rest of the week'.

'Perhaps only sincere expressions of unfavourable opinion constitute blaming. The man didn't really blame Hooper to Brown, just
as he doesn't really believe in God on Sundays.'

But we don't blame a person *to* anyone at all, though sincere
opinions may be expressed to all and sundry. Moreover, it is surely
possible to blame someone – say, a persuasive salesman for your
financial difficulties – without ever telling anyone. Blame is more
like holding an opinion than expressing it.

(7) Is blaming something we do? It is not completely clear
what is meant to contrast with what, but the following questions do
not seem to fit blame: 'When did you blame Hooper for taking the
apples? How many times did you blame him? How long did you
take to blame him? How did you blame him – quickly or slowly?
energetically or lazily? carefully or carelessly? Did you blame him
inadvertently, by accident, or was it deliberate?' Yet most of the
corresponding questions suit punishing, reproving, reprimanding,
ticking off, praising, as well as straightforward 'things that we do'
such as walking, writing, kicking a ball. Moreover, you can't try to
blame someone and fail, in the way that you could try to punish
someone, try to express an opinion or try to walk and yet fail.

'The evidence doesn't all point in the same direction, as the
following examples show: "He stopped me in the street and blamed
me for my part in the affair." "The chairman repeatedly blamed
the Moblavians for making political points in a debate on procedure." "What is Cropper doing? He is blaming the Vinland
delegation for their late arrival." These are clear cases where someone is acting in a certain way. To say such cases are misdescribed or
a misuse of the word "blame" simply begs the question, unless
independent tests for misuses can be provided.'

If these examples are taken at face value they show that there is a
sense of 'blame' which is roughly synonymous with 'censure' or
'reprove'. It is certainly not the only sense, as the previous arguments have shown. Nor is it a very common sense.

(8) Punishment may be mild or severe. This refers to the type
and degree of penalty, usually in relation to the gravity of the
offence. Thus, five years' imprisonment is normally a more severe
punishment than five months', but to give someone five years' for
murder is probably to punish him more mildly than someone who
is given five months' for dropping litter. But we don't sentence
people to so much blame, as the court sentences them to so much

punishment. When we discuss degrees of blame, whether one person is more to blame than another or how much someone is to blame, then what is in question is the division of responsibility. If someone is not exonerated altogether, he will be partly, largely or wholly blamed. However, if someone is partly punished, then the penalty has only been partly administered and suffered.

Blame is allocated and borne. One could even bear or take the blame for something without realising it, but could scarcely be punished without realising it. Punishment, but not blame, can be an expiation or atonement. It can be harsh or token. Having established that someone is fully responsible for an undesirable upshot, there is a question what punishment he deserves, but not what blame he deserves. He just gets *the* blame. If there is a proper question whether one blames Jones for this more severely than one blames Black for that, then what is wanted is a comparison of the offences. If this is a grave offence and that a trivial one, then Jones is severely blamed and Black mildly blamed. It isn't a question of anger or vehemence of expression, for blaming is not a kind of grumbling.

(9) We blame machines, weather, unforeseen occurrences and so forth for ill events, whereas we punish people only.

'This is an extended use of the word "blame". It just means that they caused the outcome. Compare an extension of the word "responsible" when we say rain was responsible for the delay or glacial movements were responsible for the scratches on the rock.'

Even if extended uses can be separated from central uses, it is perhaps significant that there is no similar 'extension' of the verb 'punish' to inanimate things.

II

'To blame someone is not indeed to impose sanctions on him; rather, it is a readiness to impose sanctions. No actual sanctions need occur, but, nevertheless, reasons that would justify actual sanctions would be needed to justify a readiness or preparedness to sanction. If it is unreasonable to jump on the table when a mouse appears, then a readiness to jump on tables when mice appear is also unreasonable. Similarly, blame is justified to the extent that actual sanctions are justified. Considerations of deterrence and reform are relevant to the latter, and so to the former, issue. Different sanctions will be appropriate in different cases – they may be formal or informal, social, legal, military and so forth. For example, if you blame Buster for a robbery this may mean that you would send him to prison if you were the judge; if you blame Stomper for a malicious foul this may mean that you would send him off the field if you were the referee; if you blame Crump for neglecting his work this may mean that you would reprove him if you met him. Blame isn't, after all, a kind of punishment, but it is a readiness to punish and, therefore, justifiable on the same grounds. It is no mystery that we blame historical characters, since that only means that we would have taken appropriate action against them if we had been in a position to do so.'

(1) The fact that people would be discouraged from certain courses of action if they were punished for them cannot in itself justify a readiness to punish them, since it takes no account of the desirability of the action. It also needs to be shown that the action is wrong, harmful, undesirable.

'Indeed; but the case is obviously the same for punishment. It is only claimed that reform and deterrence are relevant considerations.'

(2) We can blame someone for something without knowing what the appropriate sanctions would be or who the relevant official is. For example, you may blame an ice-hockey player for tripping an opponent, even though you don't know what the penalty is or who is in charge of the game. It would, therefore, be absurd to suggest that when you blamed Glassman this meant that if you were the referee you would award a two-minute penalty against him!

'Nevertheless, you must know that a trip is a foul and not a legitimate part of the game, that it is an offence against which action should be taken. To blame Glassman for tripping is to believe that appropriate sanctions, whatever they may be, should be imposed on him.'

(3) There are many reasons why you may not be prepared to impose sanctions on or censure someone whom you blame. You may be too timid. You may have a special interest in retaining his good-will. If you are a magistrate, you may be bribed. If you are an umpire, you may be partisan. Similarly, there are various reasons why you may be prepared to punish someone you don't blame. You may have a spite against him. You may want to 'encourage the others'. You may be pressed into administering a law with which you disagree.

'Perhaps the theory should be modified to meet these counter-examples. To blame someone for doing something is not to say "If I were in such a position, I would punish him or deal appropriately with him", but, rather, it is to believe that appropriate sanctions ought to be imposed on the person. This is consistent with timidity, backsliding and so forth, on the part of the person who holds the belief. However, the main consequence for justification is unaltered. If deterrent considerations are needed to justify punishing someone they will be needed to justify the belief that he ought to be punished. Hence, they will be needed to justify blame.'

(4) It isn't obvious what 'appropriate sanctions for an act' are meant to be. If these are understood as those sanctions which are in the statutes or rulebooks or which are customarily meted out, then it is quite common to blame someone for doing something without believing that such sanctions should be imposed. This will be the case whenever the accepted punishment is thought to be harsh or excessive, for example. On the other hand, if 'appropriate' sanctions are those which ought to be imposed, the original claim about blame becomes extremely vague. It amounts to this, that a person who blames someone for something believes that *some* action should be taken against him. But even this is very doubtful.

(5) You may blame someone for something without believing that he ought to be punished or that any action should be taken against him. You may think he has troubles enough or that it would damage his morale when all his efforts are needed or that the matter is too slight for action.

'Blame involves the belief that sanctions should be imposed unless there are special circumstances, such as those mentioned.'

Unless the circumstances are carefully defined, this escape-clause eliminates the explanatory force of the original claim. It amounts to this: if you blame someone then you think he ought to be punished unless he shouldn't! This is comparable to the claim that if you have a leg you can kick a ball unless you can't.

(6) A simpler view is suggested by a comparison with cases where non-human factors are blamed. When we blame the thunderstorm, the frail bridge or the icy road, this doesn't mean we are ready to punish them. However, we may well take some action to prevent recurrences, where this is practical. But the question whether we do take further action, installing lightning conductors, sacking the engineer or salting road surfaces, is certainly not answered simply

by allocating the blame. Is there any reason to suppose that when we blame people for unwanted outcomes or undesirable behaviour we have prejudged the question whether any action should be taken against them? Thus, even though we would often be ready to punish or endorse the punishment of those whom we blame, and even though the fact that we punish or recommend the punishment of someone usually reveals whom we blame, nevertheless, the mere fact that we blame someone does not in itself commit us to imposing sanctions on him. To blame Hooper is to believe he has done what he shouldn't. This is no recommendation or endorsement of sanctions against him. The question whether any sanctions would reform him or deter others is irrelevant to the justification of blame.

'But isn't an unwanted or undesirable outcome precisely one which we are prepared to prevent and discourage, if we can? The more undesirable, the more measures we are prepared to take to stop it. This is part of the meaning of such words as "undesirable".'

This may be so. But it doesn't follow that in order to vindicate the description of an outcome as unwanted we would need to show that particular measures could be taken to prevent it. Whether such measures are available and how effective they are, is quite irrelevant to the 'justification' of the description. Hence it is not relevant to the justification of blame.

Blame is no kind of punishment. It is not an expression of opinion. It is not something done for a purpose. Nor is it the opposite of praise. Nor is it justifiable by an appeal to reformative or deterrent value. Blame doesn't necessarily involve a readiness or preparedness to impose sanctions, nor a belief that sanctions ought to be imposed. To blame a person is to be of the opinion that he is responsible for an undesirable upshot, that he has done what he ought not.

14 ❧ *Mercy*

ALWYNNE SMART

I

A theory of punishment should give some account of
mercy and yet it is true to say that very little has been said about it
at all. It is commonly regarded as a praiseworthy element in moral
behaviour – something to be practised occasionally both for the good
of the one who punishes and the one who is punished. The suffering that punishment involves is unpleasant for all concerned, and if
it is possible to avoid it or lessen it without moral injustice, then it is
desirable to do so. We condemn as hard and unbending the judge
who never shows mercy and the suggestion is that the poor unfortunates whose lot it is to be judged by him are poor unfortunates
indeed. This is reflected in the fact that the opposite of merciful –
merciless – means cruel. Presumably there are occasions when it is
appropriate to show mercy to an offender, and other occasions when
it is not. What are the conditions for the appropriate exercising of
mercy, how do we decide how much mercy is appropriate, and
when is a judge[1] morally obliged to be merciful, if ever?

The contexts in which we commonly talk about and recommend
mercy are many and varied, and some seem more appropriate than
others. It is more appropriate to speak of mercy in respect of some
murderers rather than others. This is sometimes because one kind of
murder is intrinsically worse than another. Suppose, for example,
that in a particular State, the penalty for murder is death or life
imprisonment, with no provision for lesser penalties. Suppose a man
discovers that his wife is unfaithful to him, and, blind with uncontrollable anger and jealousy, he shoots her with a rifle that
happens to be lying around. Now take another case – the case of a
man who murders his wife for her money after weeks of careful

---

[1] I use 'judge' loosely to mean the person with the authority to punish
in a particular case. Where I mean a judge in the legal sense, this is
apparent from the context.

planning. We believe that coldly premeditated murder for personal gain is morally worse than heat-of-the-moment murder and that it warrants a harsher penalty. We might consider the full penalty prescribed by the law to be the right punishment, be it death or life imprisonment. It is generally felt that heat-of-the-moment murder does not warrant the same punishment and one would expect the jury to add a recommendation of mercy to its verdict. Mercy *ought* to be exercised in such a case, even if it is difficult to reach agreement on what penalty should be imposed instead. The reason why mercy ought to be exercised is that the penalty as it stands is too harsh for the particular offence. To treat these two kinds of murder as being of equal gravity and warranting identical penalties would be a great injustice, one into which the crudeness of the law would force us if there was no provision for mercy riders. The reason why the premeditated murder is thought to be worse than the spontaneously committed one is presumably that the murderer is more responsible when the crime is premeditated. Similarly, there seems to be a difference in moral gravity between a murder planned one week ahead and one where the murderer takes a year to plan and execute the slow poisoning of his victim. In the latter case the offender has more time to consider the morality of his actions; his decision is less likely to be influenced by particular events of the moment and the frame of mind he was in that week. The penalty ought to be less harsh in the first case, and where the law does not make this provision we often find a judge making the adjustment under the blanket term of 'mercy'.

It is appropriate to advocate mercy when one murderer acts under greater provocation than another. This point emerges if we consider another example, this time of two heat-of-the-moment murders where an unfaithful wife is shot in anger by a jealous husband, each crime committed by immigrants from different countries. The two murders are similar *in all respects* except that murderer A comes from a country where a wife's adultery causes a husband and his family great dishonour and humiliation, whereas in murderer B's homeland adultery is regarded as a regrettable lapse, but nothing more. Furthermore, in A's homeland murder in such circumstances is looked upon as a comparatively minor offence, almost excusable. Although both men are equally guilty in the eyes of the law, one is inclined to treat A more leniently than B because he acted under extreme provocation and could not have been expected to view his crime as seriously as we would. If the full penalty prescribed by the law was a just and appropriate punishment for murder B, it would be unduly harsh and unjust to prescribe the same penalty for murder A. Where the law made no provision for this sort of difference a fair judge would exercise mercy; a judge who didn't would be regarded as unjust.

Similarly, if A's wife had deliberately flaunted her continual adultery in front of A's friends, and B's wife had concealed her one lapse from everyone but her husband, we would think the greater provocation was a significant difference between the two murders and think it unduly harsh and unjust to prescribe the same punishment for A as for B. A should be treated more mercifully than B; a ten-year imprisonment may be a fair and desirable penalty for B, but unwarranted for A.

Likewise in manslaughter charges a great variety of relevant circumstances may be found, some of which would appear to constitute grounds for mercy. The following case might serve as an example of the uppermost limit of seriousness in such a charge. A motorist is guilty of killing a woman on a well-lit pedestrian-crossing; it is established that he was drunk and knew that he would get very drunk if he drank seventeen vodkas; he also knew that he had no brakes and that he had to drive after drinking. He habitually ignored pedestrian-crossings, drove very fast and had previous convictions for driving an unroadworthy car, drunken driving, and speeding through a pedestrian-crossing. Suppose that the full penalty of twenty years' imprisonment was the appropriate and just penalty for such a case.

Compare this with a second case where the offender wasn't drunk, knew his car was in good order, and was travelling at his normal speed of thirty-five miles per hour in such areas, and it was found that this was, in fact, a safe speed for the conditions. However, the motorist didn't slow down as he approached the pedestrian-crossing as he should have, and didn't have time to avoid the child who ran across suddenly. Perhaps two years is the fair penalty in this case, but unfortunately our imaginary legal code prescribes ten years as the minimum sentence, so the judge has to go through the necessary legal procedure to recommend mercy. Even where the law does prescribe a sufficiently wide range of penalties to cope with the cases described, the judge speaks of showing mercy where he is imposing less than the full penalty and justifies his decision by pointing out the relevant factors which make the crime much less serious than the charge suggests.

All the examples considered to date were chosen to bring out the fact that some crimes warrant sterner treatment than others because they are intrinsically worse (this is particularly so with premeditated crimes), and that we speak of exercising mercy when discriminating in favour of the lesser crimes. These cases are different from those that warrant mercy because of extenuating circumstances. Sometimes a case arises where important excuses can be made for the offender and it is appropriate to show him mercy even though the offence was not intrinsically less evil than other like cases. Take, for example, the case of the motorist whose car was in good order and who was driving at his normal, safe speed. Like the previous offender he didn't slow down as he approached the pedestrian-crossing and didn't have time to avoid the child crossing the road; it appeared that he had had some very upsetting news that day, and just didn't notice the child step out on to the crossing. While it might be argued that if a man is seriously upset he should not drive if there is a chance that it will interfere with his driving, it would nevertheless be very hard to impose the same penalty as in the previous case. If we think his emotional state prevented him from giving full attention to his driving we might also argue that it might have interfered with his judgment of his own capabilities in such a situation. In a very important sense his crime is not as great as the previous offender's, and warrants more lenient treatment. Another example of the same kind would be that of a person who was to some extent forced to commit a particular crime, for example, to provide food for his miserable children, or to avoid a threat of harm to someone else. Such cases are rarely extreme enough to be fully justified, but certainly coercion would normally be considered an extenuating factor which made the crime less grave than it would otherwise have been, all other things being equal.

We might consider now another example of manslaughter which warrants mercy for quite different reasons. This example is the case of a man who knew his car was in good condition, and was a thoroughly competent driver although inclined to speed a little. He approached the pedestrian-crossing at forty miles per hour and couldn't stop in time to avoid the child who ran across suddenly. He discovered it was his only child to whom he was devoted, and, apart from suffering great personal grief and condemnation, he estranged his wife's affections as a result of the accident. While it would be irresponsible to suggest that remorse was sufficient to absolve a man from the consequences of his crime there are sometimes circumstances in which it is appropriate to take into consideration the fact that the man has already suffered greatly as a result of the crime. In such a case we might consider it unduly harsh to impose what would otherwise be the appropriate and just penalty, and recommend mercy. The justification is that, the law aside, the man has already served part of what we consider a morally just punishment. It is not as though we are 'letting him off lightly', but simply that to impose the full penalty would be to impose a total amount of suffering quite out of keeping with the gravity of his crime. There was in this case a gap between moral justice and legal justice, the possibility of which the law acknowledges when it makes provisions for recommendation of mercy; sometimes the bridging of the gap is a simple step, sometimes it is a long and complicated legal procedure which might involve appeals to government and heads of state.

It seems then that mercy is appropriate when an offence is intrinsically less evil than another, where a person acts under provocation, and where there are extenuating circumstances such as impaired judgment, coercion and ignorance. It is sometimes appropriate where the offender has already suffered a great deal.

In each of the examples so far discussed a recommendation of mercy was necessary to avoid an injustice because the law cannot always anticipate all the significant differences that there might be between offences that look alike superficially. In some countries where murder is classed as first, second, or third degree it is no longer necessary to add a mercy rider to ensure that a heat-of-the-moment murder is treated less severely than a coldly premeditated one.

Now although it is quite normal to talk about mercy in the sort of cases I have described, what we are actually doing is redressing a potential wrong. We say there are mitigating circumstances and what we mean is that the prescribed penalty *doesn't fit* the case in question and that it would be an injustice to impose it. Sometimes it is just a case of pointing out the mitigating facts so that it is clear that the offence falls under penalty X rather than the harsher penalty Y; more often 'mercy' is just a loophole to make the law more flexible and sophisticated. Obviously for the law to be completely (morally) just and sophisticated it would have to provide for every possible gradation of a crime and prescribe the appropriate penalty, and this would be impracticable; in the final analysis it would destroy the generality of the law and reduce it to a list of specific descriptions. To avoid this, exceptions are provided for by the exercising of 'mercy'. This means that here mercy is nothing more than a way of ensuring that the just penalty is imposed and injustice avoided.

I suggest that most cases of mercy are of this sort and are simply misnamed. Furthermore, the possibility of weighing the just course of action against the merciful course of action does not come up for consideration, and the judge who rigorously applies the law and declines to exercise 'mercy' is not being just as opposed to merciful, but is unjust. Such cases cannot properly be called acts of mercy, and I have spoken of them at some length to avoid confusing them with real acts of mercy.

II

I have suggested in Part I that showing mercy often turns out to be merely fitting the punishment to the crime where the law is too inflexible and unsophisticated to do so. I now wish to discuss what I think is genuine mercy, and to examine some situations in which it is not appropriate.

One of the other things we mean when we talk about showing mercy is deciding not to inflict what is agreed to be the just penalty, all things considered. The reason for advocating mercy is that it avoids suffering and this is desirable whenever it can be morally justified. This view of mercy is a very common one and is illustrated in the Christian's cry, 'God have mercy upon us, miserable sinners.'

It is important to notice the distinctions that should be made between condoning and showing mercy. When we condone an offence we do not act merely as if it hadn't happened, but rather as if it didn't matter – in other words, as if it weren't an offence. We might ask someone in a tone of shocked disapproval, 'are you *condoning* his act?' but we should ask 'are you pardoning him?' in a quite different tone – possibly in admiration.[2] I do not wish to suggest

[2] It should be noted that total abstention from punishment is not necessarily condoning. One may acknowledge the seriousness of an offence and decide that mercy is appropriate. The amount of mercy appropriate will vary from case to case: sometimes the punishment should be reduced, sometimes completely waived.

that pardoning and showing mercy are identical – I simply mean that they both acknowledge the seriousness of the offence whereas 'condoning' doesn't. When a man exercises mercy, what he does is acknowledge that an offence has been committed, decides that a particular punishment would be appropriate or just, and then decides to exact a punishment of lesser severity than the appropriate or just one. He might say to the offender, 'I'm letting you off lightly this time!' and might reasonably expect that the privilege of merciful treatment should be an extra reason why the man shouldn't commit the same offence again in the future.

Although the suggestion, in cases of real acts of mercy, is that mercy is good in itself, it is quite clear that it would not be justified in all cases, and in some cases, in fact, would be immoral. In the case of a habitual vicious rapist who showed no signs of repentance and reform, very clear justification for merciful treatment would have to be given for it to be permissible. If the choice in such a case was between a light fine or a term of imprisonment only an irresponsible person would recommend mercy. To do so would be immoral because it would be endangering others and would probably give the rapist the impression that his crime was not so very serious after all. One ought not to be merciful at the cost of others – to do so would be to defeat what is thought to be the main point of exercising mercy, namely, to avoid suffering. If one's purpose is to avoid suffering, then mercy in the case described is futile because it permits greater suffering and on the part of an innocent party, which makes it an injustice as well.

Generally, then, it might be said that mercy is unjustified if it causes the suffering of an innocent party, is detrimental to the offender's welfare, harms the authority of the law, or where it is clear that the offender is not repentant or not likely to reform (and he may not be *likely* to reform even though temporarily repentant). Even if it will do some good, it must be clear that it will do more good than harm before it is justifiable and some may wish to contend that if it involves injury to an innocent party this should be an overriding factor.

It might also be argued that mercy is not justified if it involves unfair discrimination against others. If a judge has before him two cases which are identical in all relevant respects, and exercises mercy in one case but not in the other, he could rightly be criticised for showing favouritism and committing an injustice. If he is going to let one off lightly he ought to let the other one off lightly too, and equally lightly. The point can be seen even more clearly if we take the case of a crime committed jointly by two men whose situations showed no relevant differences at all. To show mercy arbitrarily to one and not to the other would be grossly unjust. Possibly this case would outrage us more because in the former instance of a like offence being tried in two separate cases in the same day we are likely to think that there must be some significant difference between them that we don't know about. However, if further examination showed they were, in fact, identical cases and the judge had no reason to think they weren't and gave no reason, there is no reason why we should be less shocked than in the other case. Now let us imagine that identical crimes are being tried in the same court in the same day, but by different judges. If the first judge imposed a penalty which everyone agreed was fully just both by legal and moral standards, and the second judge, knowing the full facts of the previous case, decided to exercise mercy in the case before him, we should be inclined to ask him why he had done this. If he had no reason, we should be slightly shocked, or nonplussed, at least. One of the reasons for this is that indiscriminate exercising of mercy is considered unwise because of the possibility that it might in some way harm the authority of the law. However, even if it was clear that this is not a real possibility, we should still be puzzled and try to find some explanation for the judge's actions. Without it we should feel that his discrimination was not justified. This is borne out by the fact that we do not condemn as hard and relentless the judge who does not decide, solely through benevolence, to exact less than the fair penalty; nor should the offender sentenced by such a judge feel hardly done by.

This is a real difficulty because it can be argued that the context of like cases can be extended to limit even further the number of occasions upon which one might justifiably exercise true mercy. All other things being equal, there is no reason why felonies identical in all relevant respects should be treated more leniently by one judge than by another, or more leniently on Tuesdays than Fridays, or more leniently in country towns than in large cities. Such discrimination appears irrational. This point still holds even on an international scale. If we consider, for example, the case of Eichmann being tried in Israel, and of another and equally vicious Nazi war criminal being tried in Frankfurt for a crime of the same kind and enormity, the point becomes clearer. If it is beyond dispute that the cases *are* identical in all relevant respects, even allowing for the differences between the Israeli and German legal systems, we feel that for justice to be done the offenders should be dealt with in a similar fashion. To execute Eichmann, and show mercy to his colleague in Frankfurt, and only sentence him to fifteen years in Spandau prison, seems unjust. No matter how evil the men are and how terrible the crime, it would seem that one ought not to be discriminated against in favour of the other.

The obvious way out for those of us who feel squeamish about exacting the just penalty for both offenders rather than showing mercy to one and not to the other, is to argue that some mercy is better than none at all. However, this too is unsatisfactory, because of the basic insight of justice that if one man is going to be treated leniently then all others with identical cases should be too. If this is allowed it is difficult to see where we should stop. If all identical cases of felony type-X are treated equally mercifully in 1966, to avoid unfair discrimination we should have to extend this mercy to all like cases in 1967, and all other things being equal, in 1968 and 1969 and so on, till we might say that we had changed our opinion of what is the appropriate and just penalty for this particular offence; we would consider the penalty thought fair in 1965 and earlier to have been unduly harsh. But then if the appropriate penalty for identical cases of felony type-X was changed, to be consistent, we should have to adjust proportionally our ideas of the fair penalty for cases of felony type-W and felony type-Y. Similarly we would have to adjust the penalties for the other lesser and greater felonies and in fact, for all other offences, so that they were all brought into line with our view of justice. We would talk with regret about the harsh penalties of former times and pride ourselves on our enlightenment. After this new state of affairs had persisted for some time we might again find people inclined to exercise mercy for no reason in some cases, and not in others that were the same. To remedy this sort of injustice we would have to again recommend mercy in all like cases, and the whole process would begin again and again, until finally we reached the absurd position where we imposed no penalties for offences at all. Regardless of one's view of punishment, this would be an undesirable state of affairs.

This suggests that there is something unsatisfactory about the notion of mercy as it has been discussed so far. In all the cases to date we have not found a single real example of permissible or advisable mercy. This is somewhat disquieting because it conjures up a vision of a hard, relentless judge bent on exacting the last ounce of punishment justified and unsympathetic to the suffering that punishment, by definition, entails. If one were to ignore the first part of this paper, then quite probably this reaction would be justified, but of course in a consideration of mercy we cannot ignore the sort of cases described in the first part. I think that if a judge conscientiously examined every case before him, and, where the law was too crude and inflexible to bridge the gap between legal and moral justice, exercised mercy, we would probably regard him as a very humane and merciful judge. The more so, too, if he took into account, on appropriate occasions, any deep suffering the offender had already brought upon himself. Such a judge is not being merciful but is merely showing a normal regard for morality and recognising that the legal code, as it stands, is not always sophisticated enough to cope with this gap. It would be quite unreasonable to regard such a man as hard and inhuman simply because he didn't on occasions, solely through benevolence, impose less than what was recognised to be a fair penalty. On the other hand, the judge who always observed the letter of the law and didn't take account of the occasional gap between legal and moral justice, *would* be unjust.

III

I now wish to consider examples where mercy is justified and the kind of reasons that make it justifiable. If one takes into account the limitations suggested in Parts I and II, the number of justifiable instances diminishes considerably.

The kind of cases described in Part I are probably those that first spring to mind when one thinks about mercy; as we saw, they are not genuine cases. However, there are genuine cases of mercy in which the difficulties mentioned in Part II are not serious objections. There are times, for example, where one feels obliged to show mercy not because the offender himself warrants it, but because it is necessary if we are to meet the claims that other duties have on us. The suffering of an innocent party is almost always involved when an offender has friends or family, and it is clearly not feasible to suspend punishment whenever this is so, but there are times when the suffering caused will be so great that this should be a major, even the main consideration. It might be proper, for example, to release a man on a bond where there was pretty clear indication that the warranted term of imprisonment would be the final shock that would cause his mother's breakdown. Suppose that a five-hundred-dollar fine is appropriate in a certain case and there is a good indication that such a fine would teach the offender a lesson; if, however, the imposition of such a fine would impose an intolerable burden on his wife and family, we might hesitate. If further investigation showed that the wife was an invalid and the children were frequently ill, we might, after serious deliberation, decide that out of consideration for the innocent parties we were obliged to exercise mercy and cut the fine in half. One might be tempted to think that in cases like this it might be more accurate to say we are showing mercy to the innocent sufferers rather than to the offender. But this, I feel, will not do, since there is something odd and disturbing about saying we show mercy to those who have committed no offence. In cases like these we feel that the offender is just lucky to be treated so leniently.

Let us look at another example: suppose a child does something wrong and it is desirable and proper that he should be punished in a certain manner; if it is the new stepfather's job to punish and there is a very good chance that his relationship with the child might suffer as a result, he may be wiser to exercise mercy even though it may give the child the impression that the offence wasn't important. Where supervision of the punishment imposes a great burden on a third party we might be inclined to recommend mercy too. One can also imagine without difficulty a situation where mercy is expedient – for example where a small but powerful section of the community is unreasonably antagonistic towards the existing judiciary, it might be advisable for the moment (and even imperative) to exercise mercy and thus protect the authority and stability of the law. In cases such as those described the judge has no choice – he is obliged to be lenient in order that he may prevent other evils and injustices. They are, nevertheless, genuine cases of mercy.

The passage of time is a factor which ought to be considered in an investigation of the notion of mercy. At first glance, at least, it seems to constitute a good reason for being merciful. Recently in Australia a judge declined to convict a man of a crime he committed twenty-odd years ago. The reason he gave was that he could see no point in punishing a man for a crime committed so long ago and virtually forgotten. The passing of time does seem to make a difference in this sort of case, but only a closer examination of the examples will reveal what sort of difference it makes, and why. In the case just quoted the offender is now living a contented and law-abiding life so that the punishment could have no effect on him and would probably have a bad one – one that was not commensurate with the crime committed, and which, all things considered, was unduly harsh. Some might feel that the judge ought to have imposed *some* penalty, perhaps a good-behaviour bond for example, but at least one which was considerably milder than the one which would have been appropriate had the crime been committed recently. In any event, despite the difficulties that might be encountered in trying to reach agreement on the details of the proper penalty in this case, it is clearly a case of acting 'mercifully' to avoid a potential injustice such as I described in Part I. There is no suggestion of a judge deciding, solely through benevolence, to exercise mercy.

Let us consider more closely the real significance of the passing of time. Suppose that thirty years ago Roberts robbed Smith's firm of a large sum of money; he did no damage to property or persons in doing so, and Smith died in a motor accident without hearing of the theft. Very soon after, Roberts had pangs of conscience and mailed the stolen money to the police, explaining the circumstances of the theft, but withholding his identity. He subsequently turned away from crime completely and led a normal, law-abiding life. Thirty years later he is identified as the thief, and charged. In view of the facts, the judge decides to exercise mercy. Even if Roberts had been apprehended within a few months of the crime, before the strength of his resolution to 'go straight' had had time to be tested, his case would probably have been treated with leniency. Taking all the facts of the case into account, and in view of the normal penalty when *no* restitution has been made, a one-hundred-dollar fine and three years' good-behaviour bond might be a just sentence. So after thirty years of tried and tested good faith, the crime appears considerably less serious even than when committed. In view of the offender's reform the crime is so trivial as to warrant either dismissal, a record of conviction but no penalty, or a token good-behaviour bond. The decision would depend to a large extent on one's assessment of the consequences to the authority of the law.

In any event, to ignore the moral significance of the passage of time in this case would be grossly unjust.

As so far considered this example is still not a case of genuine mercy; it is once again just a question of bridging the gap between the inflexibility of the law and moral justice. It becomes real mercy when the judge benevolently decides to impose less than the just penalty. If our reformed thief Roberts really deserved and expected a three-year bond, it would be a genuine act of mercy to dismiss the case. Even here we are inclined to ask the question 'why?', and one possible answer might be that it is a sort of 'reward'.

What begins to emerge out of this example is the significance of the differences between the utilitarian and retributivist positions on punishment in a discussion of mercy. Let us first look at the problem of the passage of time from a utilitarian point of view. Suppose that in the case just described, the judge *did* dismiss the charge even though recognising that Roberts really deserved a three-year bond, there are two possible reasons that the utilitarian might give to justify this decision. He might say that it is a sort of 'reward' for the offender's sincere and successful reform and since utilitarian reasons are the only ones open to the utilitarian, this could only mean something like 'the probable good resulting from this sort of encouragement to Roberts and similar offenders outweighs the amount of good that the imposition of a light penalty is likely to do'. If this is the utilitarian's final assessment of the situation, then he is bound to act on it, and the possible alternative of imposing a three-year bond is no longer a real alternative. The only justification of mercy open to him is that it is the course of action likely to produce most good.

The other reason a utilitarian might have given to justify mercy in the Roberts case, was that it would be kinder than imposing a three-year bond. What this presumably means is that it is kinder because it avoids pointless suffering, and of course only a person who was morally insensible would deny the strength and propriety of this claim. However, it does bring out the oddness of the notion of mercy in the utilitarian ethic. If the punishment, that is, the suffering that the three-year bond would impose on the offender, served no good purpose, then the question of imposing it wouldn't come up at all; nor consequently would the question of mercy. The utilitarian has no choice; he must recommend the course of action that produces most good, and if this means imposing a certain penalty he cannot act mercifully and impose less than that penalty. Real mercy is never a possibility for him because he must always impose what is, according to his ethic, the fully justifiable penalty. Even where there is a serious conflict of interests, and punishment is suspended because the harm it would do to others is greater than the good it will do, this cannot properly be called mercy, because there is no significant sense in which the utilitarian can say 'I *ought* to do such and such, but special considerations persuade me to act differently on this occasion'. For him, the statement 'I shall act mercifully' can *only* mean 'I shall impose a penalty less than the one which will produce most good', which in turn can *only* mean 'I shall impose a penalty less than the one which will produce most good because this action is the one which will produce most good.'

The notion of mercy seems to get a grip only on a retributivist view of punishment. It is open to the retributivist (at least most retributivists) to say that a particular crime[3] warrants such and such a punishment but that other moral considerations permit or compel him to act with mercy. Such a possibility is open to him only because his ethic is a multi-principled one, or at least is not based on only one principle.

In the light of all this, let us have another look at the example involving the passage of time. What course of action is open to the retributivist? Can he recommend mercy? Although in practice probably no one holds a *purely* retributive view of punishment (it is usually held in conjunction with deterrent and reformative considerations), the real basis of the theory seems to be that a crime is intrinsically evil over and above any undesirable consequences it might have, and as such requires vindication. The suggestion seems to be that in some way this act of requital sets things right, that it somehow erases the crime or counter-scores it in some way. Just how it would do this is not at all clear, but if this is in fact the basis of the theory, then it has some interesting consequences in the passage of time examples of mercy.

Although the retributivist, no less than anybody, would claim that we have a duty to avoid pointless suffering, deserved punishment can never be, for him, pointless suffering. Since it is merited on other grounds as well as utilitarian ones, absence of utilitarian

---

[3] I mean 'crime' in the broad sense which includes the motives and frame of mind of the offender and all the other relevant background information.

reasons for its justification is not sufficient to make the punishment pointless. So merely to point out, in the Roberts case, that the offender has been a reformed character since the crime, and that it has been forgotten or disregarded to such an extent that the law will not suffer any harm if the case is dropped, is not sufficient reason for the retributivist; the crime, as a crime, still merits punishment. In this sort of situation the thinness of the utilitarian theory really shows through.

What makes the retributivist position more reasonable in cases similar to the Roberts example is the fact that where the offender has repented, and the strength of his reform has been convincingly tested, we feel it would be unjust to punish him because he was, in effect, not the same person that he was thirty years ago. This is borne out by the fact that where the offender has not repented and reformed we are not at all inclined to dismiss the case, even though thirty years have elapsed since the crime was committed. This decision might be overridden if it was shown that it antagonised a significant section of the community to such an extent that the authority of the law suffered greatly as a result. However, such a reaction would be unreasonable and unjustified, even though we were forced to take account of it. We would be exercising mercy in spite of ourselves, so to speak.

Further light may be thrown on the significance of the passage of time in a theory of punishment, if we look at cases of murder committed a long time ago, for example thirty years ago. In cases where the offender has committed, or attempted to commit, another murder since the first one, then, barring extraordinary circumstances, we would be quite unjustified in recommending mercy. Likewise we should probably hesitate to recommend mercy if it was found that the offender had pursued a life of petty crime since the murder thirty years ago, until the present time. Where the case is one of a murderer who has genuinely repented and led a normal, law-abiding life ever since, our attitude is less clear.

Superficially, perhaps, this case looks no different in nature from our Roberts case. However, there are two things which seem to make a difference and which may account for our greater hesitancy in recommending mercy. The first is the seriousness of the crime. Murder is obviously much more serious than theft and for this reason the consequences to the authority of the law are likely to be greater if we are irresponsibly lenient. This is one very important reason why we are less inclined benevolently to impose less than the just penalty. The second reason is that most murderers do not normally go around killing people every few months the way a thief might commit robberies. Most murderers commit only one murder, so thirty years free of a repeat of the offence is not nearly as significant as thirty years free of theft for a former thief. If it was found that the offender had in fact been placed in the same sort of circumstances again and again since the murder thirty years back, then we would indeed want to recommend mercy on the grounds that he was a new person. However it seems clear that the passage of time is not, *per se*, grounds for mercy. A significant change of identity *is* grounds, but even then we may question whether this is really mercy. Since the real offender no longer 'exists', or fully exists, we are not in a position to show him mercy, just as we are not in a position to show mercy to someone who is not responsible for his crime, for example a man who didn't know what he was doing or who couldn't stop himself. There is something odd about being merciful to someone who is not an offender, unless we are thinking only of cases purely in a legal context where there may be a gap between legal guilt and moral guilt.

There seem to be two major ways of looking at the notion of mercy. In the majority of cases acts of 'mercy' are simply measures by which we ensure that the punishment fits the crime. We exercise mercy to avoid an unduly harsh penalty which an insufficiently flexible legal system would impose upon the offender. In other words we exercise 'mercy' to avoid an injustice. In cases like this there can be no contrast between the just course of action and the merciful course of action. There is some impropriety in calling cases like these cases of genuine mercy.

We also think of mercy as benevolently reducing or waiving punishment. If we regard mercy as deciding, solely through benevolence, to impose less than the deserved punishment on an offender then the answer to the original question 'when are we justified in being merciful?' must be: 'only when we are compelled to be by the claims that other obligations have on us'. I suggest that this is not so very shocking if we define mercy in the way that I think we must. I wish to suggest, too, that it is a concept which only makes strict logical sense in a retributivist view of punishment.

▣ *Bibliography*

The entries are arranged chronologically.

PLATO *Crito; Republic*, 409–10, 618; *Gorgias*, 476–9; *Protagoras*, 324; *Timaeus*, 876; *Laws*, 731, 859 ff. [Plato's views are discussed by A. W. H. Adkins, *Merit and Responsibility* (Oxford, 1961) 299 ff., and I. M. Crombie, *An Examination of Plato's Doctrines*, vol. 1 (1962) 278 ff.]

ARISTOTLE *Nicomachean Ethics*, bk v.

ST THOMAS AQUINAS *Summa Theologica*. Pars Prima Q. 48 esp. art. 5. Prima Secundae. Q. 87 (poena medicinalis § 7). Secunda Secundae. Q. 66 art. 6 and Q. 106 esp. art. 3 ff. (retributio proportionalis).

THOMAS HOBBES *Leviathan* (1651) ch. 28.

SPINOZA *Tractatus Theologico-Politicus* (1670) chs iv, xvi. *Tractatus Politicus* (1677) ch. iii.

JOHN LOCKE *Second Treatise of Civil Government* (1690) § 87 ff. *Essay Concerning Human Understanding*, ed. 1 (1690) bk II, ch. xxviii.

JOSEPH BUTLER *Sermons*, 2nd ed. (1729). Preface to *Sermons* (Selby-Bigge, *British Moralists*, §§ 196–7). *Dissertation on Nature of Virtue* (1736) (Selby-Bigge, §§ 246–7). Sermon VIII 'Upon Resentment' (not in Selby-Bigge).

FRANCIS HUTCHESON *Enquiry concerning the Original of our Ideas of Virtue or Moral Good* (1725) (Selby-Bigge, § 175). (Punishment in respect of violation of rights.)

RICHARD PRICE *Review of the Principal Questions in Morals*, ed. 1 (1758) ch. iv.

ADAM SMITH *Theory of the Moral Sentiments*, ed. 1 (1759) pt II, ch. ii.

J.-J. ROUSSEAU *The Social Contract* (1762) bk I, ch. 7 and bk II, ch. 5.

C. B. BECCARIA *An Essay on Crimes and Punishments*, by the Marquis Beccaria of Milan, with a Commentary by M. de Voltaire (Glasgow, 1770). The Italian original appeared in 1764 with the title *Dei delitti e delle pene*.

KANT *Lectures on Ethics* (1780–81). Trans. L. Infield (1930) pp. 52 ff. *Metaphysik der Sitten*, pt 1: *Metaphysische Anfangsgründe der Rechtslehre* (1797) § 49. E. English translation, *The Metaphysical Elements of Justice*, ed. and trans. John Ladd (Library of Liberal Arts) pp. 99–108.

BENTHAM *Introduction to the Principles of Morals and Legislation* (1780 and 1789) esp. chs iii, xiii–xv.

J. G. FICHTE *Grundlage des Naturrechts* (1796) pt II, bk iii, § 2. Trans. A. E. Kroeger (Philadelphia, 1869; London, 1889).

HEGEL *The Philosophy of Right* (1821) §§ 90–103 and 'Additions' in T. M. Knox's translation (Oxford, 1942) pp. 246–7.

JOHN AUSTIN *The Province of Jurisprudence Determined* (1832) lectures i, v.

SCHOPENHAUER *The World as Will and Idea*. English translation by R. B. Haldane and J. Kemp. (4th ed. 1896) vol. I, pp. 430 ff. and vol. III, pp. 402 ff. (The German edition is in two volumes. Vol. I appeared in 1819. Vol. II was added in 1844.) *Die beiden Grundprobleme der Ethik* (1841). Trans. by E. F. J. Payne (Library of Liberal Arts, 1965) ch. II, § 4.

MARX *The Holy Family* (1845) ch. 8, § 3. In *New York Daily Tribune*, 18 Feb 1853, 'On capital punishment' (reprinted in *Marx and Engels Basic Writings*, ed. L. S. Feuer, 1959).

J. S. MILL *Utilitarianism* (1863) ch. v. *Examination of Sir William Hamilton's Philosophy* (1865) ch. xxvi.

HENRY SIDGWICK *The Methods of Ethics* (1st ed. 1874. 7th ed. 1907) bk I, ch. v, § 4 and bk III, ch. v, § 7. *The Elements of Politics* (1st ed. 1891. 3rd ed. 1908) ch. viii.

F. H. BRADLEY *Ethical Studies* (1876) essay i. 'Some Remarks on Punishment', *International Journal of Ethics* (1894).

T. H. GREEN *Lectures on the Principles of Political Obligation* (T. H. Green, *Works*, vol. II, 1885).

F. W. MAITLAND 'The Relation of Punishment to Temptation', *Mind*, 1880.

SIR JAMES FITZJAMES STEPHEN *History of the Criminal Law of England*, vol. 2 (1883) chs xvii, xviii.

HASTINGS RASHDALL 'The Theory of Punishment', *International Journal of Ethics*, 1891.

J. McT. ELLIS McTAGGART 'Hegel's Theory of Punishment', *International Journal of Ethics*, 1896.

EDWARD WESTERMARCK 'Freedom, Responsibility and Punishment', *Mind*, 1894.

J. H. HYSLOP 'The Essence of Revenge', *Mind*, 1898.

BERNARD BOSANQUET *The Philosophical Theory of the State* (1899).

HASTINGS RASHDALL 'The Ethics of Forgiveness', *International Journal of Ethics*, 1900.

J. McT. ELLIS McTAGGART *Studies in Hegelian Cosmology* (Cambridge, 1901) ch. v.

G. E. MOORE *Principia Ethica* (Cambridge, 1903) pp. 213–16 (§§ 128–130).

HASTINGS RASHDALL *The Theory of Good and Evil*, vol. I (Oxford, ed. 1, 1907. ed. 2, 1924) ch. ix.

F. C. SHARP and M. C. OTTO 'A Study of the Popular Attitude towards Retributive Punishment', *International Journal of Ethics* (Apr 1910). 'Retribution and Deterrence in the Moral Judgments of Common Sense', *International Journal of Ethics* (Jul 1910).

ELLSWORTH FARIS 'Origin of Punishment', *International Journal of Ethics* (1914).

BERNARD BOSANQUET *Some Suggestions in Ethics* (1918) ch. viii.

W. C. DePauley 'Beccaria and Punishment', *International Journal of Ethics* (1925).

W. H. Moberly 'Some Ambiguities in the Retributive Theory of Punishment', *Proceedings of the Aristotelian Society*, n.s. vol. xxv (1924–5).

A. C. Ewing 'Punishment as a Moral Agency', *Mind*, 1927. *The Morality of Punishment* (1929).

W. D. Ross *The Right and the Good* (Oxford, 1930) ch. 2, appendix 2.

Archbishop William Temple *The Ethics of Punishment*. Howard League Lecture, 1930.

R. E. Hobart 'Freewill as involving Determination and inconceivable without it', *Mind*, 1934.

J. D. Mabbott 'Punishment', *Mind*, Apr 1939.

W. G. Maclagan 'Punishment and Retribution', *Philosophy*, Jul 1939.

M. R. Glover 'Mr. Mabbott on Punishment', *Mind*, Oct 1939.

W. D. Lamont 'Justice: Distributive and Corrective', *Philosophy*, 1941.

J. C. Flügel *Man, Morals and Society* (1945) chs xi, xii.

W. D. Lamont *The Principles of Moral Judgment* (Oxford, 1946) ch. viii.

E. F. Carritt *Ethical and Political Thinking* (Oxford, 1947) ch. 5.

R. W. Pickford 'Psychological Aspects of Punishment', *International Journal of Ethics*, 1947.

G. Del Vecchio *Justice* (Edinburgh, 1952). First published as *La Giustizia* (Rome, 1922).

H. D. Lewis, J. W. Harvey and G. A. Paul 'The Problem of Guilt', *Proceedings of the Aristotelian Society*, supplementary vol. xxi, 1947.

P. Nowell Smith 'Freewill and Moral Responsibility', *Mind*, Jan 1948 (esp. pp. 54–8).

C. H. Whiteley 'Nowell Smith on Retribution and Responsibility', *Mind*, Apr 1948, pp. 230–31.

F. B. Ebersole 'Free Choice and the Demands of Morals', *Mind*, Apr 1952.

H. L. A. Hart 'Justice' (a review of G. Del Vecchio's *Justice*), *Philosophy*, 1953, pp. 348–52.

A. C. Ewing *Ethics* (1953) ch. viii.

Anthony M. Quinton 'On Punishment', *Analysis*, Jun 1954.

C. W. K. Mundle 'Punishment and Desert', *Philosophical Quarterly*, Jul 1954.

Antony Flew 'The Justification of Punishment', *Philosophy*, Oct 1954.

John Rawls 'Two Concepts of Rules', *Philosophical Review*, Jan 1955.

N. Haines 'Responsibility and Accountability', *Philosophy*, Apr 1955.

J. D. Mabbott 'Professor Flew on Punishment', *Philosophy*, Jul 1955.

K. E. Baier 'Is Punishment Retributive?', *Analysis*, Dec 1955.

D. D. Raphael *Moral Judgment* (1955) ch. v, § 2.

J. D. MABBOTT 'Freewill and Punishment', *Contemporary British Philosophy*, 3rd series, ed. H. D. Lewis (1956).

C. H. WHITELEY 'On Retribution', *Philosophy*, Apr. 1956.

'Crime and Punishment', *Dublin Review*, no. 471 (summer 1956). [Articles on Punishment and Penology. Discourse by Pope Pius XII on 'The Function of Punishment'.]

MORRIS GINSBERG *On the Diversity of Morals* (1956) ch. vi.

W. B. GALLIE 'The Lords' Debate on Hanging', *Philosophy*, 1957.

DANIEL CAPPON 'Punishment and the Person', *Ethics*, 1957.

PHILIPPA FOOT 'Freewill as involving Determinism', *Philosophical Review*, 1957.

ELIZABETH LAW BEARDSLEY 'Moral Worth and Moral Credit', *Philosophical Review*, 1957.

RAPHAEL DEMOS 'Some Reflections on Threats and Punishments', *Review of Metaphysics*, 1957.

DONALD CLARK HODGES 'Punishment', *Philosophy and Phenomenological Research*, 1957.

S. I. BENN 'An Approach to the Problems of Punishment', *Philosophy*, 1958. Also as ch. 8 of *Social Principles and the Democratic State* (1959) with R. S. Peters.

H. L. A. HART 'Prolegomenon to the Principles of Punishment', *Proceedings of the Aristotelian Society*, 1959–60. Reprinted in *Punishment and Responsibility* (Oxford, 1968).

RICHARD B. BRANDT *Ethical Theory* (Englewood Cliffs, N.J. 1959) ch. 19.

ARNOLD S. KAUFMAN 'Mr Quinton on Punishment', *Analysis*, Oct 1959.

W. H. J. SPROTT 'Society and Criminology', *Howard Journal*, 1960.

ROBERT E. GAHRINGER 'Punishment as Language', *Ethics*, 1960.

ARNOLD S. KAUFMAN 'The Reform Theory of Punishment', *Ethics*, 1960.

ELIZABETH L. BEARDSLEY 'Determinism and Moral Perspectives', *Philosophy and Phenomenological Research*, 1960.

J. J. C. SMART 'Free-will, Praise and Blame', *Mind*, 1961.

LORD LONGFORD *The Idea of Punishment* (1961).

K. G. ARMSTRONG 'The Retributivist Hits Back', *Mind*, 1961.

JOEL FEINBERG 'Problematic Responsibility in Law and Morals', *Philosophical Review*, 1962.

P. F. STRAWSON *Freedom and Resentment*. British Academy, 1962.

H. L. A. HART *Punishment and the Elimination of Responsibility*. L. T. Hobhouse Lecture (1962). Reprinted in *Punishment and Responsibility* (Oxford, 1968).

P. J. FITZGERALD *Criminal Law and Punishment* (1962). *Crime, Sin and Negligence* (Leeds, 1962).

A. R. MANSER 'It serves you right', *Philosophy*, 1962.

H. J. McCLOSKEY 'The Complexity of the Concepts of Punishment', *Philosophy*, 1962.

A. C. EWING 'Armstrong and the Retributive Theory', *Mind*, Jan 1963.

I. THALBERG 'Remorse', *Mind*, Oct 1963.

DON LOCKE 'The Many Faces of Punishment', *Mind*, Oct 1963.

H. J. McCLOSKEY 'A Note on Utilitarian Punishment', *Mind*, Oct 1963.

BARBARA WOOTTON *Crime and the Criminal Law* (1963).

F. A. WHITLOCK *Criminal Responsibility and Mental Illness* (1963).

MARCUS SINGER *Generalisation in Ethics* (1963) ch. vi, § 5.

N. MORRIS and C. HOWARD *Studies in the Criminal Law* (Oxford, 1964).

JAMES M. SMITH 'Punishment: A conceptual map and normative claim', *Ethics*, 1965.

R. S. DOWNIE 'Forgiveness', *Philosophical Quarterly*, 1965.

V. HAKSAR 'The Responsibility of Psychopaths', *Philosophical Quarterly*, 1965.

GILES PLAYFAIR and DERRICK SINGTON *Crime, Punishment and Cure* (1965).

H. J. McCLOSKEY 'A Non-Utilitarian Approach to Punishment', *Inquiry*, 1965.

T. L. S. SPRIGGE 'A Utilitarian Reply to Mr McCloskey', *Inquiry*, 1965.

J. FEINBERG 'The Expressive Function of Punishment', *The Monist*, 1965.

GIORGIO DEL VECCHIO 'La Lotta contro il Delitto', *Nuova Antologia* (Rome, 1965, n. 1971).

D. F. THOMPSON 'Retribution and the Distribution of Punishment', *Philosophical Quarterly*, Jan 1966.

O. L. JENSEN 'Responsibility, Freedom and Punishment', *Mind*, Apr 1966.

GERALD DWORKIN and DAVID BLUMENFELD 'Punishment for Intentions', *Mind*, Jul 1966.

JOHN CHARVET 'Criticism and Punishment', *Mind*, Oct 1966.

ROBERT A. SAMEK 'Punishment: A Postscript to two Prolegomena', *Philosophy*, Jul 1966.

DONALD LOFTSGORDON 'Present-day British Philosophers on Punishment', *Journal of Philosophy*, Jun 1966.

NIGEL WALKER *The Aims of a Penal System*. James Seth Memorial Lecture (Edinburgh, 1966).

JAMES HEATH *Eighteenth-century Penal Theory* (Oxford, 1966). (Contains extracts from writings of Montesquieu, Hutcheson, Howard, Blackstone, Beccaria, Voltaire, Paley, Kant, Rousseau.)

J. D. MABBOTT *An Introduction to Ethics* (1966) ch. 11.

EDMUND L. PINCOFF *The Rationale of Legal Punishment* (New York 1966).

JAMES F. DOYLE 'Justice and Legal Punishment', *Philosophy*, Jan 1967.

H. J. McCLOSKEY 'Utilitarian and Retributive Punishment', *Journal of Philosophy*, 16 Feb 1967.

L. KENNER 'On Blaming', *Mind*, Apr 1967.

VINIT HAKSAR 'A Scientific Morality?', *Philosophy*, Jul 1967.

NORMAN O. DAHL '"Ought" and Blameworthiness', *Journal of Philosophy*, Jul 1967.

C. L. TEN 'Mr Thompson on the Distribution of Punishment', *Philosophical Quarterly*, Jul 1967.

S. I. BENN 'Punishment', *The Encyclopedia of Philosophy*, ed. Paul Edwards, vol. 7.

THOMAS McPHERSON 'Punishment: definition and justification', *Analysis*, Oct 1967.

WILLIAM KNEALE *The Responsibility of Criminals* (Oxford, 1967).

R. J. O'SHAUGHNESSY 'Forgiveness', *Philosophy*, Oct 1967.

JOHN PLAMENATZ 'Responsibility, Blame and Punishment', *Philosophy, Politics and Society*, 3rd series, ed. Laslett and Runciman (1967).

H. L. A. HART *Punishment and Responsibility* (Oxford, 1968).

J. E. R. SQUIRES 'Blame', *Philosophical Quarterly*, Jan 1968.

MRS ALWYNNE SMART 'Mercy', *Philosophy*, Oct 1968.

SIR WALTER MOBERLY *The Ethics of Punishment* (1968).

EDWARD H. MADDEN, ROLLO HANDY and MARVIN FABER *Philosophical Perspectives on Punishment* (Springfield, Illinois, 1968).

NIGEL WALKER *Crime and Insanity in England* (Edinburgh 1968) [Essential reading for philosophers as well as criminologists, especially ch. 5 (M'Naghten's Case and the Rules), and ch. 6 (The Rules in Action).]

TED HONDERICH *Punishment: the supposed justifications* (1969).

~ *Index*